Philanthropic Foundations at the League of Nations

This book presents a comprehensive analysis of the relations between US philanthropic foundations (in particular the Rockefeller Foundation and the Carnegie Endowment for International Peace) and the League of Nations.

Generations of students and scholars have learned that the US, having played a key role in the creation of the League of Nations in 1919, did not join the organization and stood aloof from its activities during the whole interwar period. This book questions this idea and argues that, even though the US was not a *de jure* member of the League of Nations, the financial, human, and intellectual investment of foundations brought about the *de facto* integration of the US within the League system and also modified the latter's architecture. The book describes the Americanization of the League and shows how it resulted from three strategies pursued throughout the interwar period: that of US foundations, that of the Secretariat, and that of the US federal government. The book also shows the limits of this Americanization and analyzes the role of the European experts in the coproduction of the postwar international order together with the US government.

This book will be of interest to historians and political scientists, as well as undergraduate and graduate students in interdisciplinary programs of international relations.

Ludovic Tournès is professor of international history at the University of Geneva. He has published numerous books and articles including *New Orleans Sur Seine. Histoire du jazz en France* (Fayard, 1999), *Du phonographe au MP3* (Autrement, 2008, rééd. 2011), *L'Argent de l'influence. Les fondations américaines et leurs réseaux européens* (Autrement, 2010), *Sciences de l'homme et politiques. Les fondations philanthropiques américaines en France au XXe siècle* (Garnier, 2011), *Global Exchanges: Scholarships and Transnational Circulations in the Contemporary World* (19–21st centuries), in cooperation with Giles Scott-Smith (Berghahn Books, 2017), and more recently, *Américanisation. Une histoire mondiale* (Fayard, 2020).

Routledge Studies in US Foreign Policy
Series Editors:
Inderjeet Parmar, *City University*, and John Dumbrell, *University of Durham*

This new series sets out to publish high-quality works by leading and emerging scholars critically engaging with United States Foreign Policy. The series welcomes a variety of approaches to the subject and draws on scholarship from international relations, security studies, international political economy, foreign policy analysis and contemporary international history.

Subjects covered include the role of administrations and institutions, the media, think tanks, ideologues and intellectuals, elites, transnational corporations, public opinion, and pressure groups in shaping foreign policy, US relations with individual nations, with global regions and global institutions and America's evolving strategic and military policies.

The series aims to provide a range of books – from individual research monographs and edited collections to textbooks and supplemental reading for scholars, researchers, policy analysts and students.

US Power and the Social State in Brazil
Legal Modernization in the Global South
Júlio Cattai

The United States and Greek-Turkish Relations
The Guardian's Dilemma
Spyros Katsoulas

Rhetoric, Media, and the Narratives of US Foreign Policy
Making Enemies
Adam Lusk

Philanthropic Foundations at the League of Nations
An Americanized League?
Ludovic Tournès

For more information about this series, please visit: www.routledge.com/series/RSUSFP

Philanthropic Foundations at the League of Nations
An Americanized League?

Ludovic Tournès
Translated by Arby Gharibian

LONDON AND NEW YORK

First published 2022
by Routledge
4 Park Square, Milton Park, Abingdon, Oxon OX14 4RN

and by Routledge
605 Third Avenue, New York, NY 10158

Routledge is an imprint of the Taylor & Francis Group, an informa business

© 2022 Ludovic Tournès

The right of Ludovic Tournès to be identified as author of this work has been asserted in accordance with sections 77 and 78 of the Copyright, Designs and Patents Act 1988.

All rights reserved. No part of this book may be reprinted or reproduced or utilised in any form or by any electronic, mechanical, or other means, now known or hereafter invented, including photocopying and recording, or in any information storage or retrieval system, without permission in writing from the publishers.

Trademark notice: Product or corporate names may be trademarks or registered trademarks, and are used only for identification and explanation without intent to infringe.

British Library Cataloguing-in-Publication Data
A catalogue record for this book is available from the British Library

Library of Congress Cataloging-in-Publication Data
A catalog record has been requested for this book

ISBN: 978-0-367-07529-3 (hbk)
ISBN: 978-1-03-222504-3 (pbk)
ISBN: 978-0-429-02121-3 (ebk)

DOI: 10.4324/9780429021213

Typeset in Times New Roman
by Newgen Publishing UK

Contents

List of Abbreviations   vii

Introduction: Rethinking the Relations between the
United States and the League of Nations   1
State of the Art of Research 2
The Argument of This Book 4
The Book's Structure 8

1   The United States at the Heart of the League System?   20
     The Laborious Beginnings of the LoN 21
     The Growth of the Technical Sections 23
         The Strategy of the Secretariat 23
         The Forms of US *Rapprochement* 26
         Participation in Commissions 30
     US Membership in the International Labour Organization 39
     The Permanent Court of International Justice 46
     Conclusion 50

2   A World Ruled by Science: Philanthropic Universalism   57
     The Philanthropic Project 58
     Shaping the LoN to Enable US Membership 63
     Lobbying 70
     Philanthropic Funding of the LoN 73
     Conclusion 78

3   A Global Health Policy: The Health Organization   85
     The LoN in the RF's Global Medical Project 86
     The Epidemiological Intelligence Service 91
     Study Tours by Health Experts 97
     The Limits of International Cooperation 104
     Conclusion 107

4 The International Commission on Intellectual
   Cooperation and New International Power Relations   113
   The New International Scientific Configuration after 1918 114
   US Representation at the ICIC 118
   The Marginalization of the ICIC 123
   The Crisis of Intellectual Cooperation and the Rise of the US 128
   Conclusion 133

5 From Intellectual Cooperation to Economic Expertise   139
   The Economic and Financial Organization 140
      Analysis of the World Economy 140
      The Coordination of Research 144
      Projects Funded by the RF 147
   The International Studies Conference 150
      The Assumption of Control by Foundations 150
      National Committees and Fellows 154
      From Collective Security to International Trade 159
   Conclusion 165

6 From Geneva to Princeton: The Dismantling and the
   Legacy   171
   The Bruce Reform and the Move 172
      The Bruce Reform 172
      The EFTD's Move to the US 176
      The LoN's Other Services 178
   The Coproduction of the New International Order 182
      Integration within Networks of Economic Experts 182
      Relief and Rehabilitation 186
      The Global Economy, between Liberalization and Regulation 188
      The Well-Being of Populations 191
   Conclusion 195

Conclusion   201

Archival Sources   207
Index   209

Abbreviations

ACLS	American Council of Learned Societies
AIBCR	Austrian Institute for Business Cycle Research
BSH	Bureau of Social Hygiene
CEIP	Carnegie Endowment for International Peace
CEIP-CE	European Center of the Carnegie Endowment for International Peace
CFR	Council on Foreign Relations
CIO	Congress of Industrial Organizations
ECOSOC	Economic and Social Council
EFO	Economic and Financial Organization
EFTD	Economic, Financial and Transit Department
FAO	Food and Agriculture Organization
FPA	Foreign Policy Association
GATT	General Agreement on Tariffs and Trade
GEB	General Education Board
GRC	Geneva Research Centre
HO	Health Organization
HS	Health Section
IAS	Institute of Advanced Study
IAU	International Academic Union
IBRD	International Bank for Reconstruction and Development
ICIC	International Commission on Intellectual Cooperation (ICIC)
ICO	Intellectual Cooperation Organisation
ICSU	International Council of Scientific Unions (CIUS)
IHB	International Health Board
IHC	International Health Commission
IIE	Institute of International Education
IIIC	International Institute of Intellectual Cooperation (IICI)
ILO	International Labour Organization (OIT)
IMF	International Monetary Fund
IOPH	International Office of Public Hygiene
IPR	Institute of Pacific Relations

IRC	International Research Council
ISC	International Studies Conference
LNA	League of Nations Association
LoN	League of Nations (SdN)
LSRM	Laura Spelman Rockefeller Memorial
MMF	Milbank Memorial Fund
MPPDA	Motion Pictures Producers and Distributors of America
NRC	National Research Council
PUMC	Peking Union Medical College
RF	Rockefeller Foundation
SGF	Statistique générale de la France
SOLI	Scientific Organization of Labor Institute (IOST)
UNESCO	United Nations Educational, Scientific and Cultural Organization
UNO	United Nations Organization (ONU)
UNRRA	United Nations Relief and Rehabilitation Administration

Introduction
Rethinking the Relations between the United States and the League of Nations

In October 1920, a few days after the presidential election and a few months after Congress refused to ratify the League of Nations (LoN) Covenant in March, Elihu Root informally notified the Republican candidate Warren Harding that if the "LoN according to Wilson" seemed doomed, an "Americanized LoN"[1]—in which the United States (US) would involve itself in order to gradually change the organization—struck him as highly desirable. He believed that instead of keeping the LoN at a distance, as proposed by Harding, the US should discuss with the major European powers to secure the renegotiation and "Americanization of the Treaty."[2] We are familiar with what happened next, as Harding handily won the election and moved precisely in the opposite direction, cutting all ties with the LoN.

This stance was one episode among others in the long debate surrounding ratification of the Treaty of Versailles and the LoN Covenant, which stretched from the opening of the Paris Peace Conference in January 1919 to the presidential election in November 1920. This debate has been documented in detail by historians, and its culmination in the refusal to ratify the Treaty of Versailles appears to have established, once and for all, the interpretation of US–LoN relations (or more precisely the lack thereof). This book's aim is to show that this interpretation should be revisited. Root's appeal gives pause to the historian, especially given that the notion of a lack of US participation in the LoN, which has long remained uncontested, has been challenged in recent years by a number of works emphasizing US involvement in LoN activities.[3] Conclusions remain to be drawn from this participation, with three questions in particular having received insufficient attention from historians and political scientists: what was the extent of this participation? Was it part of a strategy or accidental? And more importantly, what impact did it have on the LoN and the future of the League system? This book aims to answer these three questions. I will first argue that the US was not a *de jure* member of the LoN, but that it was *de facto* part of the League system; that its participation was massive, and occurred throughout the LoN's existence; that it was part of a strategy developed by the federal government and private actors in particular (notably the Rockefeller Foundation [RF] and the Carnegie Endowment for International Peace [CEIP]), as well as by the LoN Secretariat;

DOI: 10.4324/9780429021213-1

and that it had major consequences on the League system, contributing to the autonomization of technical sections from the Secretariat, and ultimately to the implosion and dismantling of the League system in 1940, which fostered its reconstruction and transformation into the United Nations (UN).

State of the Art of Research

The historiography for the LoN has long been poorly developed.[4] In 2001 in her classical study on the Paris Peace Conference, Margaret MacMillan wryly noted that "only a handful of eccentric historians still bother to study the League of Nations. Its archives, with their wealth of materials, are largely unvisited."[5] However, the organization has drawn increasing scholarly attention since the mid-2000s, as the end of the Cold War, globalization, and the resurgence, especially in Europe, of international problems often stemming from the territorial reorganizations following World War I, have prompted historians to take renewed interest in the LoN.[6] Since then there has been an increasing number of works on the subject, which have largely corrected the received notions regarding the organization that has prevailed since 1945. They have notably shown it was not the failure that is often described (and decried), instead stressing the initiatives that marked its history. This new research has focused on political activities,[7] but also and especially on the work of its "technical" sections, in addition to LoN-affiliated organizations, which engaged throughout the interwar period in an international effort to normalize and harmonize numerous areas such as economics,[8] health,[9] refugees,[10] minorities,[11] transportation,[12] labor,[13] social issues,[14] and drug trafficking.[15] Some aspects have generated considerable literature in recent years, such as intellectual cooperation, whose general aspects have been studied,[16] in addition to policies for artistic creation and museography,[17] along with academic and scientific activity.[18] Other questions have been the subject of recent works, such as movements in support of the LoN,[19] or development policies,[20] which demonstrate the enthusiasm it generated, and that its history extends beyond that of international organizations and expert networks, taking its place more broadly in the history of interwar societies. Other research has challenged the notion of a radical break between the LoN and the UN—which dates back to the period when the LoN's disrepute required keeping a distance from it at all costs—instead underscoring the powerful continuities that existed between the two organizations. While certain issues remain little explored, such as international justice, drug trafficking, and the role of women, a clear picture emerges from this burgeoning historiography: the LoN was a major moment in the history of international organizations, with a plethora of highly varied initiatives. This fact is all the more remarkable given that its technical activities, which were included in the Covenant almost by force, developed in a short amount of time and with limited means, and rose in importance in inverse proportion to the organization's political disrepute. They became central to LoN activity in the 1930s, ultimately continuing (for the most part) under another name as part of the UN system. US–LoN relations are among the points that have received little attention in the historiography; they are not entirely unfamiliar, having been emphasized on a number of occasions since the early 2000s,[21] although they remain poorly understood. This book is the first attempt to analyze the full US involvement in the organization, with philanthropic foundations being major actors in this involvement.

The historiography of philanthropy is too vast to summarize here.[22] The international activities of major foundations, especially the Carnegie, Rockefeller, and Ford Foundations, have been well documented over the last 30 years. This historiography is based on the incredibly rich archives of foundations, which have their blind spots, and is marked by multiple structural problems that persist today. The first is that this historiography was long structured around the dispute between liberals and Gramscians, which began in the 1970s and continues today.[23] The dispute opposes a view of foundations as apolitical organizations that are independent of power, pursuing a disinterested quest for knowledge, with another view that presents them as instruments reproducing the hegemony of the ruling class, capitalism, and the international power of the US. The opposition between these two perspectives, however relevant it may be, has tended to obscure other aspects of the history of philanthropy. The other structural problem of the historiography is that it is nation-centric, paradoxically even when it analyzes foundation activity in the world: studies on a particular country are legion, but comparative works, or those focusing on international organizations, are relatively rare.[24] Finally, the third structural problem of this historiography is that it is highly sector-specific, often focusing on a single domain such as health, biomedical research, the social sciences, or education. There are few crosscutting studies that analyze these fields together as an integral part of a global project on the part of foundations.[25] The historiography of philanthropy is therefore both very rich and very fragmented. This is partly due to the actual structure of the foundations' archives, especially those of the RF, which are organized by sector and country; one could even say, somewhat satirically, that each box could be the subject of an article or book. The historiography of philanthropy has broadened its horizons since the 2000s,[26] primarily by using the knowledge provided by global and transnational history.[27] It is not my intention to offer a detailed discussion of the various trends in transnational studies (global history, world history, transnational history, entangled history, connected history, shared history, etc.). I will simply say that it allows for moving beyond the ideological oppositions that have long structured the historiographical debate between liberals and Gramscians regarding the role of international foundations, namely by highlighting the transnational circulations they generated, as well as the complex relations between foundations and their recipients, which cannot be reduced to a dominant-dominated relationship, or to a disinterested action in the name of science. A transnational perspective provides a more accurate picture of their work in the field, without obscuring the power relations and asymmetry between the US and the rest of the world, and more precisely accounts for the complexity and evolution of situations on the ground.

This book's analysis of relations between foundations and the LoN is in keeping with this perspective. It is not a diplomatic history of relations between the US and the LoN or its member states, but an analysis of its technical activities and its key figures. It is also based on the achievements of political science and sociology, which have long emphasized the role of private actors in international relations,[28] even though works in these disciplines sometimes lack chronological depth, with most not stretching back past 1945. Yet the role of nongovernmental actors is much older, and the considerable presence of foundations in US foreign policy has long been familiar.[29] Beginning in the 1910s, they began to build a philanthropic diplomacy[30] that acted both with and alongside the federal government at the intersection of public and private spheres of action, which in the US more than elsewhere is a vast contact zone where the border between the two spheres is blurred and shifting. Analysis of the financial, human, and intellectual investment of foundations in the LoN shows that they brought about the *de facto* integration of the US within the League system and also modified the latter's architecture. It also provides a clearer understanding of the logic governing US–LoN relations.

The Argument of This Book

As we have seen, some historians and political scientists have explored US participation in the LoN, especially that of the RF. This book expands the analysis by presenting a comprehensive review of foundation participation in the League system in order to move beyond sector-based studies and to understand the overall logic of philanthropic activity as well as relations between foundations and the Secretariat. It subsequently examines the consequences of this participation in the League system, a question that has not yet been studied. Three specific topics are discussed in the following chapters. The first will show why talk of an Americanization of the LoN is justified. The second will demonstrate how this Americanization resulted from a strategy pursued throughout the interwar period by foundations, whose objective was to establish a global government of science. The third will examine the term "hegemony" in reference to the US takeover of reorganizing the international order during World War II.

The Americanization of the LoN is the first topic. While the participation of foundations in technical activities is well known, this book will deepen the analysis by showing how the US was present in all technical activities through the participation of foundations, as well as the presence of federal civil servants in all of the organization's commissions and subcommissions. I will show how this participation helped shape the League system from the early 1920s onward, especially by promoting the development of technical activities, doing so with the Secretariat's consent. While the US was not an LoN member, it was part of the League system, and influenced how it functioned on the administrative, organizational, and intellectual levels. Focusing on the transnational circulations of experts and ideas renders this process of Americanization visible, a process that would otherwise remain invisible in a simple analysis of US–LoN diplomatic relations. This participation signals that the US had become an intellectual and scientific superpower as early as the 1920s—well before becoming a military one—thanks to the development of an ecosystem of knowledge production bringing together the federal government and private actors in particular, notably universities, foundations, institutes, and organizations such as the Institute of International Education, the Social Science Research Council, and the Council on Foreign Relations (CFR), among many others. If one could say there was an Americanization of the LoN, it is because of the triple impact that foundations had on the organization: (1) they stimulated the growth of technical activities to the detriment of political activities, and helped make the organization a vast organization of expertise in new fields such as health monitoring or global economic analysis, rather than a decision-making forum for international policy; (2) they promoted the autonomization of technical sections in relation to the LoN's central administration, and helped change the League system into a series of decentralized bodies and *ad hoc* conferences rather than a unified and centralized organization; and (3) they partially or totally took control of some of these conferences and imposed their agenda, especially the International Studies Conference (ISC). It is therefore clear that foundations—and through them internationalist circles—successfully counterbalanced the traditional isolationism of the US even before 1939.[31] This activity is an unfamiliar factor in the various internal and external forces that helped undermine the coherence of the League system, and led to its implosion during the invasion of Europe in 1940. This implosion took concrete form when part of the organization moved to the US; it also contributed to the reconfiguration of the international system between 1940 and 1945, and the establishment of US leadership in this process. The creation of the UN was not solely the result of the power relations that emerged from the war, but was more broadly the result of a long-term process involving US influence over the LoN's structure from the very beginning of its history. Accordingly, the Americanization of the LoN during the interwar period prepared and facilitated the leadership established by the US during the creation of the UN.

The second topic is how this process of Americanization was implemented. It did not result, at least initially, from political pressure exerted by the federal government, but from a strategy on the part of private actors, who advanced the notion that scientific expertise had to be developed in order to solve the problems left in the wake of World War I. This idea of governing global affairs through science was present from the beginning in the culture of philanthropic foundations, especially the RF and the CEIP. It was developed throughout the interwar period and served as a basis for their participation in the activities of the LoN's technical sections. Yet it was not an invention of the interwar period, for it was present in the nineteenth century in both European and US internationalist circles. Mark Mazower has rightly emphasized that the appearance of international organizations before 1914 was not so much the work of governments, which showed little interest, but that of scientists and technicians, who beginning in the middle of the century imposed the idea that science and international coordination could solve many problems. These circles historically advanced the notion that the traditional aristocracy of diplomats negotiating at congresses be replaced by a "professionalized meritocracy"[32] of experts capable of rationally conducting the world's affairs using the natural and social sciences.

US foundations therefore did not invent the idea of governing the world through science, but they helped give it a second life after 1918, in collaboration with the internationalists within the LoN. They provided it with their financial power, US prestige after 1918, and contributions from its burgeoning university system. Foundations served as essential sponsors for technical activities. Their early and lasting support throughout the LoN's existence shows that there was nothing accidental about their participation, and that it was in keeping with a project seeking to reform global affairs through expertise, one that was methodically implemented during the interwar period. Still, it would be wrong to think that this project was strictly apolitical. While foundations were heirs to Saint-Simonianism and the dream of an "engineered world society,"[33] their project clearly had a US tinge. Inderjeet Parmar has rightly affirmed that the internationalism of philanthropic circles is inseparable from a nationalist dimension and a belief in American exceptionalism, for the funding policy of foundations was inextricable from a policy supporting scientific expertise, which was in the US national interest as philanthropists understood it, namely that of heightened US engagement in the leadership of global affairs.[34]

The combination of nationalism and internationalism naturally leads to the third topic discussed in this book, which is how to interpret US participation in the debate between liberals and Gramscians that has characterized the historiography of philanthropy. As mentioned above, this debate often leads to oversimplified positions that do not conform to reality. While the notion that foundations are apolitical organizations disinterestedly supporting science, and strictly internationalist in nature, is at best naive and at worst blind, the Gramscian prism of hegemony with its denunciatory logic is not entirely satisfactory either. While the Gramscian interpretive model clearly recognizes the formation of a philanthropic project convinced that it represented the future of humanity—and seeking to internationalize US standards by presenting them as scientific and objective—its overly systematic and ahistorical character prevents it from capturing subtle and shifting situations on the ground. In this book I argue that the Americanization of the LoN, while undeniable, should not be seen as hegemony. My critique of this view focuses on two points.

The first is that the notion of hegemony is based on a diffusionist and unilateral perspective. Hegemony-based analysis adheres to a logic that opposes the dominant and the dominated, which are conceived as reified categories, and underestimates the latter's agency. Analyzing the role of foundations in Gramscian terms tends to focus on their ideological logic, and neglects to analyze the recipients of grants, who are often reduced to passive instruments, either victims of or complicit with philanthropic policy. As a result, it tends to simplify a situation that is in reality more complex on the ground. Parmar's *Foundations of the American Century* is a good example of the value and limits of Gramscian interpretation: while the general interpretive framework is relevant, the empirical demonstration is contestable because the book relies solely on foundation archives, thereby introducing an epistemological bias that exclusively provides the standpoint of philanthropists regarding the actions described. While foundation archives, especially those of the RF, are exceptionally rich, they are also a trap for the researcher, for this wealth tends to overstate the activity of foundations and their role in the analyzed process. Source bias, a syndrome that is familiar to historians, is heightened here due to the wealth of documentation in which local actors appear exclusively as auxiliaries to philanthropic activity. This bias can only be overcome by comparing the archives of different actors in order to achieve a clear picture of the agency of local actors, as well as the numerous negotiations that took place between them and philanthropists, negotiations that are largely invisible in philanthropic archives.[35] Analysis of the relations between foundations and the LoN is a characteristic example of this interaction between donor and recipient, who are the coproducers of a project, although the asymmetry of their relations—which is emphasized by the Gramscian perspective—should obviously be taken into account, especially the power that foundations enjoyed due to their financial clout.

The second problematic aspect of hegemony-based interpretation is its overly general and teleological nature: it confuses the existence of a hegemonic project developed by philanthropic actors, which is indisputable, with the actual realization of this project, which is much more so. At first sight, one could easily conclude that the massive investment of foundations in the LoN paved the way for US hegemony over the international system, as shown by the leadership assumed by the US in constructing the UN system. However, if we adopt a long-term perspective, the realization of this hegemony is highly debatable. First, the US was never hegemonic on a global scale: during the Cold War, the entire Communist Bloc and some nonaligned countries, which is to say a large part of the world, escaped this hegemony. Second, during this period the UN was partially paralyzed by the rivalry between the US and the USSR. Third, even after the fall of the Berlin Wall, this hegemony was not realized in actual fact. In the months following the collapse of communist regimes in Europe and the USSR, one could imagine that the time had come for US hegemony through the globalization of capitalism and liberal democracy. This illusion quickly dissipated, as it became clear that the US could not control the world on its own; that it disengaged from UN peacekeeping operations starting in 1994; that it undertook military operations ending in failure (Afghanistan and especially Iraq); that its image in the world has constantly deteriorated since the mid-1990s; and that this deterioration has accelerated with Donald Trump's rise to power in 2016. If hegemony is based on the dominated accepting domination and interiorizing the dominant power's legitimacy, one could subsequently say that today the US is far from being hegemonic in a considerable part of the world.[36] It is indisputable that the US internationalist elite, to whom the foundations belonged, conceived a hegemonic project in the interwar period—whether it was carried out is another question. The role of foundations in this process remains to be clarified; the degree of their influence must not be overestimated.[37] This book intends to contribute to this debate.

The Book's Structure

This book is divided into six chapters. Chapter 1 examines the overall position of the US in the League system by considering both private actors and the federal government. Chapter 2 analyzes the international project in which foundation support for the LoN was inscribed, notably that of the RF and the CEIP. The following chapters explore the role of foundations in the technical sections, especially the Health Organization (HO) (Chapter 3), the International Committee on Intellectual Cooperation (ICIC) (Chapter 4), the Economic and Financial Organization (EFO), and the ISC (Chapter 5). The final chapter (Chapter 6) analyzes the LoN's move to the United States in 1940, and its participation in developing the postwar international order.

Notes

1 Jessup Philip C., *Elihu Root*, New York, Dodd, Mead & Co., 1938 (2 volumes), vol. 2, pp. 412–413. The manuscript was also consulted in Jessup's papers: see PCJ-LOC I/247.
2 *Ibid.*, p. 413.
3 Lavelle Kathryn, "Exit, Voice and Loyalty in International Organizations: US Involvement in the League of Nations," *International Organization*, 2, 2007, pp. 371–393; Tournès Ludovic, "La fondation Rockefeller et la naissance de l'universalisme philanthropique américain," *Critique Internationale*, 35, 2007, pp. 173–197; Bear F. Braumoeller, "The Myth of American Isolationism," *Foreign Policy Analysis*, 6–4, 2010, pp. 349–371; Rietzler Katharina, "Before the Cultural Cold Wars: American Philanthropy and Cultural Diplomacy in the Inter-War Years," *Historical Research*, 84–223, 2011, pp. 148–164; Mazower Mark, *Governing the World: the History of an Idea, 1815 to the Present*, New York, Penguin Books, 2013 [2012]; Tournès Ludovic, "The Rockefeller Foundation and the Transition from the League of Nations to the UN (1939–1946)," *Journal of Modern European History*, 12–3, 2014, pp. 323–34; Ekbladh David, "'American Asylum: The United States and the Campaign to Transplant the Technical League, 1939–1940," *Diplomatic History*, 39–4, 2015, pp. 629–660; Tournès Ludovic, *Les Etats-Unis et la Société des Nations: le*

système international face à l'émergence d'une superpuissance, Bern, Peter Lang, 2016; Tournès Ludovic, "American Membership of the League of Nations: US Philanthropy and the Transformation of an International Organization into a Think Tank," in Tournès Ludovic, Wertheim Stephen & Parmar Inderjeet (eds.), "The Birth of Global Knowledge," Special Issue of *International Politics*, 55–6, 2018, pp. 852–869.

4 See especially the works by Ghébali Victor-Yves: *La Société des Nations et la Réforme Bruce, 1939–1940*, Genève, Centre européen de la dotation Carnegie pour la paix internationale, 1970; "Aux origines de l'Ecosoc: l'évolution des commissions et organisations techniques de la Société des Nations," *Annuaire Français de Droit International*, 18, 1972, pp. 469–511; *L'Organisation internationale du travail* (*L'organisation internationale et l'évolution de la société mondiale, vol.3*, Ago Roberto & Vaticos Nicolas eds), Genève, Georg, 1987. Among other early scholarship on the League, see also *The League of Nations in Retrospect*, conference proceedings, Berlin & New York, Walter & Gruyter, 1983.

5 MacMillan Margaret, *Paris 1919. Six Months that Changed the World*, New York, Random House, 2001, p. 83.

6 See the state of the art in 2007 in Pedersen Susan, "Review Essay: Back to the League of Nations," *The American Historical Review*, 112–4, 2007, pp.1091–117; see also the website *History of the League of Nations* at www.leagueofnationshistory.org/homepage.shtml; for the most recent state of the art, see Guieu Jean-Michel & Jeannesson Stanislas, "L'expérience de Genève (1920–1946)," in Guieu Jean-Michel & Jeannesson Stanislas (eds.), Special Issue on "La Société des Nations. Une expérience de l'internationalisme," *Monde(s). Histoire, Espaces, Relations*, 19–1, 2021, pp. 9–29.

7 See inter alia *The League of Nations 1920–1946, Organization and Accomplishments, A Retrospective of the First International Organization for the Establishment of World Peace*, New York, Geneva, United Nations Publications, 1996; Stone David R., "Imperialism and Sovereignty: The League of Nations' Drive to Control Arms Trade," *Journal of Contemporary History*, 35–2, 2000, pp. 213–230; Webster Andrew, "The Transnational Dream: Politicians, Diplomats and Soldiers in the League of Nations' Pursuit of International Disarmament, 1920–1938," *Contemporary European History*, 14–4, 2005, pp. 493–518; Mazower Mark, *Governing the World… op. cit.*; Pedersen Susan, *The Guardians: The League of Nations and the Crisis of Empire*, New York, Oxford University Press, 2015; O'Malley Alanna & Jackson Simon (eds.), *The Institution of International Order: From the League of Nations to United Nations*, New York, Routledge, 2018; Gram-Skjoldager Karen & Ikonomou Haakon Andreas (eds.), *The League of Nations: Perspective from the Present*, Aahrus, Aahrus University Press, 2019; Petruccelli David, "The Crisis of Liberal Internationalism: The Legacies of the League of Nations Reconsidered," *Journal of World History*, 31–1, 2020, p. 111–136.

8 Decorzant Yann, *La Société des Nations et la naissance d'une conception de la régulation économique internationale*, Bern, Peter Lang, 2011; Cusso Roser, "L'activité statistique de l'Organisation économique et financière de la Société des Nations," *Histoire & Mesure*, 27–2, 2012, online at: journals.openedition.org/histoiremesure/4553 (accessed August 19, 2021). The seminal book in the field is Clavin Patricia, *Securing the World Economy. The Reinvention of the League of Nations 1920–1946*, Oxford, Oxford University Press, 2013.

9 Borowy Iris, *Coming to Terms with World Health. The League of Nations Health Organization*, Berlin, Peter Lang Publishers, 2009.
10 Kévonian Dzovinar, *Réfugiés et diplomatie humanitaire: les acteurs européens et la scène proche-orientale pendant l'entre-deux-guerres*, Paris, Publications de la Sorbonne, 2004; Watenpaugh Keith David, "The League of Nations' Rescue of Armenian Genocide Survivors and the Making of Modern Humanitarianism, 1920–1927," *American Historical Review*, 115–5, 2010, pp. 1315–1339.
11 Fink Carol, *Defending the Rights of Others: The Great Powers, the Jews, and International Minority Protection (1878–1938)*, Cambridge, Cambridge University Press, 2006; Ekmekcioglu Lerna, "Republic of Paradox: The League of Nations Minority Protection Regime and the New Turkey's Step Citizens," *International Journal of Middle East Studies*, 46–4, 2014, pp. 657–679.
12 Schott Johan & Kaiser Wolfram (eds.), *Writing the Rules for Europe: Experts, Cartels, International Organizations*, London, Palgrave MacMillan, 2014.
13 Van Daele Jasmien, Rodriguez Garcia Magaly, Van Goethem Geert & Van der Linden Marcel (eds.), *ILO Histories. Essays on the International Labour Organization and its Impact on the World during the Twentieth Century*, Bern, Peter Lang, 2010; Kott Sandrine & Droux Joëlle (eds.), *Globalizing Social Rights. The ILO and Beyond*, London, Palgrave MacMillan, 2013.
14 Showan Daniel P., *United States Policy Regarding League of Nations Social and Humanitarian Activities*, PhD dissertation, Pennsylvania State University, 1969; more recently, see Rupp Leila, *Worlds of Women, the Making of an International Women's Movement*, Princeton, Princeton University Press, 1998, ch. 2; Miller Carol, "The Social Section And Advisory Committee on Social Questions of the League of Nations," in Weindling Paul (ed.), *International Health Organizations and Movements*, 1918–1939, Cambridge, Cambridge University Press, 1995, pp. 154–176; Rodriguez Garcia Magaly, "The League of Nations and the Moral Recruitment of Women," *International Review of Social History*, 57–20, 2012, pp. 97–128; Eisenberg Jaci Leigh, "The Status of Women: A Bridge from the League of Nations to the United Nations," *Journal of International Organization Studies*, 2, 2013, pp. 8–24; Knepper Paul, "The Investigation into the Traffic in Women by the League of Nations: Sociological Jurisprudence as an International Social Project," *Law and History Rev*iew, 34–1, 2016, pp. 45–73; Kozma Liaz, Rodogno Davide, & Rodriguez Garcia Magaly, *The League of Nation's Work on Social Issues*, New York, United Nations Press, 2016; Rodriguez Garcia Magaly, "Beware of Pity: The League of Nations Treatment of Prostitution," *Monde(s). Histoire, Espaces, Relations*, 19–1, 2021, pp. 97–117.
15 McAllister William B., *Drug Diplomacy in the Twentieth Century: An International History*, London, Routledge, 2000; Spillane Joseph F., "Global Drug Prohibition in Local Context: Heroin, Malaria and Harm," *Diplomatic History*, 2021, dhab044, https://doi.org/10.1093/dh/dhab044 (accessed August 19, 2021).
16 Renoliet Jean-Jacques, *L'UNESCO oubliée: la Société des Nations et la coopération intellectuelle, 1919–1946*, Paris, Publications de la Sorbonne, 1999; Taillibert Christel, *L'Institut international du cinématographe éducatif: regards sur le rôle du cinéma éducatif dans la politique internationale du fascisme italien*, Paris, L'Harmattan, 1999; Pernet Corinne, "Les échanges d'informations entre intellectuels: La conférence comme outil de coopération intellectuelle à la Société des Nations," in Vallotton François (ed.), *Devant le verre d'eau. Regards croisés sur la conférence comme vecteur de la vie intellectuelle*

1880–1950, Lausanne, Editions Antipodes, 2007, pp. 91–106; Laqua Daniel, "Transnational intellectual cooperation, the League of Nations, and the problem of order," *Journal of Global History*, 6, 2011, pp. 223–247; Laqua Daniel, *Internationalism Reconfigured: Transnational Ideas and Movements between the World Wars*, London, New York, I.B. Tauris, 2011; Pemberton Jo-Anne, "The Changing Shape of Intellectual Cooperation: From the League of Nations to UNESCO," *Australian Journal of Politics and History*, 58–1, 2012, 34–50; Saikawa Takashi, *From Intellectual Co-operation to International Exchange: Japan and China in the International Committee on Intellectual Co-Operation of the League of Nations, 1922–1939*, Heidelberg, Universität Heidelberg, 2014; Pernet Corinne, "Twists, Turns and Dead Alleys: The League of Nations and Intellectual Cooperation in Times of War," *Journal of Modern European History*, 12–3, 2014, pp. 342–358.
17 Caillot Marie, *La Revue Mouseion (1927–1946): les musées et la coopération culturelle internationale*, 2 vol., Paris, Ecole Nationale des Chartes, 2011; Compagnon Antoine (ed.), *La République des lettres dans la tourmente (1919–1939)*, Paris, CNRS éditions, 2011; Ducci Annamaria, "Europe and the Artistic Patrimony of the Interwar Period: The International Institute for Intellectual Cooperation at the League of Nations," in Hewitson Mark & D'Auria Matthew (eds.), *Europe in Crisis, Intellectuals and the European Idea, 1917–1957*, New York, Oxford, Berghahn Books, 2012; Sibille Christiane, "La musique à la Société des Nations," *Relations Internationales*, 155, 2013, pp.89–102.
18 Ritzler Katharina, *Before the Cultural Cold Wars…, art. cit.*; Schroeder-Gudehus Brigitte, "La société des esprits: la coopération intellectuelle dans le cadre de la Société des Nations," in *Les scientifiques et la paix: La communauté scientifique internationale au cours des années 20*, Montréal, Presses de l'Université de Montréal, 2014; Tournès Ludovic, *Les Etats-Unis et la Société des Nations…, op. cit.*; Grandjean Martin, *Les réseaux de la coopération intellectuelle. La Société des Nations comme actrice des échanges scientifiques et culturels dans l'entre-deux-guerres*. PhD dissertation, University of Lausanne, 2018; Grandjean Martin, "A Representative Organization? Ibero-American Networks in the Committee on Intellectual Cooperation of the League of Nations (1922–1939)," in Roig-Sanz Diana & Subirana Jaume (eds.), *Cultural Organizations, Networks and Mediators in Contemporary Ibero-America*, London, Routledge, pp. 65–89; Pemberton Jo-Anne, *The Story of International Relations, Part One: Cold-Blooded Idealists*, Palgrave MacMillan, 2020.
19 Kuehl Warren F. & Dunn Lynn K., *Keeping the Covenant: American Internationalists and the League of Nations (1920–1939)*, Kent, Kent State University Press, 1997; Birebent Christian, *Militants de la paix et de la SdN. Les mouvements de soutien à la Société des Nations en France et au Royaume Uni, 1918–1925*, Paris, L'Harmattan, 2008; Guieu Jean-Michel, *Le rameau et le glaive. Les militants français pour la Société des Nations*, Paris, Presses de Sciences Po, 2008; Wertheim Stephen, "The League that Wasn't: American Designs for a Legalist-Sanctionist League of Nations and the Intellectual Origins of International Organization, 1914–1920," *Diplomatic History*, 35–5, 2011, pp. 797–836; McCarthy Helen, *The British People and the League of Nations: Democracy, Citizenship and Internationalism, c. 1918–1945*, Manchester, Manchester University Press, 2011; Hathaway Oona A. & Shapiro Scott J., *The Internationalists: How a Radical Plan to Outlaw War Remade the World*, New York, Simon & Shuster, 2017.

20 Ekbladh David, "To Reconstruct the Medieval: Rural Reconstruction in Interwar China and the Rise of an American Style of Modernization, 1921–1961," *The Journal of American-East Asian Relations*, 9–3/4, 2000, pp. 169–196; Zanasi Margherita, "Exporting Development: League of Nations and Republican China," *Comparative Studies in Society and History*, 49–1, 2007, pp. 143–169; Rodogno Davide, *Night on Earth: Humanitarian Organizations' Relief and Rehabilitation Programmes on Behalf of Civilian Populations (1918–1939)*, Cambridge, Cambridge University Press, 2021.

21 See note 3.

22 The historiography for US philanthropy is very rich and would deserve an entire chapter. For detailed bibliographies, see three seminal books: Bremner Robert H., *American Philanthropy*, Chicago, University of Chicago Press, 1988 [1960]; Friedman Lawrence J. & McGarvie Mark D. (eds.), *Charity, Philanthropy and Civility in American History*, Cambridge & New York, Cambridge University Press, 2003; Zunz Olivier, *Philanthropy in America: A History*, Princeton, Princeton University Press, 2012. See also the bibliography on the international actions of the Rockefeller Foundation at www.zotero.org/groups/222650/rac

23 The debate between these two interpretations is exemplified by a series of exchanges between Martin Bulmer and Donald Fisher in the 1980s. See the articles published in *Sociology*, 17–2, 1983, pp. 206–233 and *Sociology*, 18–4, 1984, pp. 572–579 and pp. 580–587. Among recent examples of the Gramscian interpretation, see Parmar Inderjeet, *Foundations of the American Century. The Ford, Carnegie and Rockefeller Foundations in the Rise of American Power*, New York, Columbia University Press, 2012; and the special Issue on "The Hidden Hand: How Foundations Shape the Course of History," *The American Journal of Economics and Sociology*, 74–4, 2015.

24 See, for example, Weindling Paul, "Philanthropy and World Health: the Rockefeller Foundation and the League of Nations Health Organization," *Minerva*, 35–3, 1997, pp 269–281; Tournès Ludovic, *The Rockefeller Foundation and the Transition…, art. cit.*; Levich Jacob, "The Gates Foundation, Ebola and Global Health Imperialism," *The American Journal of Economics and Sociology*, 74–4, 2015, pp. 704–742; Verna Chantalle F., "Haiti, the Rockefeller Foundation and UNESCO's Pilot Project in Fundamental Education, 1948–1953," *Diplomatic History*, 40–2, 2016, pp. 268–295.

25 See, for example, Tournès Ludovic, *Sciences de l'homme et politique. Les fondations philanthropiques américaines en France au XXe siècle*, Paris, Garnier, 2013 [2011].

26 See the numerous works coordinated by Giuliana Gemelli, including, among others, Gemelli Giuliana (ed.), *The Unacceptables: American Foundations and Refugee Scholars between the Two World Wars*, Brussels, Peter Lang, 2000; Gemelli Giuliana (ed.), *American Foundations and Large-Scale Research: Construction and Transfert of Knowledge*, Bologna, CLUEB, 2001; see also Rausch Helke & Krige John (eds.), *American Foundations and the Coproduction of World Order in the Twentieth Century*, Göttingen, Vandenhoeck & Ruprecht, 2012; Rausch Helke, "US Scientific Philanthropy' in France, Germany and Great Britain: Historical Snapshots of an Interwar Panorama," in Petersen Klaus, Stewart John, & Sørensen Michael Kuur (eds.), *American Foundations and the European Welfare States*, Odense, University Press of Southern Denmark, 2013, pp. 79–103; Rausch Helke, "The Birth of Transnational US-Philanthropy from the Spirit of War: Rockefeller Philanthropists in World War I," *Journal of the Gilded Age and Progressive Era*,

17–3, 2018, online at www.cambridge.org/core/journals/journal-of-the-gilded-age-and-progressive-era/article/birth-of-transnational-us-philanthropy-from-the-spirit-of-war-rockefeller-philanthropists-in-world-war-i/87858360A41F7F46F2AEB84AA683F95C (accessed August 19, 2021).
27 These historiographies are so rich that they deserve an in-depth presentation. There is not sufficient space here for a detailed exploration of these different perspectives (world history, global history, connected history, transnational history, etc.); among recent titles in English, see Saunier Pierre-Yves, *Transnational History. Theory and History*, Basingstoke, Palgrave MacMillan, 2013; Iriye Akira & Saunier Pierre-Yves (eds.), *The Palgrave Dictionary of Transnational History*, London, Palgrave, 2009; Subrahmanyam Sanjay, *Explorations in Connected History: From the Tagus to the Ganges*, Delhi, Oxford University Press, 2004; Conrad Sebastian, *What Is Global History?*, Princeton, Princeton University Press, 2016. For a global perspective on global history, see Iggers Georg, Wang Q. Edward, & Mukherjee Supriya, *A Global History of Modern Historiography* (Second Edition), London, Routledge, 2016; and Beckert Sven & Sachsenmaier Dominic (eds.), *Global History, Globally. Research and Practice around the World*, London, Bloomsbury Publishing, 2018.
28 See, among hundreds of titles, Kjelbaek Skjell, "The Growth of International Nongovernmental Organizations in the Twentieth Century," *International Organization*, 25–3, 1971, pp. 420–442; more recently, Keck Margaret E. & Sikkink Kathryn, *Activists Beyond Borders: Advocacy Networks in International Politics*, Ithaca & London, Cornell University Press, 1998; Boli John & Thomas George M. (eds.), *Constructing World Culture. International Nongovernmental Organizations since 1875*, Stanford, Stanford University Press, 1999; Josselin Daphné & Wallace William (eds.), *Non State Actors in World Politics*, London, Palgrave, 2001; Boli John, "International Nongovernmental Organizations," in Powell Walter W. & Steinberg Richard (eds.), *The Nonprofit Sector: A Research Handbook* (Second Edition), Yale, Yale University Press, 2006, pp. 333–352; Lee Taedong, "The Rise of International Nongovernmental Organizations: a Top-Down or Bottom-Up Explanation?," *Voluntas: International Journal of Voluntary and Non-Profit Organizations*, 21–3, 2010, pp. 393–416; more in connection with the League of Nations, see Lavelle Kathryn, *Exit, Voice and Loyalty…, art. cit*; Davies Thomas Richard, "A 'Great Experiment' of the League of Nations Era: International Nongovernmental Organizations, Global Governance and Democracy Beyond the State," *Global Governance*, 18, 2012, pp. 405–423.
29 Ninkovich Frank A., *The Diplomacy of Ideas, US. Foreign Policy and Cultural Relations, 1938–1950*, Cambridge, Cambridge University Press, 1981; Berman Edward H., *The Ideology of Philanthropy: The Influence of the Carnegie, Ford and Rockefeller Foundations on American Foreign Policy*, Albany, State University of New York Press, 1983; Berghahn Volker, *America and the Intellectual Cold Wars in Europe*, Princeton & Oxford, Princeton University Press, 2001.
30 Berghahn Volker, "Philanthropy and diplomacy in the American Century," *Diplomatic History*, 23–3, 1999, pp. 393–419; Tournès Ludovic (ed.), *L'argent de l'influence. Les fondations philanthropiques américaines et leurs réseaux européens*, Paris, Autrement, 2010.
31 Parmar, *Foundations…, op. cit.*
32 Mazower, *Governing…, op. cit.*, ch. 4, p. 1 [Ebook version].

33 *Ibid.*, ch. 4, p. 3 [Ebook version].
34 Parmar, *Foundations…, op. cit.*, pp. 65–67.
35 See an example of these lenghty negotiations in Tournès, *Sciences de l'homme…, op. cit.*
36 For a more detailed discussion on this point, see Tournès Ludovic, *Américanisation. Une histoire mondiale*, Paris, Fayard, 2020.
37 Parmar, *Foundations…, op. cit.*, pp. 2–3 and 99.

References

Braumoeller Bear F., "The Myth of American Isolationism," *Foreign Policy Analysis*, 6–4, 2010, pp. 349–371.
Berghahn Volker, *America and the Intellectual Cold Wars in Europe*, Princeton & Oxford, Princeton University Press, 2001.
Berghahn Volker, "Philanthropy and Diplomacy in the American Century," *Diplomatic History*, 23–3, 1999, pp. 393–419.
Beckert Sven & Sachsenmaier Dominic (eds.), *Global History, Globally. Research and Practice around the World*, London, Bloomsbury Publishing, 2018.
Berman Edward H., *The Ideology of Philanthropy: The Influence of the Carnegie, Ford and Rockefeller Foundations on American Foreign Policy*, Albany, State University of New York Press, 1983.
Birebent Christian, *Militants de la paix et de la SdN. Les mouvements de soutien à la Société des Nations en France et au Royaume Uni, 1918–1925*, Paris, L'Harmattan, 2008.
Boli John, "International Nongovernmental Organizations," in Powell Walter W. & Steinberg Richard (eds.), *The Nonprofit Sector: A Research Handbook* (Second Edition), Yale, Yale University Press, 2006, pp. 333–352.
Boli John & Thomas George M. (eds.), *Constructing World Culture. International Nongovernmental Organizations since 1875*, Stanford, Stanford University Press, 1999.
Borowy Iris, *Coming to Terms with World Health. The League of Nations Health Organization*, Berlin, Peter Lang Publishers, 2009.
Bremner Robert H., *American Philanthropy*, Chicago, University of Chicago Press, 1988 [1960].
Caillot Marie, *La Revue Mouseion (1927–1946): les musées et la coopération culturelle internationale*, 2 vol., Paris, Ecole Nationale des Chartes, 2011.
Clavin Patricia, *Securing the World Economy. The Reinvention of the League of Nations 1920–1946*, Oxford, Oxford University Press, 2013.
Compagnon Antoine (ed.), *La République des lettres dans la tourmente (1919–1939)*, Paris, CNRS éditions, 2011.
Conrad Sebastian, *What Is Global History?*, Princeton, Princeton University Press, 2016.
Cusso Roser, "L'activité statistique de l'Organisation économique et financière de la Société des Nations," *Histoire & Mesure*, 27–2, 2012, online at: journals.openedition.org/histoiremesure/4553 (accessed August 19, 2021).
Davies Thomas Richard, "A 'Great Experiment' of the League of Nations Era: International Nongovernmental Organizations, Global Governance and Democracy Beyond the State," *Global Governance*, 18, 2012, pp. 405–423.
Decorzant Yann, *La Société des Nations et la naissance d'une conception de la régulation économique internationale*, Bern, Peter Lang, 2011.

Ducci Annamaria, "Europe and the Artistic Patrimony of the Interwar Period: The International Institute for Intellectual Cooperation at the League of Nations," in Hewitson Mark & D'Auria Matthew (eds.), *Europe in Crisis, Intellectuals and the European Idea, 1917–1957*, New York, Oxford, Berghahn Books, 2012.

Eisenberg Jaci Leigh, "The Status of Women: A Bridge from the League of Nations to the United Nations," *Journal of International Organization Studies*, 2, 2013, pp. 8–24.

Ekbladh David, "'American' Asylum: The United States and the Campaign to Transplant the Technical League, 1939–1940," *Diplomatic History*, 39–4, 2015, pp. 629–660.

Ekbladh David, "To Reconstruct the Medieval: Rural Reconstruction in Interwar China and the Rise of an American Style of Modernization, 1921–1961," *The Journal of American-East Asian Relations*, 9–3/4, 2000, pp. 169–196.

Ekmekcioglu Lerna, "Republic of Paradox: The League of Nations Minority Protection Regime and the New Turkey's Step Citizens," *International Journal of Middle East Studies*, 46–4, 2014, pp. 657–679.

Fink Carol, *Defending the Rights of Others: The Great Powers, The Jews, and International Minority Protection (1878–1938)*, Cambridge, Cambridge University Press, 2006.

Friedman Lawrence J. & McGarvie Mark D. (eds.), *Charity, Philanthropy and Civility in American History*, Cambridge & New York, Cambridge University Press, 2003.

Gemelli Giuliana (ed.), *American Foundations and Large-Scale Research: Construction and Transfert of Knowledge*, Bologna, CLUEB, 2001.

Gemelli Giuliana (ed.), *The Unacceptables: American Foundations and Refugee Scholars between the two World Wars*, Bruxelles, Peter Lang, 2000.

Ghébali Victor-Yves, "Aux origines de l'Ecosoc: l'évolution des commissions et organisations techniques de la Société des Nations," *Annuaire Français de Droit International*, 18, 1972, pp. 469–511.

Ghébali Victor-Yves, *La Société des Nations et la Réforme Bruce, 1939–1940*, Genève, Centre européen de la dotation Carnegie pour la paix internationale, 1970.

Ghébali Victor-Yves, *L'Organisation internationale du travail (L'organisation internationale et l'évolution de la société mondiale, vol.3*, Ago Roberto & Vaticos Nicolas eds), Genève, Georg, 1987.

Gram-Skjoldager Karen & Ikonomou Haakon Andreas (eds.), *The League of Nations: Perspective from the Present*, Aahrus, Aahrus University Press, 2019.

Grandjean Martin, "A Representative Organization? Ibero-American Networks in the Committee on Intellectual Cooperation of the League of Nations (1922–1939)," in Roig-Sanz Diana & Subirana Jaume (eds.), *Cultural Organizations, Networks and Mediators in Contemporary Ibero-America*, London, Routledge, pp. 65–89.

Grandjean Martin, *Les réseaux de la coopération intellectuelle. La Société des Nations comme actrice des échanges scientifiques et culturels dans l'entre-deux-guerres*. PhD dissertation, University of Lausanne, 2018.

Guieu Jean-Michel, *Le rameau et le glaive. Les militants français pour la Société des Nations*, Paris, Presses de Sciences Po, 2008.

Guieu Jean-Michel & Jeannesson Stanislas, "L'expérience de Genève (1920–1946)," in Guieu Jean-Michel & Jeannesson Stanislas (eds.), Special Issue on "La Société des Nations. Une expérience de l'internationalisme," *Monde(s). Histoire, Espaces, Relations*, 19–1, 2021, pp. 9–29.

Hathaway Oona A. & Shapiro Scott J., *The Internationalists: How a Radical Plan to Outlaw War Remade the World*, New York, Simon & Shuster, 2017.

16 *Relations between the US and the LoN*

History of the League of Nations, online at www.leagueofnationshistory.org/homepage.shtml (accessed August 19, 2021).

Iggers Georg, Wang Q. Edward, & Mukherjee Supriya, *A Global History of Modern Historiography* (Second Edition), London, Routledge, 2016.

Iriye Akira & Saunier Pierre-Yves (eds.), *The Palgrave Dictionary of Transnational History,* London, Palgrave, 2009.

Jessup Philip C., *Elihu Root,* New York, Dodd, Mead & Co., 1938 (2 volumes).

Josselin Daphné & Wallace William (eds.), *Non State Actors in World Politics,* London, Palgrave, 2001.

Keck Margaret E. & Sikkink Kathryn, *Activists Beyond Borders: Advocacy Networks in International Politics*, Ithaca & London, Cornell University Press, 1998.

Kévonian Dzovinar, *Réfugiés et diplomatie humanitaire: les acteurs européens et la scène proche-orientale pendant l'entre-deux-guerres,* Paris, Publications de la Sorbonne, 2004.

Kjelbaek Skjell, "The Growth of International Nongovernmental Organizations in the Twentieth Century," *International Organization*, 25–3, 1971, pp. 420–442.

Knepper Paul, "The Investigation into the Traffic in Women by the League of Nations: Sociological Jurisprudence as an International Social Project," *Law and History Rev*iew, 34–1, 2016, pp. 45–73.

Kott Sandrine & Droux Joëlle (eds.), *Globalizing Social Rights. The ILO and Beyond,* London, Palgrave MacMillan, 2013.

Kozma Liaz, Rodogno Davide, & Rodriguez Garcia Magaly, *The League of Nation's Work on Social Issues*, New York, United Nations Press, 2016.

Kuehl Warren F. & Dunn Lynn K., *Keeping the Covenant: American Internationalists and the League of Nations (1920–1939),* Kent, Kent State University Press, 1997.

Laqua Daniel, *Internationalism Reconfigured: Transnational Ideas and Movements between the World Wars,* London & New York, I.B. Tauris, 2011.

Laqua Daniel, "Transnational Intellectual Cooperation, the League of Nations, and the Problem of Order," *Journal of Global History*, 6, 2011, pp. 223–247.

Lavelle Kathryn, "Exit, Voice and Loyalty in International Organizations: US Involvement in the League of Nations," *International Organization*, 2, 2007, pp. 371–393.

Lee Taedong, "The Rise of International Nongovernmental Organizations: A Top-Down or Bottom-Up Explanation?," *Voluntas: International Journal of Voluntary and Non-Profit Organizations*, 21–3, 2010, pp. 393–416.

Levich Jacob, "The Gates Foundation, Ebola and Global Health Imperialism," *The American Journal of Economics and Sociology*, 74–4, 2015, pp. 704–742.

MacMillan Margaret, *Paris 1919. Six Months That Changed the World,* New York, Random House, 2001.

Mazower Mark, *Governing the World: The History of an Idea, 1815 to the Present,* New York, Penguin Books, 2013 [2012].

McAllister William B., *Drug Diplomacy in the Twentieth Century: An International History,* London, Routledge, 2000.

McCarthy Helen, *The British People and the League of Nations: Democracy, Citizenship and Internationalism, c. 1918–1945,* Manchester, Manchester University Press, 2011.

Miller Carol, "The Social Section and Advisory Committee on Social Questions of the League of Nations," in Weindling Paul (ed.), *International Health Organizations and Movements, 1918–1939,* Cambridge, Cambridge University Press, 1995, pp. 154–176.

Ninkovich Frank A, *The Diplomacy of Ideas, US. Foreign Policy and Cultural Relations, 1938–1950*, Cambridge, Cambridge University Press, 1981.

O'Malley Alanna & Jackson Simon (eds.), *The Institution of International Order: From the League of Nations to United Nations*, New York, Routledge, 2018.

Parmar Inderjeet, *Foundations of the American Century. The Ford, Carnegie and Rockefeller Foundations in the Rise of American Power*, New York, Columbia University Press, 2012.

Pedersen Susan, "Review Essay: Back to the League of Nations," *The American Historical Review*, 112–4, 2007, pp.1091–117.

Pedersen Susan, *The Guardians: The League of Nations and the Crisis of Empire*, New York, Oxford University Press, 2015.

Pemberton Jo-Anne, "The Changing Shape of Intellectual Cooperation: From the League of Nations to UNESCO," *Australian Journal of Politics and History*, 58–1, 2012, 34–50.

Pemberton Jo-Anne, *The Story of International Relations, Part One: Cold-Blooded Idealists*, Palgrave MacMillan, 2020.

Pernet Corinne, "Les échanges d'informations entre intellectuels: la conférence comme outil de coopération intellectuelle à la Société des Nations," in Vallotton François (ed.), *Devant le verre d'eau. Regards croisés sur la conférence comme vecteur de la vie intellectuelle 1880–1950*, Lausanne, Editions Antipodes, 2007, pp. 91–106.

Pernet Corinne, "Twists, Turns and Dead Alleys: The League of Nations and Intellectual Cooperation in Times of War," *Journal of Modern European History*, 12–3, 2014, pp. 342–358.

Petruccelli David, "The Crisis of Liberal Internationalism: The Legacies of the League of Nations Reconsidered," *Journal of World History*, 31–1, 2020, p. 111–136.

Rausch Helke, "The Birth of Transnational US-Philanthropy from the Spirit of War: Rockefeller Philanthropists in World War I," *Journal of the Gilded Age and Progressive Era*, 17–3, 2018, online at www.cambridge.org/core/journals/journal-of-the-gilded-age-and-progressive-era/article/birth-of-transnational-us-philanthropy-from-the-spirit-of-war-rockefeller-philanthropists-in-world-war-i/87858360A41F7F46F2AEB84AA683F95C (accessed August 19, 2021).

Rausch Helke, "US Scientific Philanthropy' in France, Germany and Great Britain: Historical Snapshots of an Interwar Panorama," in Petersen Klaus, Stewart John, & Sørensen Michael Kuur (eds.), *American Foundations and the European Welfare States*, Odense, University Press of Southern Denmark, 2013, pp. 79–103.

Rausch Helke & Krige John (eds.), *American Foundations and the Coproduction of World Order in the Twentieth Century*, Göttingen, Vandenhoeck & Ruprecht, 2012.

Renoliet Jean-Jacques, *L'UNESCO oubliée: la Société des Nations et la coopération intellectuelle, 1919–1946*, Paris, Publications de la Sorbonne, 1999.

Rietzler Katharina, "Before the Cultural Cold Wars: American Philanthropy and Cultural Diplomacy in the Inter-War Years," *Historical Research*, 84–223, 2011, pp. 148–164.

Rodogno Davide, *Night on Earth: Humanitarian Organizations' Relief and Rehabilitation Programmes on Behalf of Civilian Populations (1918–1939)*, Cambridge, Cambridge University Press, 2021.

Rodriguez Garcia Magaly, "Beware of Pity: The League of Nations Treatment of Prostitution," *Monde(s). Histoire, Espaces, Relations*, 19–1, 2021, pp. 97–117.

Rodriguez Garcia Magaly, "The League of Nations and the Moral Recruitment of Women," *International Review of Social History*, 57–20, 2012, pp. 97–128.

Rupp Leila, *Worlds of Women: the Making of an International Women's Movement*, Princeton, Princeton University Press, 1998.

Saikawa Takashi, *From Intellectual Co-Operation to International Exchange: Japan and China in the International Committee on Intellectual Co-Operation of the League of Nations, 1922–1939*, Heidelberg, Universität Heidelberg, 2014.

Saunier Pierre-Yves, *Transnational History. Theory and History*, Basingstoke, Palgrave MacMillan, 2013.

Schott Johan & Kaiser Wolfram (eds.), *Writing the Rules for Europe: Experts, Cartels, International Organizations*, London, Palgrave MacMillan, 2014.

Schroeder-Gudehus Brigitte, "La société des esprits: la coopération intellectuelle dans le cadre de la Société des Nations," in *Les scientifiques et la paix: La communauté scientifique internationale au cours des années 20*, Montréal, Presses de l'Université de Montréal, 2014.

Showan Daniel P., *United States Policy Regarding League of Nations Social and Humanitarian Activities*, PhD dissertation, Pennsylvania State University, 1969.

Sibille Christiane, "La Musique à la Société des Nations," *Relations Internationales*, 155, 2013, pp. 89–102.

Spillane Joseph F., "Global Drug Prohibition in Local Context: Heroin, Malaria and Harm," *Diplomatic History*, 2021, dhab044, https://doi.org/10.1093/dh/dhab044 (accessed August 19, 2021).

Stone David R., "Imperialism and Sovereignty: The League of Nations' Drive to Control Arms Trade," *Journal of Contemporary History*, 35–2, 2000, pp. 213–230.

Subrahmanyam Sanjay, *Explorations in Connected History: From the Tagus to the Ganges*, Delhi: Oxford University Press, 2004.

Taillibert Christel, *L'Institut international du cinématographe éducatif: regards sur le rôle du cinéma éducatif dans la politique internationale du fascisme italien*, Paris, L'Harmattan, 1999.

"The Hidden Hand: How Foundations Shape the Course of History," Special Issue of *The American Journal of Economics and Sociology*, 74–4, 2015.

The League of Nations in Retrospect, conference proceedings, Berlin & New York, Walter & Gruyter, 1983.

The League of Nations 1920–1946: Organization and Accomplishments. A Retrospective of the First International Organization for the Establishment of World Peace, New York, Geneva, United Nations Publications, 1996.

Tournès Ludovic, "American Membership of the League of Nations: US Philanthropy and the Transformation of an International Organization into a Think Tank," in Tournès Ludovic, Wertheim Stephen, & Parmar Inderjeet (eds.), *"The Birth of Global Knowledge,"* Special Issue of *International Politics*, 55–6, 2018, pp. 852–869.

Tournès Ludovic, *Américanisation. Une histoire mondiale*, Paris, Fayard, 2020.

Tournès Ludovic, "La fondation Rockefeller et la naissance de l'universalisme philanthropique américain," *Critique Internationale*, 35, 2007, pp. 173–197.

Tournès Ludovic (ed.), *L'argent de l'influence. Les fondations philanthropiques américaines et leurs réseaux européens*, Paris, Autrement, 2010.

Tournès Ludovic, *Les Etats-Unis et la Société des Nations: le système international face à l'émergence d'une superpuissance*, Bern, Peter Lang, 2016.

Tournès Ludovic, *Sciences de l'homme et politique. Les fondations philanthropiques américaines en France au XXe siècle*, Paris, Garnier, 2013 [2011].

Tournès Ludovic, "The Rockefeller Foundation and the Transition from the League of Nations to the UN (1939–1946)," *Journal of Modern European History*, 12–3, 2014, pp. 323–334.
Van Daele Jasmien, Rodriguez Garcia Magaly, Van Goethem Geert, & Van der Linden Marcel (eds.), *ILO Histories. Essays on the International Labour Organization and its Impact on the World during the Twentieth Century*, Bern, Peter Lang, 2010.
Verna Chantalle F., "Haiti, The Rockefeller Foundation and UNESCO's Pilot Project in Fundamental Education, 1948–1953," *Diplomatic History*, 40–2, 2016, pp. 268–295.
Watenpaugh Keith David, "The League of Nations' Rescue of Armenian Genocide Survivors and the Making of Modern Humanitarianism, 1920–1927," *American Historical Review*, 115–5, 2010, pp. 1315–1339.
Webster Andrew, "The Transnational Dream: Politicians, Diplomats and Soldiers in the League of Nations' Pursuit of International Disarmament, 1920–1938," *Contemporary European History*, 14–4, 2005, pp. 493–518.
Weindling Paul, "Philanthropy and World Health: the Rockefeller Foundation and the League of Nations Health Organization," *Minerva*, 35–3, 1997, pp. 269–281.
Wertheim Stephen, "The League that Wasn't: American Designs for a Legalist-Sanctionist League of Nations and the Intellectual Origins of International Organization, 1914–1920," *Diplomatic History*, 35–5, 2011, pp. 797–836.
Zanasi Margherita, "Exporting Development: League of Nations and Republican China," *Comparative Studies in Society and History*, 49–1, 2007, pp. 143–169.
Zunz Olivier, *Philanthropy in America: A History*, Princeton, Princeton University Press, 2012.

1 The United States at the Heart of the League System?

While historians have long believed that the US did not take part in the League of Nations (LoN), recent works have suggested that this notion should be revised. It is important to go even further by identifying the logic behind this participation, which requires a different perspective on two specific issues. First, the League system must be considered in its historicity as an evolving entity. Recent advances in the historiography on the LoN have revealed that the League system was permanently under construction, including many organizations created as needs and decisions arose, amid a certain empiricism and even disorder. It is in this context of gradual construction that the US role in the League system should be analyzed. In this chapter I show that this role was an important one, even though it may seem counterintuitive given that the US was not an LoN member. However, looking more closely, the changing form of the League system was largely conditioned by its attempts to integrate the US, especially by developing its technical sections. The possibility and need of integrating the US were ubiquitous throughout the interwar period in the debates surrounding the construction of the League system.

The second issue that calls for a different approach is the notion, following on recent research, that the federal government was absent, and that US participation exclusively involved private actors. It is largely based on the premise that the US government was isolationist, and private actors internationalist. While this is not entirely false, as we will see in the following chapters, it must be put into perspective, for the government also participated actively in the LoN, although its strategy was to make this involvement as informal as possible.

These two perspectives reveal that US participation in the League system resulted from the combination of three strategies: that of the LoN Secretariat, which sought to involve the US in the organization at any cost; that of the federal government, which was aware that it could not ignore the organization, and endeavored to maintain a discrete but permanent presence; and that of private actors, who believed that the US should be involved in the LoN in order to assume its *de facto* leadership role that had emerged from World War I. This final strategy will be examined in the ensuing chapters. This chapter is divided into four sections. Section One quickly presents the creation of the LoN and the debate that led to US withdrawal. Sections Two, Three,

DOI: 10.4324/9780429021213-2

and Four will examine the joint strategies of the Secretariat and the federal government to ensure US presence in the LoN's technical sections (Section Two), the International Labor Organization (ILO)[1] (Section Three), and the Permanent Court of International Justice (PCIJ) (Section Four). They show that far from being settled once and for all in 1919, the debate surrounding US participation continued throughout the LoN's history.

The Laborious Beginnings of the LoN

On December 14, 1918, Woodrow Wilson arrived in Paris to cheering crowds for the Peace Conference that opened on January 18, 1919. In an unprecedented move in US history, the president decided to lead his country's delegation personally, an unquestionable sign of expanding executive power in a country where Congress historically had preeminence in foreign policy matters. It was also the first time that a US president had visited Europe while in office. In addition to Wilson and his advisor Colonel House, the plenipotentiaries included Secretary of State Robert Lansing and two generals, accompanied by civil servants from the Department of State and a team of experts. However, the delegation did not include members of the Senate or prominent members of the Republican Party, including those who supported the creation of the LoN. Wilson would pay a steep price a few months later for going it alone and refusing to seek out allies among Republicans. Convinced that his view was correct, the president preferred filling his delegation with technical experts rather than politicians.

While negotiations between the major powers regarding territorial reshuffling and the reparations to request from defeated powers initially drew strong opposition from various actors, those regarding the creation of the LoN announced by Wilson in his Fourteen Points proceeded fairly quickly. The president made it clear from the opening of the Paris Peace Conference that the creation of the LoN was his central concern; on January 25 he secured the creation of a commission to draft a proposed charter defining its form and remit. The project sparked neither enthusiasm nor opposition among European powers. Great Britain accepted because it was aware of its relative decline and saw this as a way to conclude an alliance with the rising power of the US, namely by establishing an Anglo-American condominium over the world; France did so because it wanted to impose very harsh measures on Germany in exchange and to ensure its future security by the US. It is noteworthy that *Président du Conseil* (Prime Minister) Georges Clémenceau chose Léon Bourgeois to represent France in the Commission. A longtime supporter of creating an international organization, Bourgeois was respected by all, but he was nearing the end of his career and had no political influence; Clémenceau had little esteem for him, and gave him no specific instructions other than to cede as many points as possible in order to provide Clémenceau with arguments for requesting more during territorial and financial negotiations. In the absence of Clémenceau and Lloyd George, Wilson dominated the debates of the commission, whose work moved along quickly: less than three months passed between its first meeting on February 3, and the final adoption of the project in the Peace Conference's plenary session on April 28.

Once the Treaty of Versailles was signed on June 28, 1919, all actors turned toward the US, aware that ratification by Congress—crucial for the LoN's future—would be difficult due to the highly animated debate that unfolded in the US in the spring when Wilson was negotiating in Paris. This debate is familiar, and there is no need to linger over it here. A simple reminder of its central moments will suffice: the principle of reservations, formulated by Elihu Root in March in an open letter to Wilson; the division of Congress into four groups (those in favor of the treaty; mild reservationists; strong reservationists; irreconcilables); Wilson's catastrophic presentation of the Treaty of Versailles in Congress on July 10; the adoption of 14 reservations by the Senate Committee on Foreign Relations in September; the national tour begun by Wilson on September 3 to defend his project before the people, which ended with his stroke on the 25th; and two votes by the Senate, held on November 19, 1919 and March 19, 1920. US ratification of the Treaty of Versailles thus involved a long sequence extending nearly a year. During this time, some of the countries that planned to participate in the LoN waited for the US vote before making a final decision. From June 28, 1919, the date on which the Treaty of Versailles was signed, until the Senate's second vote, the nascent LoN had no political or legal existence, and was unable to influence European affairs, thereby giving free rein to the Allied Supreme War Council. It was generally agreed that an LoN without the US was not of any real interest, as it was clear to everyone at the time that in the absence of the US, the major powers—France and Great Britain in particular—did not need the LoN to settle European problems. Germany took advantage of the US reluctance to delay negotiations on reparations by exploiting differences of opinion between the Allies. As a result, the entire global diplomatic game was affected by the US debate, which was closely followed throughout the world.

The 1920 election campaign began immediately after the Senate's second vote. Relations between the US and the new organization were of course one of the issues but were not central to the campaign. The Democratic Party was divided between Wilson, who continued to support his project, and some of his troops, who were opposed to it. Some Republicans supported renegotiating the treaty, while the irreconcilables wanted to cut off all relations with the League. The latter won out at the Republican National Convention in June, which nominated Warren Harding as the party's candidate. He began to attack the LoN that summer,[2] rejecting outright any collaboration between the US and the organization. However, the debate was not over in the Grand Old Party, for on October 14, 2 weeks before the election, 31 Republican figures published an open letter, signed by Nicholas Murray Butler, Charles Evans Hughes, Henry Stimson, and Herbert Hoover, among others. They argued that voting Republican was the only way to save the LoN, for if the

Democratic candidate James Cox were elected, he would continue along Wilson's intransigent path, further radicalizing opposition in the Senate and thereby killing any chance of developing subsequent collaboration between the US and the League. The 31 signatories called on Harding to renegotiate the treaty if he won the election.[3] It was in connection with this debate that Root unofficially notified Harding that he wanted the next president to secure the "Americanization of the Treaty"[4] from the great powers and joined the other signatories of the letter. After his great electoral victory, Harding clearly signaled his rejection of this option by refusing to make Root his Secretary of State.

While these events were unfolding in the US, the LoN began to function as best it could. The first Council meeting was held in January 1920, and the first General Assembly in November–December. The new organization was a wholly unprecedented attempt to create an international administration with a universal mission, whose goal was to intervene in all areas that could ensure a lasting peace. Consisting of 42 member states upon its foundation, it reached a maximum of 60 in 1934, before falling to 44 in 1946 upon its official dissolution.[5] Its institutional structure consisted of three primary bodies. The first was the General Assembly of member states, which met once per year in September, and in which all countries theoretically had the same weight due to the rule of unanimity in decision-making (Article 5 of the Covenant). The second body was the Council, consisting of a more restricted group of five permanent members (the US, Great Britain, France, Italy, Japan)—which shrank to four after the US defection—and four nonpermanent members representing smaller countries, a number that rose to 10 in 1926. The major powers did not have any particular privileges, as decisions were also made by unanimity. The third and most important body was the Secretariat General, the first true international administration, which ensured the League's functioning and managed the gradual expansion of what were referred to as the League's "technical" activities. Eric Drummond of Great Britain held the position from 1919 to 1933.

The Growth of the Technical Sections

The Strategy of the Secretariat

In the aftermath of the Senate's first negative vote in November 1919, there was great consternation at the LoN. The consequences were immediately measurable by the attitude of certain states. Latin American countries, which saw the existence of the League as a potential bulwark against US expansionism, now hesitated to join an organization that would have no control over the US. Small states, which hoped that US presence in the organization would prevent the formation of new alliance systems between European powers, were also hesitant to make the leap. The Secretariat concluded that the only way to prevent the LoN from being whittled down to nothing was to secure

US participation nonetheless. In November Drummond was convinced that US membership, even with reservations, would be preferable to its abstention.[6] The Secretariat thus implemented a strategy of integrating the US at any cost. This is why Drummond continued to inform the government of the organization's activities, and used every opportunity for the US to participate in its initiatives, which increased beginning in 1920. He pursued this course of action throughout his term as Secretary General.

The centerpiece of this strategy was the development of technical activities. While peacekeeping was at the heart of the LoN's mission, its ambition was larger, as demonstrated by Article 23, which includes a series of other objectives: "to secure and maintain fair and humane conditions of labour for men, women, and children," to "secure just treatment of the native inhabitants of territories under their control" in the colonies, to ensure "general supervision over the execution of agreements with regard to the traffic in women and children," to combat "the traffic in opium and other dangerous drugs," to provide "general supervision of the trade in arms," to "secure and maintain freedom of communications" and "equitable treatment for the commerce of all Members of the League," and finally to "take steps in matters of international concern for the prevention and control of disease." However, this article was not present in the first draft Wilson submitted to his colleagues on January 8, 1919, which included just one paragraph on improving working conditions.[7] Article 23 was added at the end of the discussion and sketched out a scope of action—simultaneously very broad and very vague—that was hardly the subject of debate during the commission's meetings, a sign that it was not the central issue. Technical activities were thus initially a minor part of the LoN project.

They were nevertheless quickly prioritized by the Secretariat, which saw their development as a way to integrate the US. Many League members believed that it was only by becoming an organization of "international cooperation"[8] in various technical domains that the League would successfully attract the US, rather than by creating a system of collective security incompatible with the country's diplomatic traditions. The Secretariat consequently established a flexible procedure that initially allowed nonmember states to take part in technical activities, making it as easy as possible, especially for the US. While they were planned urgently depending on the problems emerging in the international landscape, from the mid-1920s onward they became an important part of the LoN's work, and their importance only increased during the 1930s. Their existence was the League's true originality, due to the diverse fields of intervention and their flexibility, especially with regard to the association of nonmember states, which gave them a universality that the General Assembly of member states could never claim. To circumvent the US refusal, the Secretariat built a two-stage League system: the first stage of collective security was reserved to member states; the second one of technical cooperation was open to all. The entire structure of the League system was thus adapted to allow US collaboration after it refused to ratify the Covenant.

It is difficult to establish a chronology for the appearance of technical sections, which have a complex history, often changing names and duties.[9] Their status also varied: there were first what were known as "auxiliary" organizations (Economic and Financial Organization [EFO], Communications and Transit Organization, Health Organization [HO]), in addition to "advisory commissions" both permanent (Mandate Commission, International Commission on Intellectual Cooperation [ICIC], Opium Advisory Committee) and temporary (Preparatory Commission for the Disarmament Conference, Committee of Experts for the Progressive Codification of International Law); a third type consisted of "autonomous" organizations that had their own budget and substantial independence from the LoN, such as the ILO and the PCIJ. Finally, a fourth type included "special institutions," namely organizations under national law made available to the LoN by the governments that created them, such as the International Institute of Intellectual Cooperation (IIIC) created in 1926 by the French government, the International Institute for the Unification of Private Law and the International Educational Cinematographic Institute created by the Italian government in 1926 and 1928, respectively, and finally the International Center for Leprosy Research created by the Brazilian government in 1931. All of these bodies created numerous commissions, subcommissions, and *ad hoc* committees that called on non-LoN experts to explore specific problems; some existed solely for the duration of a meeting and subsequent report, whereas others endured and accumulated considerable documentation and expertise over the years, as demonstrated by the LoN's many publications.

The Secretariat did not spare any efforts to inform the US regarding the work carried out by these sections, notably via its Information Section led by Arthur Sweetser (1881–1962), one of the eleven US members of the Secretariat between 1922 and 1937. "A tireless promoter of strengthening ties between the US and the LoN,"[10] he worked selflessly throughout the interwar period to involve the US in the organization as much as possible. This Wilsonian at the intersection of multiple worlds (the LoN administration, the philanthropic world, the federal government) had the perfect profile for an intermediary. He was a war correspondent in Europe between 1914 and 1918, and then worked at the Press service for the US Delegation to the Paris Peace Conference, which he attended in its entirety. In 1919 he was part of the team that established the Information Section,[11] designed to raise awareness regarding LoN activities. He became its Director in 1933 and remained a member until World War II. When the Senate rejected the Treaty of Versailles, he assumed the role as intermediary "between the League of Nations and the United States."[12] All matters involving the US were transferred to him, and all Americans who wanted, for one reason or another, to contact the LoN did so through his intervention. He, no doubt, spent as much time strengthening ties with the US as he did diffusing information regarding the League's activities. The work was so important that Sweetser convinced the Secretariat to hire a collaborator in 1929, his compatriot Benjamin Gerig. The two men specialized in relations with the US, and the Information Section grew as LoN activity expanded, increasing from 3 permanent members in 1919 to 19 in 1932.[13]

After the Senate's negative vote, Sweetser believed that the focus should no longer be the controversy surrounding Article 10, but rather raising awareness about the LoN's technical activities in order to show the US public the interest of participating.[14] From that point forward, Sweetser seized every opportunity to promote this *rapprochement*. He became a member of the League of Nations Non-Partisan Association as soon as it was created. In the fall of 1922 he conceived, with the agreement of the Secretariat, a plan of association between the US and the League, which provided that the US could appoint representatives to LoN meetings and conferences, and that the decisions made during these conferences could not be imposed on the US without Senate ratification. Drummond validated the plan, and in November 1922 Sweetser set out for the US to defend it before the federal government. The plan did not have any institutional outcome, but it did materialize in reality, as US representation increased in all LoN committees in the ensuing years, as we will see later.

There are other examples of his activity, such as in May 1924, when Secretary of State Charles Evans Hughes visited Geneva, and Sweetser met with him and insisted on the need for cordial relations between the US and the League; he suggested collaborating in its technical activities, if only to prevent the US from being sidelined from a global reorganization on a basis opposed to its interest.[15] Hughes was responsive to his argument but pointed out the difficult reception such a discourse would encounter among the isolationist portion of the Republican Party, and was skeptical regarding the accomplishments of the technical sections. Sweetser, who knew his issues and had anticipated the objection, cited fifteen examples of international conventions signed in connection with the LoN, on subjects as varied as labor, freedom of transit, railway traffic, ports, commercial arbitration, the white slave trade, obscene publications, etc. While Hughes was favorably impressed by the activity of the technical sections, he kept a wait-and-see attitude due to the complexity of the domestic political situation. However, the number of American civil servants participating in meetings of the technical sections increased regularly in the following years, a sign that Hughes had received the message.

The Forms of US Rapprochement

While the LoN Secretariat quickly realized that it would be difficult to function without the US, the latter also understood it could not ignore the organization, for in the early 1920s the LoN became a forum for international meetings and negotiations in various domains. The Harding administration initially burned its bridges despite last-minute attempts by the Wilson administration, which governed between the election in November 1920 and the official transfer of power to the new team on March 1, 1921. In February, when the Mandate Commission was deciding how to organize the mandate system, Brainbridge Colby, who was still Secretary of State for a few days, sent a letter to the head of the Commission insisting that the US be consulted regarding this issue. The Secretariat sent a formal invitation, but the arrival of the Harding administration in March changed things, as it refused to have any contact with the LoN. The new Secretary of State, Charles Evans Hughes, met representatives from the major colonial powers outside of the League framework and provided his agreement for the general contours of the system, as well as the establishment of mandate classes A, B, and C.[16] The Harding administration's early days were marked by the almost total absence of communication, as the federal government did not even respond to letters sent from Geneva.[17]

Yet upon closer inspection, the US quickly adopted a more flexible stance, for in the spring of 1921 it participated in the committees and conferences created by the LoN, such as the commissions working to resolve the questions stemming from the war. The Greek Refugee Settlement Commission is a good example. In addition to the emergency investment made by US philanthropic organizations, especially the Near East Relief[18] and the American Red Cross, the State Department provided modest support for LoN's involvement in the refugee question in 1923. It participated in the committee studying the conditions for a loan that would allow Greece to absorb the flow of refugees from Turkey following the Treaty of Lausanne in 1923. In the space of a few months, 1.4 million people arrived in Greece, destabilizing the small state of barely 5 million inhabitants. Following the committee's recommendations, the question was decided in the early summer during an informal meeting of the LoN Council, to which Colonel James A. Dogan, the US representative to the Reparations Commission, was invited. The conditions for the loan, to which US banks provided a substantial contribution, were specified and were later approved by an official meeting of the LoN Council, but this time without the presence of the US. The following year the Council created the Greek Refugee Settlement Commission to administer the assistance effort in connection with the loan, presided over by Henry Morgenthau, Sr. This Wilsonian was familiar with the region's problems, as he had served as ambassador to the Ottoman Empire from 1913 to 1916, before joining the US delegation to the Peace Conference, when he advised Wilson on issues in the Middle East. He presided over the Commission until 1925, when he was succeeded by his compatriot, Charles P. Howland.[19]

This was not an isolated example, as demonstrated by the case of Norman H. Davis, Wilson's, former financial advisor who later served as Under Secretary of State and who presided in 1924 over the Commission that would decide the status of the Memel Territory.[20] Other examples include the banker Jeremiah Smith, who oversaw the bank reconstruction process in Hungary between 1924 and 1926,[21] and the American James G. McDonald, who later in LoN history presided over the High Commission for Refugees from Germany, which was created in 1933 to address the problem of German refugees fleeing Nazism.

Americans were especially present in the many permanent commissions relating to technical activities, which increased beginning in 1921. They can be divided into two categories. The first consisted of what the federal government called "American citizens without a mandate,"[22] which is to say those acting on their own initiative, with no official connection to the government. This category includes the academics that were part of commissions. While they were "without a mandate," they were not disconnected from the world of government for two reasons. First, they often also worked for the federal government and were therefore familiar with its positions and could potentially defend them in committee meetings. Second, the federal government approved their appointment to LoN commissions. This practice was apparently not used early on, but in the ensuing years—and the 1930s in particular—the appointment of "citizens without a mandate" was always done with approval from the Secretary of State. When Henry Cabot Lodge submitted the draft Treaty of Versailles with 14 reservations in 1919, the seventh reservation stipulated that the Senate would have control over the appointment of all US representatives to the Council, General Assembly, and any committee or conference organized by the League. In practice, the government would never consult the Senate on this point, hence its extreme prudence and the vague designation of "citizens without a mandate."

The second category included "state or federal civil servants in a personal capacity."[23] Once again this notion is vague, poorly concealing the fact that the individuals were often senior civil servants, evidence that they were chosen carefully. While they were mostly present as observers without a right to vote, they were well acquainted with the issues and the government's positions; they contributed to the debates, and their nationality generally commanded the attention of other participants. This is the conclusion made by Ursula Hubbard, a US member of the Secretariat who conducted a study for the CEIP in the early 1930s regarding her country's participation in the LoN: "some of America's most distinguished economists have sat on the Economic Committee. While not officially representing their government, the Committee members had such close relations with it that they could accurately present trends in official economic thought."[24]

The federal government took greater interest in the LoN, beginning with the Manchurian Incident in 1931 and bolstered its presence in technical activities. A sure sign of this came in October 1931 when a "League of Nations" section appeared in the archives of the US Consulate in Geneva. This was the very beginning of the crisis, and the Secretary of State, who planned for greater collaboration with the League, suddenly began to request all possible information regarding its activities. It was now officially on the federal government's radar. In October 1931, the Consul Prentiss Gilbert provided more detailed reports on the situation in Geneva, and with support from expanded consular services, systematically informed the Secretary of State regarding all aspects of LoN activity: the General Assembly, the administration of mandates, organizational reform projects, legal matters, border disputes, the activities of all technical sections, nothing was left out. In addition to his regular correspondence with the Secretary of State, the consul sent all sorts of documents to Washington, ranging from Assembly minutes to the conventions signed in connection with the technical sections. In 1931, approximately 2,000–4,000 documents were sent in sets of six copies to the State Department, which distributed them to other departments.[25] The consul also drafted reports on technical activities, such as those in March 1931 and April 1934[26] on the IIIC, in March 1934 on the EFO,[27] or in March 1937 on the HO.[28] In addition, in October 1931 Henry Stimson asked Gilbert to provide him with an annual summary of contributions from private US organizations to the LoN, which would henceforth be punctually prepared each fall.[29] The consul also sent some of these documents to other US representations abroad: Far East legations received documentation regarding the fight against opium, as did certain federal entities such as the Public Health Service (PHS). In short, there was steady communication from 1931 onward, with LoN activities no longer being a mystery for the US government. Gilbert played a *de facto* role as the official US representative to the LoN; he almost exclusively handled LoN-related matters, with the State Department appointing a second civil servant to the consulate to handle strictly consular affairs.

The federal government even planned to make relations with the LoN official. Franklin D. Roosevelt's assumption of power in 1933 gave renewed momentum to this process. His Secretary of State, Cordell Hull, had apparently decided to proceed with a genuine *rapprochement*, aware that it was impossible to continue sending informal representatives to the LoN on the one hand, all while feigning to ignore it on the other. The absence of an official representative to the LoN at the State Department ultimately hampered the functioning of the federal government itself. Hull therefore planned, from his very arrival, to appoint a special advisor for relations with the League and to create an embassy in Geneva to maintain relations with the means to successfully respond to the intensified communication following the Manchurian Incident, which the consulate in Geneva was not equipped to handle. In August 1933, Arthur Sweetser crossed the Atlantic to meet with Roosevelt and Hull. In September the rumor spread in Geneva and the American press that the federal government was planning to create a High Commissioner of ambassadorial rank. However, things were moving too quickly for Hull, for the Roosevelt administration was in a sensitive position, needing Congressional support to pass New Deal reforms, at a time when the US was preparing to recognize the USSR. In June 1933, a delegation attended the ILO's Annual Conference, signaling potential US membership in the organization (which would come the following year).

Given these conditions, the creation of an embassy in Geneva would surely be one initiative too many, and would rekindle Republican opposition in Congress. In September Hull officially denied any project to this end,[30] although he assured Sweetser in private that he wanted to pursue the *rapprochement* process. In the spring of 1934 there were new rumors that Hull was planning to establish closer relations with the League. During a June meeting of the CEIP Board of Directors, its president Nicholas Murray Butler declared to his trustees that "one of the most prominent figures among our politicians [referring to Hull] supports joining the League of Nations. This is excellent, and marks a major change."[31] In August, the press once again reported rumors that the federal government was planning to appoint Hugh Wilson, the current Minister of the US Legation in Bern, as High Commissioner to the LoN with the rank of ambassador. This was once again denied by Hull,[32] after which the project was seemingly abandoned. The deteriorating situation in Europe after Germany's withdrawal from the Disarmament Conference in October 1933 prompted the US to take an increasingly defensive posture. The Roosevelt administration now wanted to show that it was keeping its distance from European affairs: it was being closely watched by Congress, which against Roosevelt's advice had passed a first Neutrality Act in August 1935. When Italy invaded Ethiopia at the end of the year, the State Department did not plan to send a representative to the LoN Council, as it had done in the fall of 1931 for the Manchurian crisis. In 1936, 1937, and 1939 Congress extended and expanded the Neutrality Act, once more against the advice of Roosevelt, who wanted to support France and Great Britain in the event of conflict with Germany.

Participation in Commissions

Despite this outward distance, the US had been present in the LoN's technical activities since the 1920s, with its presence even expanding in the 1930s. This was the case for the HO, whose creation was the direct consequence of the health problems left behind by World War I. As discussed above, the LoN Covenant included health issues within the new organization's scope of action in Article 23. In July 1919, the outline for an organization devoted to health was developed at the initiative of the British, a process in which the US was involved.[33] A few months later, in February 1920, a temporary Epidemic Commission was created to combat the propagation of diseases on the outer limits of Central Europe and Russia, areas that were in total chaos at the time, with combat still raging and borders not yet stabilized. The importance of the challenges involved required an organization that would be in charge of all health matters; a project for a permanent organization was created during a meeting of experts in April 1920 in London, although the US had just rejected the Treaty of Versailles and withdrawn from the process. Despite the PHS's interest in the LoN project, the State Department did not want to risk a negative vote in Congress, and followed President Harding's line of avoiding any contact with the LoN. The US withdrawal sparked the failure of the first plan for a health organization. A replacement solution was adopted in the form of a temporary Health Committee created in August 1921, assisted by a Health Section that would serve as its executive body.

The temporary Health Committee had major ambitions: combatting epidemics and

> advising the LoN on health issues; establishing closer relations between the health services of various countries; collaborating, in matters relating to protective measures for workers, with the International Labour Office; cooperating with the Red Cross and similar societies; [...] securing the conclusion of international agreements.[34]

To do so, it planned to act in three different areas: scientific research, by deepening knowledge of the etiology of diseases and developing medical statistics; prevention, by promoting the circulation of information from one country to another; and preventive medicine, by organizing the fight against epidemics. It was made permanent in 1923 as the HO, which quickly developed its activities.

While the US did not send an official representative to sit on the temporary Health Committee, the academic Charles E.A. Winslow, who was the chairman of the Department of Public Health at Yale Medical School, was present there starting in August 1921 as the representative for the International Federation of the Red Cross Societies. In December 1921, during the Conference on the Standardization of Sera and Serological Tests, the US government sent, "in a personal capacity," the surgeon Rupert Blue, who had just stepped down as the head of the PHS. This evolution was confirmed in the summer of 1922, when the temporary committee held a new health conference in Brussels. Secretary of State Charles Evans Hughes convinced Harding of the need to participate, arguing that the conference would debate port quarantine and the inspection of immigrants, two matters that were important for the US. Harding accepted sending a representative "in a personal capacity," which required no official invitation on the part of the LoN. He chose Blue's successor as the head of the PHS, Hugh S. Cumming. Like Blue, Cumming was known for his Wilsonian sympathies, but his universally recognized expertise prompted the Republican administration to renew his appointment in 1924, 1928, and 1932. He also stayed at the head of the PHS until his retirement in 1936. In January 1923, when the president of the temporary Health Committee, Thorvald Madsen of Denmark, proposed that Cumming become a member, the Secretary of State gave his approval.[35] The HO was made permanent a few weeks later, and Cumming officially returned to the Health Committee, where he would remain until 1939 and even served as its Vice President in 1937, a promotion approved by Secretary of State Hull.[36] Of the 59 individuals of various nationalities who were members of the committee between 1921 and 1939, Cumming shared the record for longevity with Madsen.[37] Many experts accompanied him during meetings on specific topics, or replaced him when he could not attend, such that the US was always represented during meetings, sometimes even better than member countries. Still, the federal government remained prudent, and was careful for this collaboration to appear informal: if Cumming was elected Vice President of the Health Committee, it was because he had been retired from the PHS since 1936. In 1937, during the reappointment of the Health Committee, Ludwik Rajchman informed the American Consulate in Geneva that he wanted the new committee's first meeting to take place in the US, in order to expand coordination between the LoN and the PHS. This request was vetoed by Hull.[38]

The US was also well represented at the EFO. In the aftermath of the war, restarting the world economy was one of the key challenges facing the major powers. However, economic matters were not included in the objectives of peace treaties, or in the LoN Covenant.[39] As with health matters, a single paragraph in Article 23 was devoted to economic issues and actually focused more on trade-related questions. During the Paris Peace Conference, suggestions to establish international economic cooperation and create an institution to regulate the world economy were rejected by the major powers, especially the US and Great Britain. Economic questions were considered strategic, and hence part of the prerogative of states, which were reluctant to exchange information regarding their industries and agriculture with neighboring countries, who were potential competitors and sometimes even enemies.

In short, the LoN Covenant hardly mentioned economic cooperation, but the economy and health-related issues quickly became a part of international events, as inflation and viruses did not stop at borders, requiring states to collectively tackle the problem. Governments quickly understood that a return to the pre-1914 order was impossible, and that the disorder resulting from the war had to be resolved globally rather than individually, with each state in its corner. The LoN therefore addressed the issue, but had more difficulty acting than in health matters due to the complexity of the economic problems involved, as well as their political implications. In fact, it took all of the 1920s to implement concerted action. The LoN did not waste any time, as the Council held a conference in Brussels in September 1920 to find solutions for the monetary disorder following the war.[40] Thirty-nine states participated, a large majority of the states and empires of the time, including the US. The results were mixed, as participants held to a line of economic orthodoxy by reestablishing prewar liberalism—especially free trade—through the suppression of price controls, a return to the gold standard to ensure stable exchange rates, and the reestablishment of budgetary stability. Yet for the first time, the Conference also introduced, albeit hesitantly, the notion of regulating the international economy through the creation of an Economic Committee and a Financial Committee.

This gave the LoN a role in organizing the international economy: the two committees included experts appointed by the governments, supervised by the Economic Section of the Secretariat, which in the late 1920s was, under the direction of Arthur Salter of Great Britain, the largest technical section (50 people in 1929). To counterbalance the major powers, which reasoned first and foremost in terms of national interest, the committees relied on experts who were supposedly guided by scientific truth rather than their government's interest. This belief in the importance of science in implementing a global order was broadly shared by the experts associated with the LoN. In practice, this position would prove difficult to uphold, as the fact that experts were part of national administrations limited their autonomy, and turned them into "negotiators in the service of their governments."[41] The committees nevertheless developed relative autonomy and established ties with the administrations of member countries as well as other international organizations. The Economic and Financial Committees quickly emerged as an international crossroads for experts in international economics, a fairly limited circle of a few hundred people at most.[42]

One of the first actions of the Financial Committee was to guide through a loan to stabilize Austrian finances. It also helped settle Greek refugees from Turkey in 1922, by helping the Greek government contract a loan for this purpose; the Committee would do the same in 1925 so that the Bulgarian government could welcome Bulgarian emigrants from Greece. In addition to these emergency measures, it undertook long-term efforts more broadly connected to the international economy. A Committee on Double Taxation and Tax Evasion was created in May 1921. The US sent the Columbia University professor Edwin R.A. Seligman,[43] even as the Harding administration was still officially ignoring the LoN. The Committee's first report came in 1923, and the first projects for international conventions were developed in 1926.

In the meantime, the Economic Committee was working on eliminating customs barriers.[44] It created commissions and organized conferences in which the US was almost always represented, such as the Conference Relating to the Simplification of Customs Formalities (October 1923), the Second General Conference on Communications and Transit (November–December 1923), the Committee of Legal Experts on Bills of Exchange (December 1926), and the Third General Conference of Communications and Transit in 1927, to which the US sent official plenipotentiary delegates for the first time. But it was especially at the Geneva World Economic Conference that international cooperation intensified, and with it US participation. Held over three weeks in May 1927, it brought together over 150 experts from 50 countries, both member and nonmember states, including the US and the USSR. One of the ideas that elicited agreement from almost all participants was that the disorganization resulting from the war, especially the restrictions on trade, was greater than material destruction. The participants thus agreed that it was imperative to "restore free trade"[45] and eliminate the "many obstacles to international commerce,"[46] customs duties in particular, through the collective, parallel, and concerted action of nations under the auspices of the LoN rather than allow individual action on the part of states. In order to put these objectives into practice, the Economic and Financial Committees were made permanent, and the EFO was created, with its subdivision into three primary committees (economic, financial, fiscal), along with the many subcommittees that would gradually be created. It would have no decision-making power but would be a place for meeting and discussion, a place for the production and exchange of knowledge between experts and administrators.

The US government quickly grasped the interest of such a creation, and immediately accepted to be part of the Economic, Financial, and Fiscal Committees.[47] The federal government appointed high-level representatives in their area of expertise, and beginning in 1933 experts who were also close to power. In 1927 the Fiscal Committee included Mitchel B. Carroll, a tax lawyer specializing in international matters that the Commerce Department sent for the effort on double taxation. He was initially present as an observer, but his involvement grew in 1930, when his administration sent him on temporary assignment and he became an employee of the Secretariat's Financial Section, a position he held until his return to the Commerce Department in 1933.[48] He nevertheless continued to sit on the Fiscal Committee until 1937, when he was succeeded by another highly qualified figure, Thomas Jefferson Coolidge, the Vice President of First National Bank of Boston and a former Under Secretary of the Treasury.[49] The first US representative to the Economic Committee was appointed in 1928 in the person of Lucius Eastman, the former President of the Merchants Association of New York, whose appointment was renewed until 1930.[50] In 1931 he was joined by a federal civil servant, Edward Eyre Hunt, an experienced economist who had served as the Secretary of the Conference on Unemployment created by Harding in 1921, and who later represented the US at the World Economic Conference of Geneva in 1927. When Roosevelt came to power in 1933, he replaced him with James Harvey Rogers, an economics professor at Yale and advisor to the new government, who remained on the Economic Committee until 1937.[51] The changes to the Committee in that year saw the appointment of another person close to Roosevelt, Henry F. Grady. He was a professor of international trade at the University of California and head of the Division for Trade Policy at the State Department since 1934. In this latter capacity he implemented the free-trade policy initiated by Hull in 1934 in connection with the Reciprocal Trade Agreement Act (RTAA).[52] Finally, between 1927 and 1939, the Financial Committee included Norman H. Davis, an industrialist who had pursued an administrative career since World War I. He had a fine understanding of international questions, having served as Wilson's financial advisor at the Paris Peace Conference, as a member of the Reparations Commission, and as a participant in all of the major postwar conferences, from the International Conference on Electrical Communication in Washington in 1920 to the London Economic Conference in 1933, in addition to the World Economic Conference in Geneva in 1927 and the World Disarmament Conference in 1932.[53] US representation was therefore highly present in all EFO components.

It was also considerably present in the many specialized subcommittees created by the EFO. This included members of the federal government or private interests in the Committee of Legal Experts on Bills of Exchange (1926), the Convention on the Execution of Foreign Arbitral Awards (1927), the Convention on the Repression of Counterfeiting (1927), the Sub-Committee on Banking Statistics (1928), the Gold Delegation (1929), in addition to committees on the exploitation of the products of the sea (1930), trademarks (1930), agriculture (1930), and economic statistics (1931). They were also present in many other conferences: indeed, in addition to the major events of Geneva in 1927 and London in 1933, the interwar period was marked by a profusion of economic and trade conferences, such as the Conference for the Abolition of Import and Export Prohibitions and Restrictions (1927), the International Conference on Economic Statistics (1928), the International Conference on Bills of Exchange (1930), and the International Conference with a View to Concerted Economic Action (1930).

The careful consideration given to its appointed representatives reflects the importance these bodies held for the US, especially with Roosevelt's arrival in office. The archives of the US Consulate in Geneva show that the federal government chose its representatives with great care, while the Secretariat did everything possible to meet its requests. The process of designating representatives for the EFO's three permanent committees was identical each time: the LoN Secretary or the director of the relevant committee asked the State Department whether it had a candidate for the position; the latter would then propose one, who was endorsed two-thirds of the time. This was the case, for example, with the nomination of Rogers to the Economic Committee.[54] The nomination could be subject to complex negotiations between the different parts of the federal government, for instance, in 1937 with Thomas Jefferson Coolidge, who was appointed following talks between the State Department and the Treasury Department.[55] However, the Secretariat would sometimes not heed Hull's suggestions, as when Drummond reappointed Mitchell Carroll to the Fiscal Committee, who was not close to the Roosevelt administration, but who knew the League machinery well, being a Secretariat member since 1930.[56]

The Americans stood out through their remarkable diligence at the meetings of the three committees, especially beginning in the 1930s. In the fall of 1933, when the composition of these committees was renewed, the Secretariat immediately sent the agendas for coming meetings to the State Department, which in turn forwarded them to the Department of Commerce.[57] Americans were aware of the importance of these meetings and diligently ensured a permanent presence. For instance, when James Harvey Rogers could not attend a meeting of the Economic Committee in November 1933, the State Department sent Jacob Viner in his stead,[58] who at the time was an instructor at the Graduate Institute of International Studies (GIIS) in Geneva. The September 1936 meeting of the Committee was especially important, as it would address the most favored nation clause, which had been central to American trade policy since the passing of the RTAA in 1934. Rogers announced to the Secretariat that he would like to have a monetary expert at his side, should such matters be discussed at the meeting. He thus came accompanied by Leo Pasvolsky, an economist from the Brookings Institution and the Division of Trade of the State Department. When specifically monetary issues were discussed at the meetings held in June and September 1937, Rogers replaced himself with Henry F. Grady.[59] When neither of them was available in December, a civil servant from the consulate attended with written instructions from Grady.[60] Beyond its anecdotal aspect, this game of musical chairs reveals the US desire to systematically attend in order to defend its positions, as well as its deliberate strategy of bringing the most qualified expert for the issue on the agenda, even if that meant replacing him at the last minute. There were similar occurrences in other committees. For example, two Americans attended the November 1933 meeting of the Fiscal Committee: the official representative Carroll, and another colleague from the Treasury Department.[61] While other countries only sent one representative to these meetings, this tactic ultimately gave the US a leading position, as the new Fiscal Committee elected in 1937 included 15 tenured members and 3 replacements, with the US being the only country with representative in both categories.[62]

The fight against drug trafficking was another area in which the US was highly involved. It was a sensitive area, as the US had been one of the primary markets of consumption since the early twentieth century. Even before World War I, the US led the fight against drug trafficking, playing an important role in the International Opium Convention signed in The Hague in 1912, the first international agreement seeking to limit the drug trade by imposing controls on producing countries. The war interrupted this emerging cooperation, and in 1919 the British broached the issue at the Paris Peace Conference, leading to the inclusion of the fight against drug trafficking in the LoN's technical missions listed in Article 23. In December 1920, the first meeting of the General Assembly created the Advisory Committee on Traffic in Opium, which became permanent in 1922; it also sent the US an official invitation to participate, which Harding refused. Despite the federal government's hostility, prohibitionist associations pressured it to participate, especially the Federal Council of the Churches of Christ in America, the American Association for University Women, and the Foreign Policy Association. This latter association established an Opium Research Committee in 1920. When Drummond once again asked Charles Evans Hughes in October 1922 to appoint an expert to the Advisory Committee on Traffic in Opium, he consulted Harding, who this time approved the appointment of the surgeon Rupert Blue.[63]

The US would henceforth be present at the committee until World War II. It defended a position of strict control over production, seeking to keep it in line with the amount needed for medical usage. This was not the position of the British, who had considerable production in their colonial empire. The Americans attended the committee meeting in May 1923, with a six-member delegation led by Stephen G. Porter, a leader of the anti-LoN branch in Congress and the Chairman of the Foreign Affairs Committee of the House of Representatives. It included Blue and a State Department representative, Edwin N. Neuville, as well as Charles H. Brent, a bishop from the Philippines and a long-standing activist against opium trafficking who had presided over the debates at the Shanghai Opium Conference organized by the US in 1909, which led to the signing of the International Opium Convention in The Hague in 1912.[64] The Americans actively participated in the committee's discussions, and Hughes even authorized Porter to join the subcommittee that would sit during the fifth session of the committee, which was tasked with drafting the resolution to be voted on by the General Assembly in September 1923. While the US delegation did not participate in the vote at the fifth session of the committee, Porter actively helped draft it. Thanks to his presence, the US successfully placed its prohibitionist position at the center of the debates. Porter also succeeded in having the committee hold a conference in November 1924. The US was heavily involved in preparing it and sent a large delegation once again led by Porter; this was the first time US representatives attended a conference organized by the LoN in an official capacity. However, Porter's prohibitionist position, which Great Britain and India refused, led to a confrontation and prompted the withdrawal of the US delegation before the end of the conference.[65] The conference continued its work, and in February 1925 delivered the International Opium Convention, which marked a step forward compared to the convention signed in The Hague, but was not ratified by the US. The conference decided to place the entire antiopium effort under LoN supervision through the creation of a Permanent Central Opium Board. This was the other reason for the withdrawal of the US, which refused to place its antiopium policy under international management; when the Secretariat asked him to send a representative for the newly created official committee in September 1928, Secretary of State Frank Kellogg refused.

The US nevertheless accepted to be part of another commission created by the General Assembly in November 1925 to study poppy farming in Persia, and to determine how other crops could replace it in an effort to dry up the market. Its management was entrusted to Frederic A. Delano, the former Vice Governor of the Federal Reserve Board. It conducted a study in Persia between March and June 1926 before submitting its report.[66] While the Persian government paid for part of the expenses arising from its work, John D. Rockefeller, Jr.'s Bureau of Social Hygiene (BSH) funded at least half of the mission.[67] Prohibitionist associations continued to act, especially the Foreign Policy Association, which conducted an investigation into the conditions of opium production and sale—notably in colonial empires—in order to base the US position on statistical data for production, which the major powers, Great Britain in particular, were reluctant to make public. It was conducted by Herbert L. May, a member of the Foreign Policy Association's Opium Research Committee.[68] The investigation, which was probably also funded by the BSH, lasted over a year and took its author to Great Britain and the Middle East; its results were published in 1927, and debated in the Advisory Committee on Traffic in Opium, before which May was heard.[69] In September 1928 when Kellogg refused to send a State Department representative to the Permanent Central Opium Board, the Foreign Policy Association used its network to have the New Zealand representatives to the LoN propose May's appointment to the committee. The Council subsequently elected him.

While May was not a federal civil servant, he immediately contacted the State Department after his appointment and kept it informed of his activity. During this time, the government continued to be present in the Advisory Committee on Traffic in Opium, albeit in a reserved manner due to Porter's intransigent position. His death in 1930 unblocked the situation, as the US adopted a more flexible stance. In 1931 it took part in the conference held in Geneva that resulted in a convention, in which countries committed to limiting production and controlling their trade, all under the authority of a third organization created for this purpose, the International Narcotics Control Board.[70] The US ratified the convention in 1932 and pressured other signatories to do so as well. The following year, when it was time to renew the composition of the Permanent Central Opium Board, the LoN Council invited the US to take part in the election. The US had to sit on the Council in order to do so. The precedent of the Manchurian crisis (during which the US sat on the Council) facilitated the procedure, and on October 12, 1933 the Minister of the Bern Legation, Hugh Wilson, sat around a table with other member states to elect a new Permanent Central Opium Board, for which May was reappointed.[71] The procedure did not spark opposition, especially due to the lack of publicity surrounding it; it was once again used in 1935, 1938, and 1939 during the Central Board's later elections. May would also be appointed to the International Narcotics Control Board, and remained in Geneva until 1939. Under his initiative, the US cooperated closely with the LoN on opium until the late 1930s.

The Social Questions Section was also marked by US presence. It was created in January 1922 to address prostitution, the publication of obscene materials, and child protection. The first LoN action in the field dates back to the International Conference on White Slave Traffic held in Geneva in June 1921. The US, which was contacted to send representatives, initially did not respond. But the following year, during the creation of the Advisory Committee on the Traffic of Women and Children, the government accepted to send Grace Abbott, the director of the Children's Bureau at the Department of Labor. She was a figure from the reform movement, who before working for the federal government was part of the settlement movement, working with Jane Addams to develop Hull House in Chicago. She later directed the Immigrant Protective League and distinguished herself in the fight for legislation governing child labor. She therefore had broad experience in the field when she joined the Department of Labor in 1917, with the management of the Children's Bureau falling to her in 1921. She used her contacts at associations combatting prostitution in major US cities, as well as those she had abroad. Her activity was in keeping with the internationalization of the network of "moral reformers"[72] that had begun to spread across the globe in the final decades of the nineteenth century. Her appointment to the Advisory Committee on the Traffic of Women and Children, where she remained until 1934, was well received by the reform movements campaigning for international engagement on the part of the federal government.

When Harding appointed her, he did not have a precise program to apply, and gave her no instructions; she therefore applied her own program, and participated actively in the committee. While she refused to be elected as its Vice President, she went well beyond what her status as an observer allowed in principle, for she voted with the representatives of member states to recommend a global investigation on prostitution in order to establish reliable statistics. Taking no notice of the delays at the State Department regarding whether to participate in the investigation, Abbott contacted private sources, especially the BSH, which granted her $75,000 in funding in 1923 to carry it out. The committee assembled to develop the program was placed under the leadership of William F. Snow, the former California Director of Public Health, and the Director of the American Social Hygiene Association at the time.[73] The committee conducted a study in 112 cities in 28 countries in Europe and the Americas, including the US, with the cooperation of the State Department and the Department of Labor, and in 1927 published a report that prompted the LoN to undertake a similar investigation for Asia in 1929. As the Department of Labor was little inclined to pay, the BSH once again funded the effort, which totaled $125,000. As done previously, a committee was created to oversee the investigation, and the Secretariat invited the US to take part, with Grace Abbott predictably being selected. The federal government also accepted the inclusion of the Philippines in the investigation. The committee visited 44 cities and ports in the Middle East and Far East between November 1930 and March 1932, providing a precise description of the traffic of women and children. Following publication of the final report, the LoN held a conference in Bangkok in February 1937, to which the State Department sent Anne Guthrie, a member of the Young Women's Christian Association of the Philippines, as representative. The process was brought to a standstill due to the deteriorating situation in the region following Japan's invasion of China.

US presence in technical sections was therefore important from the early 1920s until World War II. Intellectual cooperation, which will be discussed in Chapters 4 and 5, is another example.

US Membership in the International Labour Organization

The history of the International Labour Organization (ILO) offers an even better illustration of US participation in the League system than technical sections. Unlike the technical activities mentioned in Article 23 of the Covenant, the issue of labor was the subject of lengthy discussions during the Paris Peace Conference. It was included in the first proposal drafted by Wilson, for whom it was very important, as he saw social issues as being crucial to the Russian Revolution that had just broken out in 1917. The Wilsonian project was partly a response to the Russian Revolution: by establishing an organization specializing in labor, it sought to counter revolutionary demands and avoid the spread of Bolshevism outside Russia. That is why the original proposal stipulated that the LoN "establish and [...] maintain reasonable hours and humane working conditions for all individuals," and appoint "commissions to study the conditions of industry and labor from the international point of view and make decisions on this subject, including extending and improving the conventions in effect."[74] This original formulation would be rewritten, before ultimately being included as Article 23 of the Covenant. The issue of labor was seen as so important that on January 25 the plenary session of the Paris Peace Conference also decided to create a specific commission directed by Samuel Gompers, the president of the American Federation of Labor (AFL), and a member of the Council of National Defense created by Wilson in 1916 to coordinate war production. Gompers wanted to adopt a labor charter that would serve as a Bill of Rights of sorts for the working class, but did not support creating an international organization tasked with writing laws for working conditions.[75]

The true driving force behind the Commission on International Labour Regulation was actually the British unionist George Barnes, who was replaced in this role by the historian and member of the Inquiry James Shotwell when Gompers left the commission's presidency in April. Shotwell was favorable to a permanent organization, and used all his energy to advance the project. On April 11, the commission adopted the act creating the ILO, which became Part XIII of the Treaty of Versailles. It opens with a preamble including the essence of the Labor Bill of Rights championed by Gompers and listing its goals, especially recognition of the right to union organizing and a decent salary, the establishment of a maximum number of working hours in a workday or workweek, the introduction of union freedom, the creation of old-age and disability pensions, and the implementation of professional and technical education.[76] The rest of the act describes the operation of the ILO, which would establish social justice, the basis for international peace. While the US was not the only actor behind the creation of the ILO, it played an important role in the process. The creation was made official during the International Labor Conference that opened on October 29, 1919 in Washington. It was held in a somewhat surrealistic context, at a time when challenges to the treaty were in full swing:[77] the Senate's first negative vote came on November 19, when the conference was still in session. Woodrow Wilson, who had just recovered from his stroke, personally opened the conference on October 29,[78] before giving way to his Labor Secretary William B. Wilson, who presided until its end.

From the beginning, ILO leaders adopted a similar strategy to that of the LoN, seeking to establish ties with the US, whose absence from the ILO was even more problematic than at the LoN, for it was the world's leading industrial power. It was also a laboratory for changing relations in the world of work, especially because relations between employers and employees were diametrically opposed to those in Bolshevik Russia, and highly different from those of most European countries, where revolutionary movements were thriving in 1919. In short, the US was seemingly evolving toward a reformist model of social organization, halfway between radical conservatism and proletarian revolution. This path broadly matched both the philosophy of the ILO and the project that Albert Thomas, the first director of the International Labour Office, attempted to promote. His objective was to involve the US in the ILO's activities as much as possible.

The first manifestation of this strategy was the creation, in May 1920, of an ILO office in Washington, which would be led by Americans throughout the interwar period.[79] ILO leaders began to travel more to the US: in December 1922 Thomas crossed the Atlantic to meet with labor, employer, and philanthropist circles in order to raise awareness regarding *rapprochement*, emphasizing that the ILO was independent of the LoN, and that participation in ILO activities in no way signaled LoN membership (whereas the opposite was not true, for LoN membership automatically entailed ILO membership). This strategy of establishing distance from the Geneva-based organization irritated Secretary General Drummond. For the time being, Thomas considered his trip as a success, for the US Chamber of Commerce at one point considered sending a delegation to the next International Labor Conference, and Secretary of Commerce Herbert Hoover evoked the possibility of US membership in the ILO. None of these vague hopes materialized for the time being. During the ensuing years it was the Deputy Director of the International Labour Office, Harold Butler of Great Britain, who made these trips and pursued relations with the US, notably because of his mastery of English. During his first trip in 1926, he was more careful than Thomas not to offend Drummond, although his goal was the same: pleading the ILO's cause in union and employer circles, in an attempt to "dispel the belief that [it] is a branch of the Third International."[80] He returned there in 1929 and 1930.

Albert Thomas's strategy of *rapprochement* with the US also sought to keep the LoN as distant as possible. This was not self-evident, as the ILO was in theory subordinate to the LoN, even if only for its budget, which had to be approved by the General Assembly. The latter sought, throughout the interwar period, to limit the room for maneuver available to the ILO, with which it had a struggle over legitimacy from the very beginning. While the LoN grappled until the mid-1920s with the problems arising from ratification of the Treaty of Versailles, as well as the definition of its remit, the ILO started to work and produce results in late 1919 by developing a number of international conventions. While the ILO's room for maneuver was limited due to this relation of subordination, Thomas and Butler systematically sought to enlarge it.

On the US side, the government quickly understood that it was in its interest to participate in the ILO's commissions, as was the case with the technical sections of the LoN. The federal government was actually represented right from the beginning.[81] This was true of the Permanent Committee on Migration created in 1919, in which the US participated without interruption beginning in 1921, with the organization receiving a $6,000 subsidy from the National Bureau of Economic Research in 1925 to supplement statistics on migration. In July 1922, the government officially sent the head of the

Biochemistry Division from the Bureau of Animal Industry at the Department of Agriculture to take part in the Advisory Commission on Anthrax.[82] In 1922 the US sat on the Advisory Committee on Industrial Hygiene, which worked on occupational diseases; the academics Alice Hamilton (Assistant Professor in the Industrial Medicine Department at Harvard Medical School) and Charles E.A. Winslow (founder of the Department of Public Health at Yale Medical School) were official members of the committee and were assisted by collaborators from the Department of Labor and representatives from insurance companies. Finally, in 1927, a US representative joined the commission on indigenous labor, which focused on labor in the colonies. Experts participated in these conferences, such as in August 1930 when the federal government officially sent Albert E. Russell, Assistant Surgeon at the PHS, to the ILO's Conference on Silicosis in Johannesburg.[83] There was permanent collaboration and information exchange between the organization and the federal government. The Departments of Labor and Commerce provided their data to the International Labour Office, received its reports and publications, responded to its surveys, and provided contributions, such as when the organization sent a questionnaire to 33 countries as part of a study on labor migration, or when it collaborated with the Federal Bureau of Labor Statistics to produce a study on the cost of living in fourteen European cities commissioned by Henry Ford and supported by the Twentieth Century Fund.[84] In fact, in the late 1920s there were already close ties between the US and the ILO, as demonstrated in 1929 when a resolution at the AFL Annual Meeting asking President Hoover for unofficial American representation at the International Labour Office was almost brought to a vote.[85]

The crisis changed the ILO's mission, and bolstered its strategy of collaborating with the US. While the central goal of Albert Thomas's activity was social justice, that of his successor Harold Butler (Thomas died in May 1932) was fighting the Depression, which for the ILO meant expanded collaboration with the US. The ILO also had other, and even more urgent reasons, to seek US membership. In the early 1930s it had to ease the growing tensions within the organization, which in the eyes of its leaders threatened its very survival. The primary source of tension was its domination by European countries and the frustration of other countries, which did not have access to its governing bodies due to opposition from the major powers. Some states envisioned withdrawing from the ILO, such as Latin American countries, which during the Conference of the Pan-American Union held in December 1933 in Montevideo proposed creating a Pan-American labor organization. To counter this growing discontent, the ILO adopted an amendment to Article 393 of its constitution in 1933, which increased the number of non-European states on the Board of Directors.[86] In 1932 Harold Butler redoubled his efforts to secure US membership, which became the central issue during his term as director. He believed this membership was key for the ILO's survival, not only because the struggle against the global Depression could not dispense with the participation of the world's leading industrial power, but also because US membership would truly de-Europeanize the organization and change power relations.

For the US, the crisis also marked a turning point in its relations with the ILO, with the federal government showing increased interest in its activities. In 1931, the Department of Labor seriously considered sending an attaché to Europe.[87] At the same time, the US Consul in Geneva, Prentiss Gilbert, was asked by the State Department to send all possible information to Washington on the social legislation in effect in different countries, as well as its consequences on the cost of production. He in turn directly addressed Harold Butler to obtain this information.[88] The Department of Commerce also took interest in the ILO.[89]

The election of Franklin D. Roosevelt as President of the US in November 1932 and the implementation of the New Deal signaled the country's imminent membership. The process was initiated in the late spring of 1933, with enthusiastic participation from the US delegation at the International Labour Conference. At that time the ILO had consolidated its autonomy from the LoN and enjoyed a growing reputation, whereas the League, which was discredited due to its impotence during the Manchurian Incident, saw its reputation decline. In June 1934 Butler officially invited the US to join the ILO, an initiative that did not please the new LoN Secretary General, Joseph Avenol, who was not consulted and saw it as a real snub, as the LoN had never succeeded in securing US membership. The Roosevelt administration spared no efforts to make this invitation a reality. Frances Perkins, the Secretary of Labor, and Francis B. Sayre, the Under Secretary of State, launched a lobbying campaign among members of Congress and with public opinion, insisting that membership would promote the implementation of the New Deal. In June 1934 Congress responded to the invitation with a positive vote. The administration was prudent, choosing a procedure that was less risky than the one reserved for traditional treaties: it requested ratification via a joint congressional resolution that required only a simple majority in Congress. This was easily secured, as it passed in the House of Representatives by a large majority, and garnered unanimous support in the Senate.[90]

The question arises as to why the Roosevelt administration was so eager to finalize this membership, and why it received such a large majority at a time when the US rejected any idea of LoN membership and when the membership process for the PCIJ—which was also underway at the time and hardly attracted the president's interest—proceeded via the much riskier procedure of a treaty that culminated with the Senate's rejection in January 1935. It is clear that between the membership to these two institutions, Roosevelt chose the first, with his reasons for doing so being connected to the domestic situation rather than his internationalist opinions. It appears that membership was closely linked to implementation of the New Deal, whose first measures took effect in March 1933, including those designed to combat unemployment, restart the economy, and bolster purchasing power by raising salaries in particular, especially via the National Industrial Recovery Act of May 1933.[91]

Roosevelt and his team were aware that these measures would increase the cost of labor; if similar measures were not taken in other countries, the US industry would become less competitive in relation to its European competitors. Incidentally, an increase in salaries—and hence in standard of living—in European countries would be beneficial for the US industry, which would see its export opportunities increase. Roosevelt's team saw the international harmonization of standards of living and social legislation as a *sine qua non* for the US to emerge from the crisis. As the harmonization of international standards for working conditions had been central to ILO activity since its creation, membership would allow the US to influence this process, especially to harmonize standards of living upward rather than downward. In late 1933 this reasoning became the leading argument of Frances Perkins, who advocated membership with Roosevelt.[92] At this time the International Labour Office was debating a convention making the 40-hour workweek the universal standard to be reached by all countries.[93] Perkins believed that such a convention would intrinsically increase the cost of labor throughout the world, and thus preserve the competitiveness of US industry. From this point of view, ILO membership was no doubt the first sign of a voluntarist strategy of internationalizing US standards of living, with the Marshall Plan and the developmental aid policy crafted after 1945 by the federal government's New Dealers representing the next steps.

For all that, interpreting ILO membership as part of a strategy to export the American way of life only provides a partial explanation. For even before serving as a sounding board for New Deal principles, the ILO was clearly seen by the Roosevelt administration as a way to give them legitimacy in the eyes of Americans, at a time when they were highly contested domestically. While the US was the industrialized country with the highest standard of living, it also lagged behind in terms of social legislation. This was true of both union rights and social insurance, due to the reluctance of employers and the country's federal structure, in which social legislation was a matter for the states, which did not want to lose competitiveness by implementing measures that would drive companies away to neighboring states. While employee rights came to the forefront in the mid-1910s due to tragic events, for which the Ludlow Massacre remains the symbol, it did not translate into legislation. It was the crisis and the implementation of the New Deal that once again made them a key concern for the federal government. Still, when the government wanted to enact measures to raise salaries, increase union rights, and expand unemployment insurance, it was met with opposition from employers, who served as a headwind for the New Deal's philosophy.

With this in mind, ILO membership was the first sign of Roosevelt's desire to renew social relations at a time when the measures for the Second New Deal had not yet been passed (they would be in the spring of 1935). Joining the organization would attest to the federal government's support for a philosophy of social justice as defended by the ILO since its very beginnings, one that had been rejected by Roosevelt's predecessors. Membership had another advantage for the president: it was a symbolic gesture toward the AFL, which was wary of him, but whose support he needed for the New Deal. By promoting it as the representative organization for US unionism at the ILO, Roosevelt also probably tried to bolster its legitimacy, which was being challenged by some of its members, who would break with it and found the Congress of Industrial Organizations (CIO) in 1938. Membership also reflected Roosevelt's stance of promoting independent unionism, a solution long advocated by the ILO, and a repudiation of the principle of company unions defended by some US employers. This stance was confirmed in 1935 by a leading measure of the Second New Deal, the National Labor Relations Act (Wagner Act) passed in July 1935, which affirmed the right of workers to unionize and the duty of the state to respect this right. In a few years this law gave rise to mass unionism, as the number of unionized employees rose from three million in 1933 to nine million in 1939. While ILO membership was not responsible for this increase, it helped legitimize the principle of independent unionism among the American population. The relevance of Roosevelt's strategy was emphasized by some observers, who during the debate preceding US membership stressed that the creation of the ILO and its convention-based activity coincided with a decrease in labor conflict and strikes between 1919 and 1929,[94] thereby lending legitimacy to the organization's activity in the eyes of Americans.

Membership brought an immediate sea change within the League system. It gave greater legitimacy to the ILO in relation to the LoN, to which the US had clearly indicated it would not join. More generally, it gave greater importance to the technical organizations within the League system, to the detriment of the General Assembly, which was sinking into discredit. Finally, it strengthened the ILO's financial independence, for it came with a financial contribution that was as substantial as Great Britain's[95]—but did not depend on the LoN's Fourth Commission to approve the ILO's budget—in an effort to avoid any organic link between the US and the League. In other words, one could see US membership as a turning point in the ILO's organizational evolution, and especially as an important step toward its financial autonomy, a disposition that did not exist in 1919 but that would be established with the creation of the UN system in 1945.[96]

The first concrete consequence of membership was the arrival of US civil servants in the organization. The President had a completely free hand in making these appointments: as the congressional resolution relating to membership was silent on the subject, Roosevelt appointed those whom he saw fit, without consulting with the Senate.[97] In April 1935 when Germany's departure from the ILO took effect and left a vacancy for the Deputy Director of the International Labour Office, Roosevelt named John G. Winant, who had just completed his term as the Governor of New Hampshire, and who despite being a member of the Republican Party was close to Roosevelt's ideas and well-acquainted with social issues. His trial by fire came during the International Labor Conference, which voted on the convention that made the 40-hour workweek the universal objective. The US delegation played an important role in this vote.[98] Winant did not stay at the ILO for very long. In August 1935 Roosevelt signed the Social Security Act, with a Social Security Board being created to implement it, and Roosevelt calling on Winant to serve as its president. He resigned two years later to once again take his position as Deputy Director of the International Labour Office. When Butler completed his term in late 1938, Winant succeeded him at the head of the International Labour Office. His arrival translated into greater US influence, for throughout his term (1939–1941) the director made very few important decisions without consulting the State Department,[99] thereby breaching the principle of independence that had been methodically maintained by Thomas and Butler.

The Permanent Court of International Justice

Along with the ILO, the PCIJ was the other organization of the League system that had autonomy from the LoN. Its creation was provided for in Article 14 of the Covenant. Unlike the Permanent Court of Arbitration (PCA) founded in 1899, which actually involved the creation of *ad hoc* courts based on the disputes arising between states, the new institution had to be truly permanent and include full-time judges: its role would not be one of finding compromise between two countries during a dispute, but formulating rules of international law applicable to all. Finally, it would issue decisions on questions referred by the LoN Council or General Assembly, thereby making it a central piece of the League system.

The Secretariat also did everything in its power for the US to join. It was with this in mind that a few days before the Senate's second vote Drummond invited Elihu Root to join the Committee of Jurists preparing the court's Statute.[100] In addition to Root's universally recognized expertise, the move was designed to win over US internationalists hostile to the LoN in its current form, but who were favorable to international cooperation based on law. Root hesitated but accepted, while the State Department completely lost interest in the matter.[101] He left for Europe in June to contribute to the Committee of Jurists, assisted by James Brown Scott, the Director of the CEIP's Division of International Law and the Secretary of its Board of Directors, of which Root was the president. The two men did not have a government mandate but were acting as private citizens, with their travel expenses being paid by the CEIP.[102]

Root played an important role in drafting the statute, although his influence has sometimes been overestimated.[103] In particular, he was behind three major provisions adopted by the Committee of Jurists. The first was the adoption of the principle of compulsory arbitration. From the committee's very first meeting, he insisted that this principle, which had already been affirmed during the Second Hague Conference in 1907, serve as the starting point for the discussion, with his colleagues approving. The second point was the process for electing judges, which he helped sketch out with his British colleague Lord Phillimore. The two men proposed that the court include 15 judges elected from a list proposed by the PCA, for which each state would indicate four nationals. Each of these four-person national groups could then propose four names in turn, with only two being nationals from their state. The LoN Council and Assembly would elect judges from the final resulting list with absolute majority voting. Finally, the third point where Root had important influence was the Committee adopting the principle of a Third Hague Conference to codify international law.

However, the project of the Committee of Jurists did not receive unanimous support, which derailed the Secretariat's strategy. The principle of compulsory arbitration was met with opposition, especially on the part of the British, while the project for a conference to codify international law was not popular within the Secretariat, as Drummond believed the resulting rules would undermine the legitimacy of the Treaty of Versailles, and thereby the authority of the LoN. There were many members of the Secretariat— Wilsonian Americans in particular—who suspected Root was turning the Court into an organization tailored-made for the US, one that would ultimately short-circuit the LoN. It was surely to dispel such suspicions that Root publicly declared in August that the Court would not be able to uphold the international system on its own, and that it must be backed by the LoN.[104] The Secretariat indicated that the unitary nature of the League system was non-negotiable, and refused the principle of such a conference. In December 1920 the LoN Assembly came to a decision on the plan proposed by the Committee of Jurists. It ratified the proposed election mechanism but refused two elements. The first was the principle of compulsory arbitration, which the British managed to replace with a clause allowing states not to adhere to this principle (it would become Article 36 of the Court's Statute). The second was the convening of a conference to codify international law. However, the General Assembly adopted a provision allowing a state that was not an LoN member to join the Court, a provision that—in the very words of the recorder of the Third Commission of the General Assembly—"signifies the United States could adhere to the Statute."[105] For this vote the General Assembly reaffirmed the unitary nature of the League system and the LoN's preeminence over the Court, all while opening a path for US membership to the latter.

But Harding, who had been elected a month earlier, did not share this logic of *rapprochement*. In the spring of 1921 he forbade US judges at the PCA, of which Root was a member, from proposing candidates for the new Court: when the Secretariat officially addressed them, they were required to refuse. But the Secretariat found another solution, as Harding's measure did not prevent other states from proposing US candidates on their list of four names. Five countries thus transmitted to the Secretariat a list including Root, who nevertheless declined the opportunity to join the Court. He had personal reasons for doing so, as accepting would involve settling in Europe, which the 76-year-old gentleman did not want to do. However, his legitimacy in the Republican Party was also a consideration, as this nomination would put Root in a difficult position with the Harding administration.[106] When informed of the refusal, the countries that had put him on their list chose the other US judge at the PCA, John Bassett Moore. The election of judges by the General Assembly and the Council took place in September 1921. Moore was among those elected, and sat on the Court until his retirement in 1928. The Secretariat's strategy had partially succeeded: it did not secure US participation, but a US judge was elected nevertheless. This would be the case throughout the interwar period, for when Moore retired, he was replaced by the former Secretary of State Charles Evans Hughes, who remained there until 1930, when he returned to the US to serve as the Chief Justice of the Supreme Court. His successor at the Court would be Frank Kellogg, who had also succeeded him at the State Department, and who would remain in The Hague until 1935. Finally, Manley O. Hudson was appointed in 1936, and remained in this post until 1946, when the PCIJ became the International Court of Justice. The activity of these judges has not yet been studied in detail, although their very presence bears witness to US involvement in the development of international law during the interwar period.

The court met for the first time in January 1922, and began its activity immediately. That same year, the Secretariat continued to work with its US representatives on a strategy for the US to join the Court. Moore and Hudson developed a project to this end. Hudson had contributed to the LoN Covenant before joining the LoN's Legal Section in August 1919, while also serving as a professor at Harvard University. He held the two positions until 1922, after which he only spent the summer months in Geneva until 1933.[107] In August 1922 Moore and Hudson submitted a project to Drummond consisting of four proposals: (1) that the US be represented during the debates preceding the election of judges by the Council and the General Assembly, even if it did not vote; (2) that US judges at the PCA take part in designating candidates; (3) that the US could, at any moment, withdraw from its membership in the Court; and (4) that its membership in the Court does not entail membership in the LoN.[108] In short, they developed an exceptional made-to-measure status for the US. The project, which was approved by Drummond, was sent to the State Department in September, with triangular negotiations being held in the ensuing weeks between the Secretariat, the US government, and the British government.

In September 1922 Root submitted a project to Drummond that would circumvent Senate approval via the procedure of executive agreement, which allowed the president to transpose into US law an agreement signed with another country without the required two-thirds Senate majority to ratify a treaty. Root's plan was to have the LoN Council and General Assembly officially invite the US to participate in electing judges, and then sign an executive agreement with the President that would be presented to Congress, where it would only need a simple majority to pass. This proposal ran into problems: first, Drummond believed that circumventing the Senate would weaken the agreement's legitimacy; second, the LoN Legal Section vetoed it, as it believed that the election of judges was reserved for LoN member states, and US participation in the election would entail an amendment of the Covenant.

President Harding softened his stance in February 1923, and indicated he was ready to submit the Court's Statute to the Senate in accordance with the normal procedure for ratification. He was isolated within his own party, as the repeated scandals of his early term left him in a difficult position, while the midterm elections in November 1922 sent an even more isolationist Republican majority to Congress. The division within the Republican Party was always stark between internationalists (Root, Hughes, Butler, Hoover, Taft) and isolationists, who were led by Henry Cabot Lodge. To preserve the party's unity, Harding reversed course in June, suddenly asking, as a precondition to ratification, that the Court and the League become two totally separate entities, a solution that would involve a global renegotiation of the Covenant unacceptable to the Secretariat. He died two months later of pneumonia contracted during a trip to Alaska.

From that point forward, the ratification process for the Court's Statute got bogged down, a victim of divisions within the Republican Party as well as a lack of coordination among internationalist circles. It was not until January 1926 that Harding's proposal from February 1923 came to a vote in the Senate. As was the case with the passage of the Treaty of Versailles, the vote included conditions, which were taken from the Moore-Hudson project, and made even further exceptions by requesting that the Court's Statute not be changed without US consent and especially that the Court not hear a case involving the US without the latter's agreement.[109]

Immediately after the vote, the federal government submitted the decision to the Court's member states, and a conference was held in September 1926 by the signatories to examine the US proposals. The US government refused to attend, to avoid giving the impression that it was participating in a conference organized by the LoN. After discussion, the conference accepted the first proposals, and revised the Statute to establish equality among its members: the ability to withdraw from the Court at any time was henceforth available to all members. However, participants were reluctant to accept that the court consults the US before issuing a judgment on an international dispute involving the country, believing that this would impinge upon the independence of judges. Dissatisfied by the conference's response on a point it deemed crucial, the Coolidge administration suspended the membership process.

It took until the signing of the Kellogg-Briand Pact in August 1928 for the federal government to accept the resumption of negotiations. A Committee of Jurists was created in January 1929, with Root among its members. It provided its conclusions in August, and a second conference of signatories was held in September, which adopted a slightly different Statute than that of 1926: the article on disputes involving the US was watered down, as it provided for consultations between the Council and the US government to determine whether US interests would truly be affected in the relevant disputes.[110] Overall, the US got what it wanted, as the act gave it latitude to participate in the Court's activities, but to withdraw if the least decision went against its interests. In other words, the Secretariat made all of the necessary concessions to provide the US with a made-to-measure Statute. The agreement was immediately adopted by the LoN General Assembly, and then signed by President Hoover in December 1929. However, ratification would once again get bogged down, for a number of reasons. First, the economic crisis relegated foreign issues to the background of US policy. Second, in 1932 the federal government initiated the membership process for the ILO, and simultaneous membership in the Court risked giving the impression that the US was joining the League system, thereby reviving the anger of isolationists. Third, the new Secretary General in July 1933, Joseph Avenol, was in less of a hurry than Drummond to secure US membership. Finally, the League's growing discredit starting in 1932 tempered internationalist ardor in the US, including among Democrats. As a result, despite the large Democratic victory in the November 1934 midterm elections, the Senate rejected Court membership in January 1935, with seven votes lacking for the two-thirds majority. Despite its many attempts, the Secretariat never succeeded in having the US join.

Conclusion

While the failure to ratify membership in the Court clearly shows the limits of US participation in the League system, it should not overshadow an important fact: even though the US passed neutrality laws in the mid-1930s, and manifestly distanced itself from the LoN's political bodies, it was in reality increasingly present in the League system, with its presence continuing to grow until the late 1930s, as we will see in Chapter 6. Its increasingly deep involvement ran parallel to the organization's political discredit and the development of its technical activities, which in the 1930s became central to LoN activity. This chronology shows that the development of technical activities was closely linked to US presence, not only because the Secretariat developed them to promote US integration, but also because the US made decisive contributions to their development, especially through the support of private actors, notably philanthropic foundations, which we will now examine.

Notes

1 The acronym ILO will be used for the International Labour Organization. In order to avoid confusion, the International Labour Office will be designated by its full name rather than its acronym, which is also ILO.
2 Fosdick to Sweetser, August 26, 1920, AS-LOC 31.
3 Berdahl Clarence A., "The United States and the League of Nations," *Michigan Law Review*, 27–6, 1929, p. 620.

4. *Ibid.*, p. 413.
5. Walters Francis P., *A History of the League of Nations*, New York, Oxford University Press, 1952, pp. 64–65.
6. Drummond to Fosdick, November 22, 1919, RBF-PU 1/2.
7. Link Edward S. (ed.), *The Papers of Woodrow Wilson*, vol. 53 (November 9, 1918–January 11, 1919), Princeton, Princeton University Press, 1986, pp. 655–687.
8. Deibel Terry, *Le Secrétariat de la Société des Nations et l'internationalisme américain*, Washington, Carnegie Endowment for International Peace, 1972, p. 46.
9. For a more precise description, see Ghébali Victor-Yves, "Aux origines de l'Ecosoc: l'évolution des commissions et organisations techniques de la Société des Nations," *Annuaire Français de Droit International*, 18, 1972, pp. 469–511. See also the *League of Nations Yearbook*, Genève, 1920–1927, 1931, 1936, 1938.
10. Ostrower Gary B., "American Ambassador to the League of Nations-1933: A Proposal Postponed," *International Organization*, 25–1, 1971, p. 53.
11. Sweetser to Drummond, 1929, Arthur Sweetser personal file, LON S889. As the documents of the League of Nations are in English and French, the references in this book are in both languages, depending on the language of the original document consulted.
12. Pierre Comert (Director of the Information Section) on Sweetser, November 30, 1923, Arthur Sweetser personal file, LON S889.
13. Gilbert to Stimson, September 23, 1932, NARA RG 84/415.
14. Deibel, *Le Secrétariat…, op. cit.*, p. 56.
15. Arthur Sweetser, Interview with Secretary Hughes, May 1924, AS-LOC 32.
16. Berdahl Clarence A., "International Affairs: Relations of the United States with the Council of the League of Nations," *American Political Science Review*, 26–3, 1932, p. 498.
17. Ninkovich, *The Wilsonian Century…, op. cit.*, p. 90.
18. Rodogno Davide, "Beyond Relief in the Near East. The Ideology and Practices of an American Humanitarian Organization in the Aftermath of the First World War," *Monde(s). Histoire, Espaces, Relations*, 5, 2014, pp. 45–64.
19. Hubbard Ursula, *La collaboration des Etats-Unis avec la Société des Nations et l'Organisation internationale du travail, des origines à 1936*, Paris, Centre européen de la dotation Carnegie, 1937, p. 684.
20. Norman H. Davis Papers, Library of Congress, lcweb2.loc.gov/service/mss/eadxmlmss/eadpdfmss/2012/ms012065.pdf, accessed August 30, 2021.
21. Peterecz Zoltan, *Jeremiah Smith, Jr. and Hungary 1924–1926. The United States, the League of Nations, and the Financial Reconstruction of Hungary*, Berlin & New York, Walter & Gruyter, 2013.
22. Hubbard, *La collaboration…, op. cit.*, p. 673. This book was based on State Department archives. The categories mentioned in the following pages are those used by the federal government.
23. *Ibid.*, p. 673.
24. *Ibid.*, p. 775.
25. Distribution of documents, 1931, NARA RG 84/405. The list is 400 pages long, with each page containing up to 10 items.
26. Gilbert to Hull, April 16, 1934, NARA RG 84/442.
27. Gilbert to Hull, March 7, 1934, NARA RG 84/441.
28. Gilbert to Hull, March 20, 1937, NARA RG 84/496.

29 Gilbert to Stimson, December 9,1931, NARA RG 84/404; Gilbert to Stimson, January 6, 1932, NARA RG 84/416; Gilbert to Hull, January 31, 1934, NARA RG 84/437; Gilbert to Hull, January 29, 1935, NARA RG 84/452.
30 Ostrower, *American Ambassador...*, *art. cit.*
31 Meeting of the Administrative Board of the European Centre, June 18, 1934, CEIP III/105/3.
32 *Journal de Genève*, August 14, 1934; *New York Herald*, August 14, 1934, BIT XR61/1/3.
33 Showan Daniel P., *United States Policy Regarding League of Nations Social and Humanitarian Activities*, PhD dissertation, Pennsylvania State University, 1969, p. 41 sq; on the beginnings of the Health Organization, see also Borowy Iris, *Coming to Term with World Health. The League of Nations Health Organization*, Berlin, Peter Lang Publishers, 2009, ch. 1.
34 SDN. Section d'Information. *L'Organisation d'hygiène de la Société des Nations*, Genève, 1923, p. 10.
35 Showan, *United States Policy...*, *op. cit.*, p. 49.
36 Gilbert to Hull, January 27, 1937, NARA RG 84/496.
37 See the complete list of its members in Borowy, *Coming to terms...*, *op. cit.*, pp. 470–471; it appears that Cumming joined the Committee in 1923 (Showan, *United States Policy...*, *op. cit.*, p. 49), and not 1924 as mentioned in Borowy.
38 Gilbert to Hull, January 21, 1937; Hull to Gilbert, February 3, 1937, NARA RG 84/496.
39 Halperin Jean, "La conférence économique internationale de 1927," in *The League of Nations in Retrospect*, Berlin & New York, Walter & Gruyter, 1983, p. 343.
40 Mouton Marie-Renée, "Société des Nations et reconstruction de l'Europe: la conférence de Bruxelles (24 septembre-8 octobre 1920)," *Relations Internationales*, 39, 1984, p. 325.
41 Farquet Christophe, "Expertise et négociations fiscales à la Société des Nations, 1923–1939," *Relations Internationales*, 142, 2010, p. 8.
42 Bussière Eric, "L'Organisation économique de la SdN et la naissance du régionalisme économique en Europe," *Relations Internationales*, 75, 1993, p. 303.
43 The Relations between the United States of America and the League of Nations under the Harding Administration, anonymous, July 1922, AS-LOC 31.
44 Dennery Etienne, *Le nationalisme économique contemporain*, Institut des hautes études internationales et Centre européen de la dotation Carnegie, 1932.
45 SDN, Conférence économique internationale, Genève, 1927, Rapport définitif, Genève, mai 1927, p. 13.
46 *Ibid.*, p. 9.
47 Clavin Patricia, *Securing the World Economy. The Reinvention of the League of Nations 1920–1946*, Oxford, Oxford University Press, 2013, p. 38.
48 Mitchell Benedict Carroll, League of Nations Search Engine (LoNSEA), www.lonsea.de/pub/person/5121, accessed August 30, 2021.
49 Gilbert to Hull, June 24, 1937; Hull to Bukknell, September 6, 17, and 23, 1937, NARA RG 84/493.
50 Hubbard Ursula, *La Collaboration...*, *op. cit.*, p. 584.
51 James Harvey Rogers Papers, Yale University Library, archives.yale.edu/repositories/12/resources/4463, accessed August 30, 2021.
52 Henry F. Grady Papers, Harry S. Truman Library & Museum, www.trumanlibrary.gov/library/personal-papers/henry-f-grady-papers, accessed August 30, 2021.

53 Norman H. Davis Papers, Library of Congress, findingaids.loc.gov/db/search/xq/searchMfer02.xq?_id=loc.mss.eadmss.ms012065&_faSection=overview&_faSubsection=did&_dmdid=, accessed August 30, 2021.
54 Gilbert to Hull, September 14, 1933; Hull to Gilbert, September 23, 1933; Gilbert to Hull, October 12, 1933, NARA RG 84/428.
55 Gilbert to Hull, June 24, 1937; Hull to Bukknell, September 6, 17, and 23, 1937, NARA RG 84/493.
56 Drummond to Gilbert, May 22, 1933; Gilbert to Hull, May 26, 1933; Hull (Philipps acting) to Gilbert, June 9, 1933; Hull to Gilbert, September 20, 1933, NARA RG 84/426; Gilbert to Hull, January 19, 1934, NARA RG 84/441.
57 Gilbert to Hull, October 30, 1933, NARA RG 84/428.
58 Hull to Gilbert, November 6, 1933, NARA RG 84/428.
59 Henry Grady report sent to Hull by Gilbert, June 16, 1937, NARA RG 84/493.
60 Hull (Welles acting) to Bukknell, November 8, 1937; Bukknell to Hull, November 9, 1937; Hull to Bukknell, November 18, 1937, NARA RG 84/493.
61 Gilbert to Hull, November 6, 1936, NARA RG 84/482.
62 Financial Committee list of members sent to Hull, October 8, 1937, NARA RG 84/493.
63 Showan, *United States Policy...*, op. cit., p. 226.
64 Lowes Peter D., *The Genesis of International Narcotics Control*, Geneva, Droz, 1966, p. 97.
65 McAllister William B., *Drug Diplomacy in the Twentieth Century: An International History*, London, Routledge, 2000, pp. 50–78.
66 SDN. Commission d'enquête sur la production de l'opium en Perse. Rapport au Conseil, Genève, 1926.
67 DeNovo John A., *American Interests and Policies in the Middle East, 1900–1939*, Minneapolis, University of Minnesota Press, 1963, p. 288.
68 Anslinger Harry J., "Herbert L. May," *Bulletin on Narcotics*, 15–2, 1963, pp. 1–7, www.unodc.org/unodc/en/data-and-analysis/bulletin/bulletin_1963-01-01_2_page002.html, accessed August 30, 2021.
69 SDN. Commission consultative du trafic de l'opium et autres drogues nuisibles. Procès-verbal de la dixième session (extraordinaire), 28 septembre-8 octobre 1927, p. 36.
70 *Annuaire de la Société des Nations*, Genève, Payot et Cie, 1936, p. 170.
71 Showan, *United States Policy...*, op. cit., p. 284.
72 Tyrrell Ian, *Reforming the World: The Creation of America's Moral Empire*, Princeton, Princeton University Press, 2010.
73 Limoncelli Stephanie A., *The Politics of Trafficking. The First International Movement to Combat the Sexual Exploitation of Women*, Stanford, Stanford University Press, 2010, p. 77.
74 Conférence des préliminaires de paix. Commission de la Société des Nations, première séance du 3 février 1919, annexe I: projet de Pacte.
75 Tillman Seth P., *Anglo-American Relations at the Paris Peace Conference of 1919*, Princeton, Princeton University Press, 1961, p. 305.
76 Miller Spencer, Jr., "American Labor's Relation to the International Labor Organization," *Annals of the American Academy of Political and Social Science*, 166, 1933, pp. 155–161.
77 Tortora Manuela, *Institution spécialisée et organisation mondiale: étude des relations de l'OIT avec la SdN et l'ONU*, Bruxelles, Bruylant, 1980, p. 57.

78 Myers James, "American Relations with the International Labor Office, 1919–1932," *Annals of the American Academy of Political and Social Science*, 166, 1933, pp. 135–145.
79 Hidalgo-WeberOlga, *La Grande-Bretagne et l'Organisation internationale du travail (1919–1946). Une nouvelle forme d'internationalisme*, Louvain-la-Neuve, Academia—L'Harmattan, 2017.
80 Butler to Pinckney S. Tuck (American Consulate, Geneva), September 16, 1926, BIT XR 61/1/3.
81 See the complete list in Myers, *American Relations…, art. cit.*
82 Berdahl Clarence A., "Relations of the United States with the Assembly of the League of Nations," *The American Political Science Review*, 26–1, 1932, pp. 99–112.
83 Myers, *American Relations…, art. cit.*
84 Hanna Hugh S., "The International Cost-of-Living Inquiry," *Annals of the American Academy of Political and Social Science*, 166, March 1933, pp. 162–167; de Grazia Victoria, *Irresistible Empire: America's Advance through Twentieth Century Europe*, Cambridge, Harvard University Press, 2005, pp. 75–95.
85 Miller, *American…, art. cit.*
86 Hughes Stephen & Haworth Nigel, "A Shift in the Centre of Gravity: The ILO under Harold Butler and John G. Winant", in Van Daele Jasmien, Rodriguez Garcia Magaly, Van Goethem Geert & Van der Linden Marcel (eds.), *ILO Histories. Essays on the International Labour Organization and its Impact on the World During the Twentieth Century*, Bern, Peter Lang, 2010, p. 294.
87 Gilbert to Butler, February 5, 1931, BIT XR 61/1/3.
88 Gilbert to Butler, February 6, 1931, BIT XR 61/1/3.
89 Gilbert to Butler, February 6, 1931, BIT XR 61/1/3.
90 Ostrower Gary, "The American Decision to Join the International Labor Organization," *Labor History*, 16–4, 1975, p. 501; *The United States and the International Labor Organization (1889–1934)*, PhD thesis, Fletcher School of Law and Diplomacy, Tufts University, 1960.
91 Patel Kiran Klaus, *The New Deal. A Global History*, Princeton, Princeton University Press, 2016.
92 Ostrower, *The American Decision…, art. cit*, p. 499.
93 The convention would be adopted by the International Conference of Labor in 1935 ("Bureau international du travail," *Bulletin Officiel*, 20–3, 13 août 1935, p. 73).
94 Ratzlaff C.J., "The International Labor Organization of the League of Nations: its Significance to the United States," *American Economic Review*, 22–3, 1932, p. 455.
95 "Bureau international du travail," *Bulletin Officiel*, 20–1, 30 avril 1935, p. 17.
96 Tortora, *Institution spécialisée…, op. cit.*, p. 36.
97 Gathings James A., "Appointment of American Delegates to the International Labor Organization," *The American Political Science Review*, 29–5, 1935, pp. 870–871.
98 Bellush Bernard, *He Walked Alone: A Biography of John Gilbert Winant*, La Haye-Paris, Mouton, 1968, p. 112 sq.
99 Hughes Stephen & Haworth Nigel, *art. cit,* p. 306.
100 Root to Drummond, March 11, 1920, SDN 21/R1299/88/472.
101 Deibel, *Le Secrétariat…, op. cit.*, pp. 38–46.

102 Dunne Michael, *The United States and The World Court, 1920–1935*, London, Pinter Publishers, 1988, p. 29.
103 *Ibid.*, ch. 2.
104 Deibel, *Le Secrétariat…, op. cit.*, p. 67.
105 Cited in Hudson Manley O., *La Cour permanente de justice internationale*, édition française, Paris, A Pedone, 1936, p. 244.
106 On the details of this episode, see Jessup Philip C., *Elihu Root…, op. cit.*, vol. 2, ch. XLVI, pp. 425–427; and The Relations between the United States of America and the League of Nations under the Harding Administration, anonymous, July 1922, AS-LOC 31.
107 Manley Ottmer Hudson Papers, *Harvard University Library*, hollisarchives.lib.harvard.edu/repositories/5/resources/4473, accessed August 30, 2021.
108 Deibel, *Le Secrétariat…, op. cit.*, p. 119.
109 Hudson, *La Cour permanente…, op. cit.*, p. 248.
110 *Ibid.*, p. 258.

References

Bellush Bernard, *He Walked Alone: A Biography of John Gilbert Winant*, La Haye-Paris, Mouton, 1968.
Borowy Iris, *Coming to Term with World Health. The League of Nations Health Organization*, Berlin, Peter Lang Publishers, 2009.
Bussière Eric, "L'Organisation économique de la SdN et la naissance du régionalisme économique en Europe," *Relations Internationales*, 75, 1993, pp. 301–313.
Clavin Patricia, *Securing the World Economy. The Reinvention of the League of Nations 1920–1946*, Oxford, Oxford University Press, 2013.
de Grazia Victoria, *Irresistible Empire: America's Advance through Twentieth Century Europe*, Cambridge, Harvard University Press, 2005.
Deibel Terry, *Le Secrétariat de la Société des Nations et l'internationalisme américain*, Washington, Carnegie Endowment for International Peace, 1972.
DeNovo John A., *American Interests and Policies in the Middle East, 1900–1939*, Minneapolis, University of Minnesota Press, 1963.
Dunne Michael, *The United States and the World Court, 1920–1935*, London, Pinter Publishers, 1988.
Farquet Christophe, "Expertise et négociations fiscales à la Société des Nations, 1923–1939," *Relations Internationales*, 142, 2010, pp. 5–21.
Ghébali Victor-Yves, "Aux origines de l'Ecosoc: l'évolution des commissions et organisations techniques de la Société des Nations," *Annuaire Français de Droit International*, 18, 1972, pp. 469–511.
Halperin Jean, "La conférence économique internationale de 1927," in *The League of Nations in Retrospect*, Berlin & New York, Walter & Gruyter, 1983.
Hidalgo-Weber Olga, *La Grande-Bretagne et l'Organisation internationale du travail (1919–1946). Une nouvelle forme d'internationalisme*, Louvain-la-Neuve, Academia—L'Harmattan, 2017.
Hughes Stephen & Haworth Nigel, "A Shift in the Centre of Gravity: The ILO under Harold Butler and John G. Winant," in Van Daele Jasmien, Rodriguez Garcia Magaly, Van Goethem Geert & Van der Linden Marcel (eds.), *ILO Histories. Essays on the International Labour Organization and its Impact on the World During the Twentieth Century*, Bern, Peter Lang, 2010, p. 293–312.

Limoncelli Stephanie A., *The Politics of Trafficking: The First International Movement to Combat the Sexual Exploitation of Women*, Stanford, Stanford University Press, 2010.

Link Edward S. (ed.), *The Papers of Woodrow Wilson*, vol. 53 (November 9, 1918–January 11, 1919), Princeton, Princeton University Press, 1986.

Lowes Peter D., *The Genesis of International Narcotics Control*, Geneva, Droz, 1966.

McAllister William B., *Drug Diplomacy in the Twentieth Century: An International History*, London, Routledge, 2000.

Mouton Marie-Renée, "Société des Nations et reconstruction de l'Europe: la conférence de Bruxelles (24 septembre-8 octobre 1920)," *Relations Internationales*, 39, 1984, pp. 309–331.

Ninkovich Frank A., *The Wilsonian Century: U.S. Foreign Policy Since 1900*, Chicago & London, Chicago University Press, 1999.

Ostrower Gary B., "American Ambassador to the League of Nations-1933: A Proposal Postponed," *International Organization*, 25–1, 1971, pp. 46–58.

Ostrower Gary, "The American Decision to Join the International Labor Organization," *Labor History*, 16–4, 1975, pp. 495–504.

Patel Kiran Klaus, *The New Deal. A Global History*, Princeton, Princeton University Press, 2016.

Peterecz Zoltan, *Jeremiah Smith, Jr. and Hungary 1924–1926. The United States, the League of Nations, and the Financial Reconstruction of Hungary*, Berlin/New York, Walter & Gruyter, 2013.

Rodogno Davide, "Beyond Relief in the Near East. The Ideology and Practices of an American Humanitarian Organization in the Aftermath of the First World War," *Monde(s). Histoire, Espaces, Relations*, 5, 2014, pp. 45–64.

Showan Daniel P., *United States Policy Regarding League of Nations Social and Humanitarian Activities*, PhD dissertation, Pennsylvania State University, 1969.

Tillman Seth P., *Anglo-American Relations at the Paris Peace Conference of 1919*, Princeton, Princeton University Press, 1961.

Tortora Manuela, *Institution spécialisée et organisation mondiale: étude des relations de l'OIT avec la SdN et l'ONU*, Bruxelles, Bruylant, 1980.

Tyrrell Ian, *Reforming the World: The Creation of America's Moral Empire*, Princeton, Princeton University Press, 2010.

2 A World Ruled by Science
Philanthropic Universalism

While the US government was quite present in League of Nations (LoN) commissions, some private actors, philanthropic foundations in particular, were even more so through their funding and participation in technical activities. This was especially the case for the Rockefeller Foundation (RF) and the Carnegie Endowment for International Peace (CEIP), which were the two most involved in the LoN's work. In doing so they adhered to an intellectual, scientific, and geopolitical logic; despite being internationalist organizations, on a basic level they were also US organizations campaigning for their country's greater engagement on the international stage. What was distinctive about their activity compared to that of governmental representatives is that it was guided by a faith in the boundless power of science and by the objective of establishing rational government of global affairs. In doing so, these foundations were inextricably linked to the geopolitical and geoscientific emergence of the US. Their project helps understand the process by which the US became an intellectual and scientific superpower in the 1920s, well before becoming a military superpower, which only occurred during World War II. This is clearly demonstrated by the nature of the philanthropic project, as well as the importance of the financial and technical investment of foundations in the LoN, an investment intended to integrate the US within the organization as much as possible, and more broadly within the international system.

This chapter is divided into four sections. The first analyzes the philosophy of the universalist philanthropic project of governing the world through science and shows how it saw the LoN as one means for achieving this objective, namely by funding the expertise of its technical sections working on the global problems of the interwar period. This project was in accordance with the LoN's goal of integrating the US. The convergence of these two objectives enabled the rapid development of the technical sections, which were barely mentioned in the Covenant, and ultimately transformed the LoN into an organization very different from the one envisioned by Wilson. The second section shows how foundations wanted to shape the LoN to enable US participation, a strategy clearly illustrated by the career of James T. Shotwell and his multiple attempts to adapt the shape of the League system to US geopolitical objectives. The third section analyzes the US lobbying efforts

DOI: 10.4324/9780429021213-3

conducted by foundations to promote greater participation in the LoN; this effort proved unsuccessful, as the country did not join the organization, but it helped make US participation in global affairs a subject of debate throughout the interwar period. Finally, the fourth section provides an overview of foundation funding for technical sections, especially on the part of the RF and the CEIP. It shows the depth of philanthropic engagement, as well as its importance for the LoN.

The Philanthropic Project

The interest of philanthropic foundations in the LoN was in keeping with the emergence of scientific philanthropy in the US. Traditional charitable activity was accompanied in the late nineteenth century by new organizations seeking to solve the problems of contemporary society by using scientific analysis to treat them at the root and find lasting solutions. The major foundations created at that time (General Education Board, 1902; Carnegie Foundation for the Advancement of Teaching, 1905; Russell Sage Foundation, 1907; RF, 1913, among others) were financed by industry magnates who quickly amassed colossal fortunes. The common feature of these organizations, which acted in very different sectors, was their belief in the omnipotence of science, as well as their investment in teaching, scientific research, and expertise based on work in the field. Between the 1900s and 1930s, their activity played a decisive role in transforming the US university system.

Their interest in the sciences was also demonstrated by their activity outside the US and prompted some of them to fund universities and research centers in many countries. Their funding of LoN activities was part of this general policy framework, as we will see in detail in the following chapters. The project underpinning this funding inextricably linked the advance of science and the emergence of the US as a leading scientific power, at a time when major European countries (notably Germany, France, and Great Britain) were the leaders in this area. From this point of view, scientific philanthropic universalism was also the product of US nationalism, as well as the ambition to make US standards global standards.[1]

The representatives of philanthropic circles active on the international scene in the first half of the twentieth century thought highly of their mission and were convinced they embodied a new cosmopolitan elite that was the heir to the Enlightenment, one that would succeed the aristocracy of the European spirit in conducting world affairs. These men (there were very few women in the major foundations) shared the objective of modernizing the world and making the principles of liberal democracy universal, thereby enabling a global state of mind to emerge.[2] Their goal was a rational organization of global society entrusted to a small group of experts who, thanks to science, could overcome the "unpredictability of traditional diplomacy"[3]—dependent on circumstances and the personality of decision-makers—as well as the particular interests of states by promoting a genuinely universal view of the world. They saw science, which was founded on precise facts rather than volatile opinions, as being intrinsically apolitical and hence as a source of peace, with objective analysis of problems reconciling diverging interests through indisputable conclusions. It was on this basis that foundations engaged with the LoN, which they saw as the first attempt to manage global affairs.

The CEIP was characteristic of this state of mind. It was founded in 1910 by Andrew Carnegie with the goal of establishing world peace through international law, which must be built on a solid basis, namely field studies that could scientifically resolve disputes between countries, thereby establishing unquestionable international arbitration. Recourse to scientific expertise thus represented, from the very outset, one of the pillars of the CEIP's working method. The organization was structured in divisions, each in charge of a specific area of activity: the Division of Intercourse and Education led by Nicholas Murray Butler, which promoted international exchange and propaganda in favor of peace; the Division of International Law, led by James Brown Scott, which published legal texts on international arbitration and planned seminars to help develop international law[4]; and the Division of Economics and History led by John Bates Clark, which conducted scientific studies on the causes of wars and how to avoid them.

In Switzerland in 1911, Clark brought together a research committee of academics, politicians, and journalists from 11 countries (Austro-Hungarian Empire, Italy, Belgium, Denmark, France, Germany, Great Britain, Holland, Japan, Switzerland, and the US) to conduct a joint study on the causes of wars since 1815. The project had barely begun when World War I broke out, with the new situation prompting its creator to change the objectives, which would henceforth be how to assess "the economic cost of the war [that had just broken out] and the disturbances it would cause for the forward march of civilization."[5] However, the evolution of the conflict toward a total war soon prevented any international collaboration and interrupted the project.

It was resumed after the conflict under the leadership of the historian James T. Shotwell, who would deepen this approach based on scientific analysis. Shotwell was born in Canada in 1874 and studied at the University of Toronto before specializing in medieval history at Columbia University, where he became a lecturer in 1903 and professor in 1908, after a long sojourn in Europe. When the US joined the war in April 1917, he put his academic knowledge in the service of the war effort and was appointed Chairman of the National Board for Historical Service, a branch of the Committee on Public Information. In the fall he was sought out by Colonel House to join The Inquiry, a collective of specialists created to prepare for peace negotiations and support the work of the US delegation. The group included over 150 experts, primarily academics from all backgrounds and disciplines: geographers, historians, economists, political scientists, and sociologists, among others. The Inquiry provided analyses to the State Department and the president in an effort to help the federal government determine its position and played an important role in developing the 14 points. It was Shotwell who came up with the name,[6] which symbolized the importance of research and the social sciences in the general reorganization process envisioned by Wilson. Shotwell quickly became one of the group's key members, being selected as one of the four members of the Research Committee that coordinated the working team.[7] In a revealing fact, he was also the organization's highest-paid member. It was thus logical that he was among the 21 members selected in late 1918 to join the delegation accompanying Wilson to the Paris Peace Conference, where they would play a key role. Initially considered simple purveyors of empirical data to enlighten diplomats, they were thrust into the heart of the negotiations due to the complexity of the issues involved, as well as Wilson's desire to circumvent Lansing and the State Department, who looked unfavorably on these amateur diplomats developing the US position in their stead and doing so with Wilson's blessing. While the president made the final decisions, as the conference progressed the 21 members of The Inquiry took on the status of a "little State Department."[8] The Inquiry was an important moment in Shotwell's career and a landmark in formulating a culture of scientific expertise, which he would help develop within the CEIP.

In the fall of 1917, while he was in the middle of preparing his team, Shotwell was approached by John Bates Clark to join the Division of Economics and History in order to revive the collective project on war. Shotwell, who was absorbed in his work, refused. Clark renewed his proposal in January 1919,[9] which this time was accepted. As the context had changed since 1914, Shotwell reconfigured the project, which became an economic and social history of the Great War, an effort whose nature was not very different from that of the specialists in The Inquiry. Once the Paris Peace Conference was finished, the historian set out to work, convening in Paris in the fall of 1919 the same experts called on in 1911. National editorial committees were created to study the various aspects of the war in each country, which, taken together, would provide a general view of the conflict. Shotwell established his headquarters in London and often visited Europe in the ensuing years. The editorial undertaking mobilized a global network of academics, administrators, and politicians gathered in 11 national editorial committees (France, Belgium, Great Britain, Italy, Germany, Austria, Hungary, the Netherlands, Russia, Scandinavian countries, Romania, Yugoslavia). It led to as many national series, which were later joined by a Czechoslovak series personally coordinated by President Thomas Mazaryk. The result of this long-term collective effort was considerable, leading to the publication of at least 173 volumes between 1921 and 1937.[10] The endeavor perfectly symbolizes the CEIP's intellectual project; its participation in LoN activities, which I will examine in the following chapters, was in keeping with the same logic of developing scientific expertise to solve post–World War I problems.

The other emblematic organization of scientific philanthropic universalism was the RF. Created in 1913 "to promote the well-being of mankind throughout the world,"[11] it quickly began activities in many countries outside of the US and the American continent: it organized health campaigns to eradicate certain diseases (tuberculosis, ankylostomiasis, malaria, yellow fever, etc.) in Central America, South America, and Europe; provided support to create and develop public health administrations on all five continents; and offered support for medical instruction and scientific research in biomedicine and the social sciences in the Americas, Europe, and Asia.[12] Its first major accomplishment outside of the US was funding Peking Union Medical College (PUMC), which opened in 1921 with the objective of introducing scientific medicine to China by reproducing the model of Johns Hopkins University.[13] There were many others, as the foundation funded a series of institutions for medical instruction and research during the interwar period, with the stated objective of supplanting the European medical model, especially the French clinic tradition and German scientific research. As with the CEIP, the RF's engagement in the LoN, which I will discuss later, was in keeping with this certainty that science could solve humanity's problems. The RF was not the only organization of this type founded by the Rockefeller family; there were many others that had specific objectives and were also founded on the principle of scientific expertise. This was especially true of the Bureau of Social Hygiene (BSH)—created in 1911 by John D. Rockefeller, Jr. to conduct research on prostitution, crime, and juvenile delinquency—which as we have seen funded certain LoN projects, as well as the Laura Spelman Rockefeller Memorial founded in 1918, which was merged into the RF in 1929. The general reorganization of the Rockefeller philanthropic world that year integrated most of the boards that had been created since the early twentieth century (General Education Board, Laura Spelman Rockefeller Memorial, International Education Board) within a single RF now structured into five divisions (International Health, Medical Sciences, Natural Sciences, Social Sciences, Humanities). Far from a purely administrative process, this reorganization reflects the coming of age of philanthropic universalism. The unifying principle of the foundation's activity was not just health, as it was in 1913, but science, with the foundation's purpose now being "the advancement of knowledge"[14] through scientific research, in an effort to "rationalize life"[15] and control human behavior. It is striking that the foundation's growing investment in LoN activities during the 1930s corresponded with the maturity of this project to reconfigure fields of knowledge on a global scale.

Science had a major role in the foundation's project from the very beginning of its activity, as personified by its first president George E. Vincent, a man steeped in positivist culture who believed that its mission was to promote global exchange of ideas by supporting research and granting fellowships for scientists to travel the world. Vincent saw them as the reincarnation of the sixteenth-century merchants of light described by the philosopher Francis Bacon.[16] This reference was not random, for the idea of a society led by science was central to Bacon's work. By citing him Vincent explicitly situated the RF within a tradition dating back to Renaissance Humanism and expressed his ambition to build a new world through scientific research and the international circulation of knowledge.

Raymond B. Fosdick's career offers a good illustration of the Rockefeller philanthropic project during the interwar period. Born in 1883, he was part of the East coast's social reform circles in the early twentieth century. In 1908 he earned a doctorate in law and served as Commissioner of Accounts for New York City. In 1912 he became the Democratic Party treasurer for Woodrow Wilson's electoral campaign, whose student he was at Princeton University and whom he admired unconditionally. In 1917 he was head of the Commission on Training Camp Activities for the US army in France, and then took part in the Paris Peace Conference as an advisor to General Pershing, before being appointed in May 1919 by Wilson as Under-Secretary-General for the LoN, alongside Jean Monnet, to assist Eric Drummond in his organizational work. He left the LoN in 1920 and became the personal lawyer for John D. Rockefeller, Jr. in 1921, joining the Board of Trustees of the RF and serving as its president in 1936. He was thus a major figure in the Rockefeller world. Fosdick pursued at the RF what he was unable to pursue at the LoN, playing a decisive role in the foundation's massive participation in LoN activities, as we will see later.

Fosdick's conception of the world and the LoN's role within it, as well as the role of the RF in organizing the world, are clearly described in *The Old Savage in the New Civilization* (1928), a collection of conferences he gave to various audiences, students in particular. They demonstrate Fosdick's profound knowledge of European culture and his keen awareness of the decisive break that World War I represented in world history. Taking place on a continent seen by many as embodying the height of civilization, it broke Fosdick's belief in continual progress, which he shared with many Americans of his generation deeply influenced by the evolutionism of the British sociologist Herbert Spencer.[17] For him the war showed that humans were now capable of bringing about their own downfall, given the proliferation of scientific methods mobilized to kill and destroy during the conflict. The contemporary world was characterized, according to Fosdick, by an exponential belief in scientific discoveries and the development of a mechanistic civilization. The central challenge was to determine how humanity—that "old savage"—would use the scientific progress characteristic of modern civilization: would they make it an instrument of progress or use it to destroy humanity? For Fosdick, the solution to this dilemma was to train an enlightened elite that could use science wisely so that it could contribute to a "new Renaissance"[18] like the one that had marked early modern times. Fosdick believed that history was led by minorities, with majorities generally being wrong: it was the latter, he said, that approved sending witches to the stake or supported the institution of slavery in the US or prevented teaching evolutionist doctrine in the Southern US during the 1920s. At the time of his writing, "probably the majority of Americans oppose our joining the League of Nations."[19]

Fosdick believed that his generation was facing an unprecedented challenge that it had to meet: controlling scientific progress that it could not stop and using it to build "greater quality of life"[20] for the entire world population. Bringing this project to fruition called for someone who mastered all knowledge, such as Aristotle, whom Fosdick took as an example. However, in the contemporary world no one person could master the sum of scientific knowledge, as was the case in Greek Antiquity. The undertaking therefore required a "collective intelligence" led by those who could mobilize the full resources of knowledge and technology and act on a global scale. This description actually corresponded, in Fosdick's mind, with the international policy implemented by the RF since 1913, as well as with the structure of the LoN, which was "a parliament of nations." The latter was also an example of the "application of intelligence on a global scale,"[21] an organization of "social engineering conceived on planetary terms" that would organize the collective rules for the international society of the future. Fosdick believed these two organizations were on the right side of history and promoted their *rapprochement* during the interwar period.

Shaping the LoN to Enable US Membership

In Chapter 1, I discussed the LoN Secretariat's strategy of establishing closer ties between the US and the LoN. Philanthropic foundations also implemented strategies of *rapprochement* throughout the interwar period, reflecting the continuity of the philanthropic project in this direction. The initiatives launched by Shotwell were characteristic of these strategies, which would profoundly transform the League system. Shotwell's objective, pursued with constancy over nearly two decades, was to adapt the League system to allow the US to be associated with it, but without renouncing its tradition of nonentanglement in foreign policy. It shows that US relations with the LoN had a much deeper influence on the actual form of the international organization than is usually stated.

Shotwell was very active during the Paris Peace Conference, especially in the discussions that led to the creation of the International Labour Organization (ILO). Yet he also sought, very early on, to develop the activities provided for in Article 23 of the Covenant and to give the League system the flexibility it needed to integrate the US. In March 1919 he was concerned about the growing opposition to the LoN project in US public opinion and among politicians, an opposition that could result in Congress rejecting the treaty. He therefore proposed to his colleagues a number of amendments to the Covenant.[22] The proposed amendment to Article 1 stipulated that

> states who are not members of the League of Nations can join as associate members if they participate in the regular conferences held under the auspices of the League of Nations. These associate members assume no obligations other than those arising from the decisions made by the conference they participated in.

To supplement this possibility, he broadened the LoN's institutional scope, which initially included the General Assembly, Council, and Secretariat, by proposing an amendment to Article 2, stipulating that LoN activity would be conducted not only by these three bodies but also "by regular conferences on specific subjects of international interest." Finally, he proposed an amendment to Article 23 that describes the objectives of the LoN in the "non-political" domain, adding that "to carry out these goals and other similar targets of the League of Nations, regular conferences will be held in which all states willing to accept the quality of associate member for the specific objectives planned can participate." Seeing a potential US rejection of the LoN in its current form, Shotwell proposed changing its institutional architecture by creating an associate member status and a system of regular conferences to develop technical activities. The underlying idea was to allow nonmember states—those that decided not to ratify the Covenant, the US in particular—to nevertheless take part in the League's activities when these took the form of conferences open to all countries. For Shotwell, this expansion of the institutional scope would also allow the association of the vanquished powers while awaiting their integration as full-fledged members, in addition to powers that were "less completely developed, halfway between civilized countries and colonial dependencies."[23]

Shotwell's proposal was rejected by Wilson, which is hardly surprising, as its philosophy was to make the LoN a series of specialized conferences rather than a "universal parliament,"[24] as the president wanted. Shortly after the rejection of the LoN Covenant in Congress, Shotwell reiterated this proposal in a pamphlet that had little impact in the US[25] but established a principle that would be taken up and developed in the ensuing years by philanthropic foundations, which would promote international commissions and conferences as a way to develop ties between the US and the LoN. While the status of associate member was not created *de jure*, the development of technical sections and their opening to nonmember countries led *de facto* to the result hoped for by Shotwell: the association of nonmember countries, notably the US.

Shotwell continued to shape the LoN to enable US membership after 1919 as well. The discussions surrounding collective security gave him an opportunity. In the fall of 1923, the LoN General Assembly adopted the Cecil-Réquin Plan, under which member states would sign a mutual assistance treaty defining any war as a crime, stipulating that each signatory would have to provide military assistance to any participating country that was attacked, and entrusting the LoN Council to designate the aggressor. Following the session, the Secretariat sent the proposed treaty to the governments of member states. There was strong initial opposition because the project would increase the Council's power and risked driving the US further away from the LoN out of fear of being dragged into a new conflict.

Shotwell, who was in Europe working on the *Economic and Social History of the World War*, was approached by Colonel Réquin to determine how to change the treaty in order to secure US acceptance. He assembled a committee to study the question upon his return to the US in January 1924. Its members included part of the team from The Inquiry, in particular David Hunter Miller, Isaiah Bowman, and John Bates Clark; two generals, the American representative to the Supreme War Council, Tasker H. Bliss, and the former Military Chief of Staff, James G. Habord; and academic figures that were part of the Carnegie network including Henry S. Pritchett, the former President of the Massachusetts Institute of Technology and the President of the Carnegie Foundation for the Advancement of Teaching; Frederic Keppel, Wilsons's former Assistant Secretary of War in 1918 and President of the Carnegie Corporation of New York at the time; and Stephen Duggan, a professor of international law at the City College of New York and the Director of the Institute of International Education.

The team assembled by Shotwell had no official mandate but consisted of individuals that had held political office. Shotwell also sought out the advice of members from the European editorial committees of the *Economic and Social History of the World War*.[26] After months of work, in June 1924 the group produced a "Draft Treaty of Disarmament and Security,"[27] which represented a "Declaration to make war of aggression illegal."[28] Article 1 identifies a war of aggression as an "international crime," defining it as an instance where a state enters into war "for reasons other than its defense" (Article 2). In this case, "The Permanent Court of International Justice [...] would have jurisdiction to issue a decision as to whether an international crime [...] had been committed" (Article 3). Article 5 of the draft treaty introduced a first novelty compared to the Cecil-Réquin plan by providing a legal definition for aggression, which was indispensable for characterizing the violation of international law. The principle was simple: when two countries have a dispute, they must submit it to the PCIJ, and the country refusing to do so will be designated the aggressor. The proposal also stipulated that the future mutual assistance treaty could be signed by states that were not LoN members and proposed initiating a process for arms controls. Its second novelty was the notion of "permissive sanctions": as the aggressor country is considered as having *de facto* lost all its right, protections, and diplomatic immunity on the territory of signatory countries, the latter are free to adopt, at their discretion and with no collective obligation, the sanctions they deem appropriate, whether they be diplomatic, economic, or military. The principle of sanctions that were both automatic and flexible was clearly intended to garner the assent of the US, which was allergic to any notion of a binding alliance.

In July Shotwell sent the document to Drummond,[29] who distributed it to members of the Council, and then to all member states. Once it was made public, what would henceforth be called the Shotwell Plan sparked immediate interest in the US, where it was featured on the front page of *The New York Times*, whose director Nicholas Murray Butler knew well, while even some opponents of the LoN declared their support for the principle. In Europe, reactions were more mixed. In September the draft treaty was debated at the

LoN General Assembly in front of Shotwell and part of his team, who had made the trip to Geneva. The proposal was discussed, as were the responses from the 25 governments to the Cecil-Réquin plan, as well as another plan submitted by the government of New Zealand.[30] Beyond the proposal itself, the central issue under discussion was amending the LoN Covenant to make Article 10 more flexible and to give the PCIJ a more important role in order to allow the US to join the League system. When he opened the debates on September 5, the head of the French government, Edouard Herriot, immediately emphasized this point:

> we continue to hope that the United States [...] will not refuse to provide its fraternal collaboration, especially if it sees that we have made the greatly productive and just notion of arbitration central to our organizations. Elite Americans have already sent formulations that deserve our full attention.

Herriot also emphasized the contribution of the Shotwell Plan: "it is also important to mention, alongside the remarkable work of M. Beneš, a comment regarding the definition for cases of aggression."[31] The Shotwell Plan was thus at the heart of the discussions surrounding the draft treaty of mutual assistance; and the resolution adopted on September 6 by the General Assembly gave the Third Commission (on Disarmament) a mandate to examine this draft treaty with two essential objectives:

> to study, with a view to possible amendments, the Covenant's articles relating to the resolution of disputes; and to examine the limits in which the terms of Article 36, Paragraph 2 of the Statute of the Permanent Court of International Justice [the one excluding compulsory arbitration] could be clarified to facilitate acceptance of this clause.[32]

This clearly involved modifying the LoN Covenant.

In October the draft treaty was adopted as the Geneva Protocol. It identified a war of aggression as an international crime, following the Cecil-Réquin Plan in this regard. Shotwell's definition of aggression was also added:

> any State shall be presumed to be an aggressor [...] if it has refused to submit the dispute to the procedure of pacific settlement provided by Articles 13 and 15 of the Covenant as amplified by the present Protocol, or to comply with a judicial sentence or arbitral award or with a unanimous recommendation of the Council.[33]

However, the reference to the PCIJ was less emphatic than in the Shotwell Plan, for its decisions regarding disputes between states were only advisory: the principle of compulsory arbitration had once again been refused. The fear of member states that the PCIJ would supplant the Council helped water down the Shotwell proposals. As to the planned sanctions, they no longer had the flexibility ascribed to them under the Shotwell Plan, and once again became compulsory, in keeping with the Covenant. In short, the draft treaty did not change the Covenant's logic, especially the obligation of solidarity on the part of all states in the face of an aggressor, whereas the Shotwell Plan sought to circumvent the consequences of Article 10 by suppressing the automatic nature of sanctions while promoting compulsory arbitration. As a result, the vote in favor of the draft treaty was simultaneously a personal victory for Shotwell as well as a failure, for the LoN's logic remained the same, making any form of US membership impossible. The Protocol would be nipped in the bud by the change of majority in the British House of Commons one month after the signature, as the Conservative Party returned to power, and Stanley Baldwin's new government refused to ratify it. However, even though Shotwell's initiative did not succeed, it was not appreciated by the State Department, for upon returning to the US the diplomat and historian was summoned by Secretary of State Charles Evans Hughes, who accused him of violating the Logan Act. This federal law dating back to 1799 forbade US citizens from engaging, on their own initiative, with foreign governments. Shotwell responded to the Secretary of State's veiled threat to prosecute him by archly stating that the Logan Act could not apply to an individual who had established contacts with the LoN, for the latter had not been recognized by the US.

Despite the reprimand by Hughes and the British refusal to ratify the Protocol, Shotwell did not abandon his plan. Relying on the French and German editorial committees for the *Economic and Social History of the World War*, he created committees on both sides of the Rhine to reflect on how to proceed with the Shotwell Plan. These committees debated together during 1925 and played a role, along with French and German diplomatic authorities, in negotiating the Locarno Treaties, one that yet remains to be clarified.[34] As these negotiations were coming to a close in September 1925 (the treaties would be signed on October 16), Shotwell once again attended sessions of the General Assembly, which was discussing whether to hold a conference on disarmament. At the request of multiple delegates, he drafted a memorandum to be included in the discussions, which led to the Council's decision to create a preparatory commission for the conference. The LoN sent an invitation to both member and nonmember states, the US included. As the latter accepted the invitation, Shotwell reactivated the committee that had drafted the plan in 1924, while the new President of the CEIP, Nicholas Murray Butler, officially offered his services to the State Department. The new Shotwell Committee would draft a number of notes used by the US delegation during meetings for the preparatory commission in May 1926.

At the same time, the diplomat and historian also began to work on a draft antiwar treaty with his colleague Joseph P. Chamberlain, a professor of public law at Columbia University. The project took up the fundamental principles from the 1924 plan, namely the definition of the aggressor, and the replacement of automatic sanctions with permissive sanctions. But it was even more ambitious, for while the 1924 plan involved only LoN member states, the new plan was conceived from the outset as a global treaty to complement the League system with an additional, less binding—and thereby more universal—legal system.[35]

A few months later, in the spring of 1927, during a series of conferences held in connection with the Carnegie Chair for International Relations at the Deutsche Hochschule für Politik in Berlin, Shotwell relied on the example of Locarno—the first manifestation of a collective security system on the European scale—to outline a future global Locarno. It was clear that the US government would never take such an initiative, and so it had to come from the European powers. Once his conferences were finished, Shotwell left for Geneva, where he discussed his project with the German Minister for Foreign Affairs, Gustav Stresemann, and the Director of the ILO, Albert Thomas. The three men agreed that it would be preferable for the initiative to come from France rather than Germany, which could be accused of once again pursuing an expansionist policy.

Thomas tried to arrange a meeting for Shotwell with the French Minister of Foreign Affairs, Aristide Briand.[36] In March Shotwell wrote to his friend Arthur Fontaine, President of the ILO Board of Directors, to share his idea for a global Locarno and to suggest that the French government take the initiative of proposing it to the world in order to show its commitment to international peace. Fontaine forwarded the letter to Briand, who accepted to meet with Shotwell. If the archives of the French Ministry for Foreign Affairs include no trace for the beginnings of the pact, this is not because it was "a personal initiative by Briand"[37] undertaken without consultation with his advisors, but because it was actually Shotwell's idea, who wanted to proceed as discreetly as possible. There is also no trace in the Shotwell papers preserved at Columbia University. He visited the minister's office on March 22 accompanied by Albert Thomas and reiterated his idea for a treaty renouncing war as an instrument of national policy. Briand showed interest and asked Shotwell for a memorandum on the subject. The historian was aware that this time he was violating the Logan Act by discussing the plan with the French minister and therefore refused to provide a written document bearing his signature. He suggested Briand issue a declaration for the 10th anniversary of the US entry into the war and accepted to write a list of arguments the minister could develop before the Paris bureau of the Associated Press. Briand accepted the principle, and Shotwell drafted a note that he sent to Alexis Léger, Briand's chief of staff. The text proposed a pact whose signatories would renounce war "as an instrument of national policy"[38] and would adopt the principle of collective security born in Locarno, but without being required to issue sanctions against the aggressor of another signatory country, but simply by abstaining from trading with it. For Shotwell, it was a question of extending to the rest of the world the principle of collective security created to solve the French-German problem, all while softening it in order for the US to join.

Briand's agenda was different than Shotwell's, for the minister had a French-German rather than global view of problems, and his preoccupation was not collective security but rather the security of France. He therefore transformed Shotwell's proposal into a bilateral pact. When he forwarded his message on April 6, Briand used the substance of Shotwell's arguments—notably the expressions "war outside the law" and "abjure it as an instrument of national policy" from the memorandum—but he proposed a French-American pact rather than a global one. His initiative fell flat, as the US press hardly mentioned it, and the federal government did not even respond. Upon his return to the US, Shotwell tried to attract attention to the project. He informed Butler of his role and drafted a letter that the CEIP President signed and sent to *The New York Times*, which published it on April 25 under the title "Briand proposes eternal peace with US."[39] The federal government was annoyed by the proposal, which did not at all match its diplomatic agenda, and used the pretext that Briand's proposal was addressed to the people of the US rather than its government in order not to respond. Having learned from the group of the CEIP's role in the affair, Coolidge and his Secretary of State, Frank Kellogg,[40] considered prosecuting Butler and Shotwell under the Logan Act, but ultimately reconsidered. They were aware that their initiative was a response to a movement in American public opinion favoring international peace, one that they could not ignore. Peace movements had been developing since the early 1920s, with some of their initiatives enjoying genuine success with the people, a sign that it was not as isolationist as is often believed. For instance, the National Committee on the Cause and Cure of War, "the largest women's peace organization," organized over 10,000 local meetings in 1928, at which petitions supporting the Kellogg–Briand Pact were signed.[41] Riding the wave of this broad-based movement, the CEIP increased its lobbying efforts, especially with the mainstream press, with a number of articles being published in *The New York Times* in the spring of 1927 in support of Briand's initiative. Forced to take a position, Kellogg ultimately responded to the French proposal in June, over two months after the appeal, but changed it in turn. As he did not want a bilateral pact that would commit the US to ensure France's security, he proposed a global pact that took up Shotwell's original idea. The US counter-proposal was not suitable for Briand, but he could not backtrack: the pact, which was signed in August 1928 and took effect the following year, included just two articles, stipulating that the signatories abjured war as a means of national policy and committed to resolving their disputes peacefully. Despite being very vague, the treaty nevertheless raised hopes among internationalists that the US would more actively engage in global affairs. For Shotwell and Butler, it indisputably opened the way for greater cooperation between the LoN and the PCIJ.

The CEIP henceforth put all of its energy into promoting the Pact of Paris with members of Congress, the press, intellectual circles, and public opinion.[42] This activism earned Butler the Nobel Peace Prize in 1931, but instead of traveling to Stockholm to accept the prize, he chose to address the entire world by giving his acceptance speech on the radio in December 12. He proposed measures such as arms control, and especially expanded authority for the PCIJ and the LoN, measures he believed were now possible thanks to the Pact of Paris.[43] His argument appeared the following day in *The New York Times*. Butler repeated it a few months later in a radio speech entitled "The Global Problem" delivered on July 2, 1932, with the election in full swing; Butler declared that a hermetic boundary between Europe and America was no longer possible in an interdependent world and that the US had to unambiguously engage in global affairs. A new organization had to reflect this new world, one for which international institutions—the LoN and the PCIJ in particular—served as pillars.[44] Butler was in Great Britain a few days later for a conference on US public opinion and international affairs at the Royal Institute of International Affairs in London. He stated that because of the importance of public opinion in the US—with the separation of powers system requiring congressional approval for international agreements and a lengthy ratification process—it was surely preferable that the US had not joined the LoN, for that would have seriously disrupted its functioning. He immediately added that the US should collaborate "without reservations,"[45] a clear allusion to the 14 reservations of 1919.

The Pact of Paris was, from this point of view, the culmination of the CEIP's activity—and especially that of Shotwell—to change the League system. This activity was ambiguous, as it simultaneously sought to bring the US closer to the LoN as well as changed its architecture and spirit by emphasizing international law and the PCIJ's role to the detriment of the strictly political role played by the LoN, which was central to the Wilsonian project. From this perspective the CEIP's activity was firmly in keeping with the legalist fraction of the internationalist movement, for which Root and Butler had been important representatives since the early twentieth century, and whose activity they continued through the CEIP. Additionally, if in Shotwell's mind the Pact of Paris was indeed intended to supplement the LoN, one can also wonder whether it was not meant to replace it. It is impossible to answer this question, for the pact, after momentarily raising hopes of outlawing war, disappeared amid the torment of the 1930s, swept aside by the rise of totalitarian regimes and international tension. Still, despite the evolving international situation, Shotwell did not abandon his efforts to bring the US and the League system closer all while making the latter more flexible, as we will see later in his activity as part of the ICIC.

Lobbying

Lobbying was another important strategy used by foundations and took its place within the internationalist movement's broader effort during the interwar period for the US to take part in global affairs.[46] This effort involved interventions in the media, as mentioned above, as well as and especially support for associations advocating US membership in the LoN. Raymond

Fosdick played an important and pioneering role in this regard. In 1919 his position was one of Wilsonian orthodoxy: in November, a few weeks after the Senate Committee on Foreign Relations formulated its 14 reservations, he believed that the LoN Covenant was an ensemble, and adopting the reservations would hollow out the meaning of US membership in the League.[47] Following the failure of ratification, his position became difficult, for he found himself in the situation of ensuring adherence to a Covenant that his own country refused.[48] Wilson's poor state of health deprived the Democratic Party of a leader and clear course of action, and Fosdick, who was no longer able to contact the president or even the State Department,[49] concluded that his presence at the LoN was a liability for the Democratic Party, as it provided arguments to the treaty's opponents. He therefore submitted his resignation to Drummond on January 19, 1920,[50] two months before the Senate's second vote.

His efforts in support of the LoN did not stop, for upon his return to the US in April, he publicly criticized the country's present isolation and poor image in Europe following the rejection of the treaty, denouncing the withdrawal of the world's richest country into itself at a time when Europe was bankrupt and the problem of debt was a ticking bomb. Given these conditions, only US participation in the LoN could resolve the European situation.[51] During the debates that marked the 1920 election, Fosdick continued to defend Wilson's endeavor. Like the former president, he framed the debate in moral, philosophical, and even religious terms: the LoN held the promise of a new "way of life for the human race" and provided a unique opportunity to "build a better and healthier civilization," with most of its activities being "in tune with the spirit and ends of the teaching of Christ"; whatever its form, the LoN was indispensable for "saving humans from themselves."[52]

While Root was chiefly interested in the legal dimension of international problems, Fosdick saw the LoN as a whole, emphasizing the many domains in which it had intervened since its creation. The fight against epidemics, refugee aid, trafficking in women and children, the opium trade, and disarmament were so many areas in which "the human family needs the leadership"[53] that the LoN could provide. It could help resolve conflicts between states; its true role was even greater, namely the well-being of peoples, the fight against the enemies of humanity, and the source of new hope in a world shattered by the war.[54] Under these conditions, the debate surrounding the removal of Article 10, which crystallized most of the opposition to the Covenant, struck him as being secondary, given the issues faced by the postwar world. The most important thing was for the US to participate in the LoN in order to make it viable and prevent it from becoming an instrument for vengeful imperialism, as with France, or for the restoration of imperialism, as with Great Britain. While Root's position was marked by a strict legalism and resolute attachment to the separation between American and European affairs, Fosdick's internationalist messianism saw the LoN as a global undertaking, and the world as a broader whole, one in which a hermetic boundary between America and

Europe made no sense. Yet he was no longer an unconditional Wilsonian, as he was aware that the president's intransigence was partly responsible for his failure. He therefore felt, in September 1920, that Article 10 could be removed without altering the Covenant's spirit.[55] While a year earlier he refused to consider reservations, his evolution on the matter was clear and swift, as his position was now fairly similar to that of the CEIP and the arbitrationist movement.

Fosdick became involved in pro-LoN associations. In the spring of 1920 he intensified initiatives defending the organization, creating an LoN News Bureau in August to inform the US public regarding the League's activities, especially by transmitting to the press the information he continued to receive from Geneva. His activity quickly increased, and in late 1922 the Bureau merged with the League of Nations Non-Partisan Association, which in turn became the League of Nations Association (LNA) in 1930.[56] In addition to disseminating information regarding League activities and publishing informational brochures,[57] the LNA advocated throughout the interwar period for US membership, as well as for Senate ratification of the international conventions signed by the League. To facilitate its activity he opened a bureau in Geneva in 1929, which allowed him to be in constant contact with the League, and notably with its Information Section. Fosdick was one of its leaders until World War II, serving as its president from May 1933 to June 1935. His arrival at the head of the association seemingly coincided with its intensified lobbying activities in Congress, the State Department (Fosdick and Cordell Hull had good relations), and the White House.[58] In fact, Hull asked Fosdick to become his special advisor at the State Department for the LoN. Fosdick declined the offer due to his health, but especially because Roosevelt's hostile declarations regarding the LoN during the election campaign risked putting him in a difficult position with the pro-LoN movement.[59] He thus continued to act via the LNA, and of course via the RF.

In June 1935 Shotwell became the president of the LNA and held this position until World War II.[60] The CEIP had provided financial support for the association since 1924 and collaborated with its lobbying activity. It included 30,000 members at the time, even though it was not particularly well known beyond internationalist circles. The two organizations worked together during the 1930s, exchanging publications, organizing conference tours across the US,[61] and publishing editorials in the press. This was especially true in 1929–1930 when the LNA organized an information campaign for the 10th anniversary of the LoN, with financial support from the CEIP.[62] While this lobbying effort did not translate into US membership in the LoN, it helped diffuse the internationalist position among public opinion and politicians, paving the way for US involvement in global affairs during World War II.[63]

The CEIP's lobbying activity in support of the LoN also proceeded indirectly, especially through the educational efforts on international issues that it conducted on multiple levels. This was firstly true in universities. In 1919, in cooperation with the Institute of International Education (IIE),[64] it established an important network of International Relations Clubs[65] to strengthen international intellectual exchange and counterbalance the traditional isolationism of the US. To this end, the IIE helped develop university exchange programs and the teaching of international issues at a time when history and law curricula were almost exclusively centered on the US. The idea behind the creation of International Relations Clubs was to provide university libraries with publications regarding international issues and to collect them in dedicated sections. These included CEIP publications, especially the journal *International Conciliation*, along with the courses taught at The Hague Academy of International Law and other documents relating to international law.[66] The clubs also tried to have students interested in these topics meet to debate international problems. The system enjoyed relative success judging by the increasing number of clubs listed by the CEIP, which rose from 79 in 1923 to 1,316 in 1941.

Lobbying also involved diffusion with the general public in the form of regular communication efforts. For instance, in September 1926, when the CEIP organized a visit to Europe for over 60 professors—who spent four days in Paris, three in The Hague, and three weeks in Geneva to study how the LoN functioned—the CEIP's European Centre[67] held a lunch in Geneva for the 125 participants of the Pan-American Congress of Journalists, an opportunity to present the activities of the LoN and to promote coverage of the organization in US newspapers.[68] CEIP activity also took the form of in-depth work, especially through the creation of International Mind Alcoves, which were created before World War I and developed after 1918.[69] They functioned on the same principle as the International Relations Clubs but did so in public libraries. A few dozen works suitable for the general public were selected for different age categories. There were also children's stories by writers of various nationalities, along with general works on international matters. The selection included a book by the British journalist Henry Wilson Harris, published in 1927 and entitled *What the League of Nations Is*.[70] These books were selected and purchased by the CEIP. The formula quickly achieved success, for in 1927 there were 130 alcoves throughout the US, primarily in small and medium-sized cities, a number that rose to 1,174 in 1941. While it is difficult to quantify their impact, it was most likely substantial.

Philanthropic Funding of the LoN

The most concrete manifestation of support by philanthropic foundations for the LoN was clearly their participation in its activities, financial participation in particular. A number of them, especially the Rockefeller boards and the CEIP, funded the LoN's technical activities throughout the interwar period and became crucial partners, notably through their support for the HO, the EFO, and the International Institute of Intellectual Cooperation (IIIC). This support was essential, for the LoN faced budgetary shortfalls throughout its history, as well as an increasingly large gap between the expansion of its technical activities and the growing reluctance of governments to increase their contribution. Beginning in the 1930s, the economic crisis halted the growth of the League's budget, with a significant portion of its organizational restructuring during this period resulting from the need to reduce costs.[71] It subsequently had to seek out external funding to ensure the development and even the survival of its technical activities, with the support of foundations once again proving decisive. Without them much of the LoN's technical activities would simply not have been possible.

The Rockefeller boards were by far the most involved. To support his struggle on behalf of the League, Fosdick found an important ally in Rockefeller philanthropy. He came in contact with it in 1913 when John D. Rockefeller, Jr., who had just created the BSH, entrusted him with conducting an investigation of European police forces, for which he spent a number of months in Europe.[72] Upon his return to the US in 1920, Fosdick partnered to create the Curtis, Fosdick & Belknap law office, one of whose first clients was John D. Rockefeller, Jr., for whom Fosdick became personal lawyer and advisor. The two men were very different by virtue of their personal background and political leanings, as Fosdick was a Democrat and fervent internationalist, while the son of the founder of Standard Oil was a Republican.[73] Yet mutual respect and trust quickly developed between the two men. In September 1919 even before the treaty's first refusal, Fosdick sent a memo to Rockefeller, Jr. explaining why it was in the interest of the US to support the LoN in one form or another, in order to protect the world and America from chaos,[74] for the economic situation in the US was closely linked to that of Europe. Fosdick believed that US participation in the LoN was essential for global economic coordination. Fosdick thus acted as a relay in the US for Drummond's strategy of involving the country in the LoN despite the failure of ratification.

In spite of his distrust of the League, the younger Rockefeller was convinced by Fosdick's arguments and, in 1921, invited him to join the RF Board of Trustees, of which Fosdick quickly became an influential member, climbing the ranks to become president in 1936. He played a decisive role in the foundation's involvement with the LoN. Fosdick also convinced Rockefeller, Jr. to support the LNA using his personal funds, to the tune of $10,000 per year from 1930 onward.[75] All in all, as we will see in the ensuing chapters, Rockefeller philanthropies played a major role in the life of the LoN throughout the interwar period. When the RF was developing its activities in Europe in the early 1920s, it even considered establishing its European office in Geneva, before ultimately deciding on Paris, where it opened in 1923.

Between 1922 and 1945, the RF provided a total sum estimated between $2.9 and $3.5 million, primarily to the HO (at least $2 million between 1922 and 1937), the EFO (at least $800,000 between 1931 and 1946), and the IIIC (at least $140,000 between 1932 and 1939). There were also the grants provided by the BSH to the Section for Social Problems to conduct studies on the traffic in women and children ($235,000 between 1923 and 1931),[76] as well as to the Advisory Committee on Traffic in Opium to fund the 1926 study in Persia. There was also the personal gift of $2 million given by John D. Rockefeller, Jr. in 1927 for a building for the LoN library,[77] whose documentary collection developed enormously beginning in 1919, cramping its initial location. In 1926, Andrew Carnegie's widow, Louise Whitfield Carnegie, offered $5,000 to continue paying the salary for one of its librarians, a gift that was followed by a $10,000 grant from the RF for the same purpose, apparently on the express and personal decision of Fosdick.[78] The $2 million personal gift by Rockefeller, Jr. enabled the construction of a new building in 1936, which today occupies an entire wing of the Palace of Nations. There were also the few hundred dollars given between 1935 and 1937 by the RF to pay a librarian's salary when the LoN budget could no longer contend with the increase in its documentary activities. In total, somewhere between $5.3 and $5.8 million was given by Rockefeller philanthropies to the LoN between 1922 and 1945, making it the highest recipient of Rockefeller grants among non-US organizations.

In addition to this funding, there were much smaller gifts from other foundations. The CEIP provided direct grants, which can be estimated at a few thousand dollars given to the LoN in 1924 and to the IIIC in 1932. The Woodrow Wilson Foundation provided $25,000 in 1930 to erect a bronze commemorative monument in honor of the president at the entrance to the LoN building to mark the League's 10th anniversary. The Milbank Memorial Fund (MMF) gave $5,000 in 1935 to allow US experts to participate in meetings of the Health Section (HS).[79] There were also grants from many other organizations, such as the American Relief Administration, which provided $100,000 for refugee relief activities in 1922; the American Red Cross, which provided £10,000 the same year; the American Association of Social Hygiene, which gave $5,000 in 1925; the American Council of Education, which gave $9,000 in 1928; and the Richmond Virginia Friends of the LoN Association, which in 1925 provided $1,500. Finally, there were occasional gifts made by individuals, such as the one by James Forstall (Forrestall?), who gave approximately $5,000 in 1931 to fund the publication of books,[80] along with $10,000 from another American donor who remained anonymous.[81]

Organizations linked to the LoN also received support, although much less, from foundations or other private organizations. In 1925 the International Labour Office created the Scientific Organization of Labor Institute (SOLI), which received at least $50,000 from the Twentieth Century Fund until 1934; the latter also funded at least two studies conducted by the International Labour Office, in the amount of $41,000. Rockefeller, Jr. also contributed $60,000 between 1927 and 1930 to fund SOLI,[82] while the Industrial Relations Counselors created by Rockefeller, Jr. and Fosdick in 1921 funded a 1930 study by the International Labour Office in the amount of $12,000. Finally, there was the preferential rent offered by the CEIP to the LoN to house the PCIJ in a wing of the Carnegie-funded Peace Palace in The Hague, where the court relocated in November 1921. Carnegie had hoped that the Paris Peace Conference would be held at the Peace Palace and wrote to this effect to Wilson in late 1918, although in vain.[83] Housing the PCIJ was a significant consolation prize that provided legitimacy to the philanthropist's endeavor, and the temporary rental lease that ended in 1921 was renewed the following two years, before a final agreement was signed in 1924.[84] The CEIP also made part of the Palace staff, which was compensated from its own funds, available to the PCIJ. In total, between 1922 and 1945, including all of the funding listed above, private US organizations of all sizes most probably gave the LoN between $5.6 and $6.6 million.

To assess the impact of this funding, it is important to compare it to the LoN's total budget. If we include all of the organizations under its purview (the ILO and PCIJ), along with building maintenance costs, staff salaries, retirement pensions, and of course current operating expenses, it varied between 21 million gold francs (or Swiss francs) per year in 1921, and 33 million at its highest level in 1932, and then 21 million in 1940 and 14 million in 1944.[85] However, for a clearer picture of the proportion represented by the US contribution, it is important to base the comparison on the Secretariat's budget, which included activities and salaries but excluded the cost of buildings, pensions, and associated organizations. This budget was 11.7 million Swiss francs in 1921, rising to 19 million at its peak in 1932, before stabilizing around an average of 15 million in the 1930s. Throughout the period, the proportion of salaries varied between 44% (in 1923) and 70% (in 1935) of the budget. Excluding salaries, it amounted to approximately 7 million gold francs per year in the 1920s, and 5 million in the 1930s. The Secretariat's total expenses (including salaries) between 1921 and 1945 can be estimated at approximately 270 million gold francs.[86] If we subtract salaries, which amounted to an estimated 50% during the period, we are left with an "activities" budget of 135 million gold francs, or $26 million.

Now, if we consider the $5.5 to $6.6 million provided by private American organizations, we should subtract: the $2 million from the personal gift by Rockefeller, Jr. and the gift from the Woodrow Wilson Foundation, as they were provided to build or embellish a building; the gift from the BSH, as it was apparently used by the Permanent Central Opium Board, whose budget was separate from the Secretariat's;[87] and the $110,000 given by the Twentieth Century Fund and Rockefeller, Jr. to the International Labour Office, whose budget was also separate. One could thus say that private US organizations gave the Secretariat a sum ranging between $3.4 and $4.5 million, which we will arbitrarily fix at $3.9 million for the purposes of calculation. It represented 15% of the Secretariat's $26 million budget for total expenses (excluding salaries) between 1922 and 1945. By comparison, the largest contributor to the LoN, Great Britain, provided 9.4% of the organization's total expenses for 1925, with the second contributor being France at 8.3%.[88] While comparison has its limits, as member state contributions also included salaries, building maintenance, and activities, this proportion gives an idea of the level of US participation. If we consider only technical activities, the US was definitely one of the primary contributors, and probably even the leading one. I would even go so far as to say that its contribution, which was already considerable, was even larger for the budgets of certain sections. For example, in some years the HS, EFO, and IIIC saw 40% of their budget come from US funding (excluding salaries). If we focus on the level of projects undertaken by these sections (such as the HS's epidemiological information effort), the American contribution is sometimes close to 100%, which means that some of the projects of the technical sections would not have existed without US financial support, as there were no funds earmarked for them.

It should be noted that this funding, especially that of the RF, was multiyear (generally provided for three or five years), unlike the allocations from states, which were paid on an annual basis and could always be subject to decrease. In addition to being a godsend, this funding allowed technical sections to develop a real long-term policy, one of the LoN's major contributions. This is surely one of the reasons why the US contribution did not generate any opposition during the LoN's history, with a few exceptions, such as in 1934 when Salvador de Madariaga of Spain expressed reservations regarding the renewal of funding from the RF.[89] But these were isolated examples, as US funding was generally always welcome, all the more so as it was a way for the League to involve the US in the organization. It was, beginning in the 1920s, one of the major factors in the growth of technical activities.

Funding projects that did not materialize also bear mentioning. This was the case for the ILO, where the RF tried to promote the development of expertise activities as it had with the LoN. Its objective was to make the ILO a laboratory of ideas to develop international policies for combatting the crisis. In early 1934, an economic expert at the International Labour Office, Percival Martin of Great Britain, to whom the RF had awarded fellowships in 1927 and 1932, drafted a proposal to study economic stabilization in agriculture and industry as well as the social consequences thereof, which led in the spring of 1934 to a visit from the Associate Director of the RF's Social Science Division, John Van Sickle, who was interested in the topic. At the same time, the foundation had just provided significant funding to the LoN's EFO and envisioned creating a synergy between the two organizations.[90]

The project never materialized due to hesitation on the part of Edmund Day, the Director of the Social Science Division, since the EFO and the International Labour Office were rivals, and the initiative was not sure to succeed.[91] Most especially, US membership in the ILO was taking shape, and the RF did not want to be seen as engaging in entryism, which could rekindle the isolationist fraction in Congress and scuttle Roosevelt's plans.[92] The situation remained unresolved until September 1934, when US union representatives traveled to Geneva to meet with Harold Butler to finalize the terms of the membership that Congress had approved in June. Butler enthusiastically informed them of a possible RF grant for an International Labour Office project. To his great surprise, the news infuriated the unionists, especially John Lewis, president of the powerful United Mine Workers, who retorted that "Rockefeller money is tainted money"[93] and that it would be scandalous for the International Labour Office to accept it, a gesture that would not be understood among US labor circles.[94] Butler, who burned his fingers once, hesitated to pursue negotiations with the foundation due to fear that union opposition would derail US membership, which he deemed vital for the organization's survival. When the president of the foundation, Max Mason, was informed of the affair by his officers,[95] he decided to halt all funding proposals to avoid disrupting the membership process.

In the ensuing years, all of the foundation's funding proposals for the ILO failed for the same reasons. While it granted a few more fellowships to members of the International Labour Office, this involved individual funding that was smaller in scope. Major proposals failed one after another, as in April 1937 when the foundation tried to issue a $75,000 grant for a comparative study on the effects of national economic policy on the standard of living of workers. The hostility of unions remained intact, which suspected the foundation of wanting to fund the study to slow or halt programs developed by the International Labour Office. Polemics erupted when news of the grant became public; after months of tumult, in December 1937 the RF decided to cancel the funding. John Winant once again sought funding in January 1938, unsuccessfully as well. It was not until the spring of 1939 that a small grant was issued for a conference on the social consequences of arms production programs. The outbreak of war prevented it from being held; the grant was absorbed by the ILO's general accounts and never repaid to the RF.[96]

Conclusion

All told, the involvement of philanthropic foundations in the LoN was early, permanent, and massive. It was not occasional funding but a sustained and long-term collaboration, which was based on an intellectual convergence between the LoN project and that of the philanthropic foundations representing the internationalist movement. While the lobbying efforts of US foundations did not, to all appearances, meet with success, for the US did not join the organization, they nevertheless played an indisputable albeit difficult-to-quantify role in the retreat of isolationism, which took the specific form of discreet but increasing US participation in LoN activities. This collaboration was of course not without its ambiguities, for the LoN's internationalism and philanthropic universalism did not have the same objectives, as we will see in the details of RF and CEIP support for the LoN's technical sections. The fact remains that foundation support was decisive in developing technical activities throughout the interwar period, as we will now examine by closely analyzing the projects supported by foundations in the fields of health, economics, and intellectual cooperation (Chapters 3, 4, and 5).

Notes

1. On international activities of US philanthropic foundations and their connections with the process of American international expansion, see Tournès Ludovic, *Américanisation. Une histoire mondiale*, Paris, Fayard, 2020, ch. 6.
2. Ninkovich Frank A., *The Wilsonian century. U.S. Foreign Policy Since 1900*, Chicago & London, Chicago University Press, 1999, p. 44.
3. De Benedetti Charles, "James T. Shotwell and the Science of International Politics," *Political Science Quarterly*, 89–2, 1974, pp. 379–395.
4. *Conciliation Internationale*, n°2, 1912, p. 85.
5. Dotation Carnegie pour la paix internationale, *Histoire économique et sociale de la guerre mondiale*, Paris, Presses Universitaires de France, 1926, p. 3.
6. Shotwell James T., *At the Paris Peace Conference*, New York, MacMillan, 1937, p. 8.
7. *Ibid.*, p. 30; Gelfand Lawrence, *The Inquiry, American Preparation for Peace 1917–1919*, New Haven, Yale University Press, 1963, p. 53 and 69.
8. Shotwell James T., *At the Paris Peace Conference*, op. cit., p. 18.
9. *Ibid.*, p. 125.
10. Chatriot Alain, "Une véritable encyclopédie économique et sociale de la guerre," *L'Atelier du Centre de recherches historiques*, 2009, acrh.revues.org/413, accessed August 30, 2021; Harold Josephson mentions 300 monographs but does not provide a list (Josephson Harold, *James T. Shotwell and the Rise of Internationalism in America*, London, Associated University Press, 1975, pp. 103–115). See also Barros Andrew, "Setting out on a Long Irenic Campaign: The Carnegie Endowment for International Peace Prepares the Construction of a Peaceful World Order, 1910–1920," in Ingram Norman & Bouchard Carl (eds.), *Beyond the Great War: Making Peace in a Disordered World*, Toronto, Toronto University Press, forthcoming in 2022.
11. Rockefeller Foundation, *Annual Report*, 1913–1914, p. 7.
12. For the context of its creation and its first international actions, see Tournès Ludovic, *Sciences de l'homme et politique. Les fondations philanthropiques américaines en France au XXe siècle*, Paris, Garnier, 2013 [2011], chs. 1 & 2.
13. Bullock Mary Brown, *An American Transplant: The Rockefeller Foundation and Peking Union Medical College*, Berkeley, University of California Press, 1980; Bullock Mary Brown, *The Oil Prince's Legacy: Rockefeller Philanthropy in China*, Stanford, Stanford University Press, 2011.
14. Rockefeller foundation program and policy. Advancement of knowledge, January 3, 1929, RF 3/900/22/166.
15. RF Minutes, April 11–12, 1933, RF 3/900/21/158a.
16. Tournès Ludovic, "La fondation Rockefeller et la naissance de l'universalisme philanthropique américain," *Critique Internationale*, 35, avril-juin 2007, pp. 173–197.
17. Fosdick Raymond B., *The Old Savage and the New Civilization*, New York, Doubleday, Doran, 1928, p. 27.
18. *Ibid.*, p. 59.
19. *Ibid.*, p. 86.
20. *Ibid.*, pp. 177–178, for this and the following quotation.
21. *Ibid.*, p. 195, for this and the following quotation.

22 Shotwell James T., *Hors du gouffre*, Paris, Hachette, 1937 [translated from *On the Rim of the Abyss*, New York, Macmillan, 1936], p. 428.
23 *Ibid.*, p. 3.
24 *Ibid.*, p. 8.
25 Kuehl Warren F. & Dunn Lynn K., *Keeping the Covenant: American Internationalists and the League of Nations (1920–1939)*, Kent, Kent State University Press, 1997, p. 45.
26 De Benedetti Charles, "James T. Shotwell and the Science of International Politics," *Political Science Quarterly*, 89–2, 1974, p. 386.
27 Bouchard Carl, "Le 'plan américain' Shotwell-Bliss de 1924: une initiative méconnue pour le renforcement de la paix," *Guerres mondiales et conflits contemporains*, 202–203, 2001, pp. 203–225.
28 SdN. *Journal Officiel*, supplément spécial n°23. Actes de la cinquième Assemblée, annexes aux actes de la troisième Commission, Genève, 1924, p. 169. This document contains the text of the American project.
29 Webster Andrew, "The Transnational Dream: Politicians, Diplomats and Soldiers in the League of Nations' Pursuit of International Disarmament, 1920–1938," *Contemporary European History*, 14–4, 2005, p. 507.
30 *International Conciliation*, 201, August 1924, p. 339.
31 SdN. *Journal Officiel*, supplément spécial n°23. Actes de la cinquième Assemblée. Compte rendu des débats, huitième séance plénière (5 septembre 1924), Genève, 1924, pp. 53–54.
32 *Ibid.*, Compte rendu des débats, onzième séance plénière 6 septembre 1924, Genève, 1924, p. 80.
33 *Ibid.*, Protocole pour le règlement pacifique des différends internationaux adopté par l'Assemblée le 2 octobre 1924, Procès-verbaux de la troisième Commission, annexe 12, Genève, 1924, pp. 189–194. See the English version of the text at www.refworld.org/docid/40421a204.html, accessed August 30, 2021.
34 Josephson, *James T. Shotwell…, op. cit.*, p. 131. There is no information in the Shotwell papers at Columbia University. Box 21, which pertains to the Locarno Treaties, is practically empty. Politically sensitive information may have been destroyed or removed to avoid any legal action under the Logan Act.
35 On the Pact, see Chamberlain Waldo, "Origins of the Kellog-Briand Pact," *The Historian*, 15, 1952, pp. 77–82; Ferrell Robert H., *Peace in Their Time, the Origins of the Kellog-Briand Pact*, New Haven, Yale University Press, 1952; Shotwell James T. "The Pact of Paris: With Historical Commentary," *International Conciliation*, 243, 1928, pp. 443–532.
36 Josephson, *James T. Shotwell…, op. cit.*, pp. 156–162.
37 Bariéty Jacques, "Le Pacte Briand-Kellog de renonciation à la guerre," in Bariéty Jacques & Fleury Antoine (eds.), *Mouvements et initiatives de paix dans la politique internationale (1867–1928)*, Bern, Peter Lang, 1987, p. 358.
38 See the complete text of Shotwell's note and its comparison with Briand's declaration to the Associated Press in Chamberlain, "Origins…," *art. cit.*
39 Nicholas Murray Butler, "Briand Proposes Eternal Peace with US," *New York Times*, April 25, 1927.
40 Murphy Kevin C., *Uphill All the Way: The Fortunes of Progressivism, 1919–1929*, PhD dissertation, Columbia University, 2013, p. 617.
41 Susan Zeiger, "Finding a Cure for War: Women's Politics and the Peace Movement in the 1920s," *Journal of Social History*, 24–1, 1990, p. 69 and 83 (note 11).

42 Howlett C. F., "Nicholas Murray Butler's Crusade for a Warless World," *The Wisconsin Magazine of History*, 67–2, 1983–1984, pp. 99–120.
43 Radio address by Nicholas Murray Butler, delivered on December 12, 1931, www.nobelprize.org/nobel_prizes/peace/laureates/1931/butler-acceptance.html, accessed August 19, 2021.
44 "Le problème mondial," broadcast statement, July 1932, CEIP-CE VII/223/3. The argument would be repeated by Butler in several broadcast speeches: see for example, "The family of nations," Columbia Broadcasting System, November 11, 1934, CEIP-CE VII/223/4.
45 Nicholas Murray Butler, "American Public Opinion and International Affairs," *International Affairs*, 11–15, 1932, pp. 618–632.
46 Josephson, *James T. Shotwell…, op. cit.*; Kuehl & Dunn, *Keeping…, op. cit.*; Parmar Inderjeet, "The Carnegie Corporation and the Mobilisation of Opinion in the United States' Rise to Globalism, 1939–1945," *Minerva*, 37–4, 1999, pp. 355–378; Parmar Inderjeet, *Foundations of the American Century. The Ford, Carnegie and Rockefeller Foundations in the Rise of American Power*, New York, Columbia University Press, 2012, ch. 2.
47 Fosdick to Drummond, November 7, 1919, RBF-PU 1/1.
48 Fosdick to Drummond, November 14, 1919, RBF-PU 1/2.
49 Fosdick to Drummond, February 13, 1920, RBF-PU 1/9.
50 Fosdick to Drummond, January 19, 1920, RBF-PU 1/9.
51 Fosdick's interview upon his arrival to the US, unidentified newspaper clipping, April 11, 1920, RBF-PU 2/1.
52 Statement by Raymond B. Fosdick, September 23, 1920, requested by Democratic National Committee, to be handled through agency of Federal Council of Churches, RBF-PU 2/6.
53 *Ibid.*
54 *Ibid.*
55 Fosdick to Sweetser, September 20, 1920, RBF-PU 2/6.
56 On the LNA, see De Benedetti Charles, *Origins of the Modern American Peace Movement, 1915–1929*, Millwood, KTO Press, 1978; Kuehl & Dunn, *Keeping…, op. cit.*, pp. 40–47.
57 See numerous examples in CEIP VI/245/3.
58 Accinelli Robert D., "Militant Internationalists: The League of Nations Association, The Peace Movement, and U.S. Foreign Policy, 1934–1938," *Diplomatic History*, 4–1, 1980, pp. 19–38.
59 Fosdick to Sweetser, March 22, 1933, AS-LOC 31.
60 Josephson, *James T. Shotwell…, op. cit.*, p. 215; Purposes and Program of the League of Nations Association, November 1, 1938, CEIP-CE VI/167/25.
61 Janet Wallace (Carnegie Endowment) to Mary W. Fry (League of Nations Association), April 6, 1929, CEIP VI/245/3.
62 See the detail of this campaign in CEIP VI/226/2.
63 Parmar, "The Carnegie Corporation…," *art. cit.*; Parmar Inderjeet, "Engineering consent: The Carnegie Endowment for International Peace and the Mobilisation of American Public Opinion, 1939–1945," *Review of International Studies*, 26–1, 2000, pp. 35–48.
64 Institute of International Education, *Annual Report*, 1920, p. 12.
65 On these clubs, see Kuehl & Dunn, *Keeping…, op. cit.*, pp. 64–65.

66 Babcock to Gilbert Gidel (Secretary of the Curatorium of the Academy of International Law), March 18, 1929; Lyon-Caen to Babcock, May 12, 1929, CEIP-CE I/1/1.
67 On the European Centre, see Tournès Ludovic, "La Dotation Carnegie pour la paix internationale et l'invention de la diplomatie philanthropique," in Tournès Ludovic (ed), *L'argent de l'influence. Les fondations américaines et leurs réseaux européens,* Paris, Autrement, 2010, pp. 25–44.
68 Réunion du conseil d'administration du Centre Européen, October 25, 1926, CEIP III/105/3.
69 Rosenthal Michael, *Nicholas Miraculous. The Amazing Career of the Redoubtable Dr. Nicholas Murray Butler*, New York, Columbia University Press, 2006, p. 244.
70 Carnegie Endowment for International Peace, *Yearbook*, Washington, 1927, p. 50.
71 Ranshofen-Wertheimer Egon F., *The International Secretariat: A Great Experiment in International Administration*, Washington, Carnegie Endowment for International Peace, 1945, p. 223.
72 Fosdick Raymond B., *European Police Systems*, New York, The Century Co., 1915.
73 Fosdick Raymond B., *Chronicle of a Generation. An Autobiography*, New York, Harper & Brothers Publishers, 1958, pp. 215–216.
74 Raymond B. Fosdick to John D. Rockefeller, Jr., September 4, 1919, in Fosdick Raymond B., *Letters on the League of Nations*, Princeton, Princeton University Press, 1966, pp. 29–34.
75 Kuehl & Dunn, *Keeping..., op. cit.,* p. 46.
76 Hubbard Ursula, *La collaboration des Etats-Unis avec la Société des Nations et l'Organisation internationale du travail, des origines à 1936*, Paris, Centre européen de la dotation Carnegie, 1937, p. 725.
77 Tournès Ludovic, "Comment devenir une superpuissance intellectuelle? La fondation Rockefeller et la documentation scientifique," in Hauser Claude, Loué Thomas, Mollier Jean-Yves & Vallotton François (eds), *La diplomatie par le livre. Réseaux et circulation internationale de l'imprimé de 1880 à nos jours*, Paris, Nouveau monde éditions, 2011, pp. 165–180.
78 Sweetser to Drummond, April 9, 1926, AS-LOC 14.
79 Gilbert to Hull, January 29, 1935, NARA RG 84/452.
80 Gilbert to Stimson, December 9, 1931, NARA RG 84/404. It might be a wrong spelling of James Forrestall, future Secretary to the Navy (1944) and Secretary of Defense (1947); during the 1930s, Forrestall worked for the investment bank Dillon, Read & Co.
81 Hubbard, *La collaboration..., op. cit.,* p. 725.
82 Cayet Thomas, *Rationaliser le travail, organiser la production. Le Bureau international du travail et la modernisation économique durant l'entre-deux-guerres*, Rennes, Presses universitaires de Rennes, 2010, p. 70 and 76 (note 24).
83 Link Edward S. (ed.), *The Papers of Woodrow Wilson*, vol. 53 (November 9, 1918– January 11, 1919), Princeton, Princeton University Press, 1986, p. 32 et 67.
84 Déclaration du 28 novembre 1921, LON 21/R1308/17482/17482.
85 The LoN's general budget was drawn up is gold francs, but expenses were recorded in Swiss francs. The two currencies are considered as having the same value, and I used the 1920 exchange rate of 5.18 gold francs for $1 in order to simplify calculation (Société des Nations. Administration financière et répartition des dépenses, Genève, 1927, p. 16). For the details of the annual budget, see Ranshofen, *The International Secretariat..., op. cit.,* p. 224.

86 Ranshofen, *The International Secretariat...*, *op. cit.*, p. 224.
87 *Ibid.*, p. 225.
88 SDN. Répartition des dépenses pour le septième exercice (1925), Mémoire du Secrétaire général, Genève, 1925.
89 Gilbert to Hull, January 29, 1935, NARA RG 84/452.
90 Van Sickle memorandum, February 4, 1934; Van Sickle to Day, March 23, 1934; Van Sickle memorandum, June 14, 1934, RF 2–1934/100/93/741.
91 Day to Van Sickle, November 14, 1933, RF 2–1933/100/78/623.
92 Day to Butler, March 29, 1934, RF 2–1934/100/93/741.
93 Kittredge to Van Sickle, September 3, 1934, RF 2–1934/100/93/741.
94 Memorandum of conversation with Mr. E.E. Day, J. Van Sickle & Miss Walker of the Rockefeller foundation, March 18, 1936, BIT XR 61/4/25.
95 Strode to Mason, September 4, 1934, RF 2–1934/100/93/741.
96 See the entire episode in RF 1.1/100/108/973 to 978.

References

Accinelli Robert D., "Militant Internationalists: The League of Nations Association, The Peace Movement, and U.S. Foreign Policy, 1934–1938," *Diplomatic History*, 4–1, 1980, pp. 19–38.

Bariéty Jacques, "Le Pacte Briand-Kellog de renonciation à la guerre," in Bariéty Jacques & Fleury Antoine (eds.), *Mouvements et initiatives de paix dans la politique internationale (1867–1928)*, Bern, Peter Lang, 1987, pp. 355–367.

Barros Andrew, "Setting out on a Long Irenic Campaign: The Carnegie Endowment for International Peace Prepares the Construction of a Peaceful World Order, 1910–1920," in Ingram Norman & Bouchard Carl (eds.), *Beyond the Great War: Making Peace in a Disordered World*, Toronto, Toronto University Press, forthcoming in 2022.

Bouchard Carl, "Le 'plan américain' Shotwell-Bliss de 1924: une initiative méconnue pour le renforcement de la paix," *Guerres mondiales et conflits contemporains*, 202–203, 2001, pp. 203–225.

Bullock Mary Brown, *An American Transplant: The Rockefeller Foundation and Peking Union Medical College*, Berkeley, University of California Press, 1980.

Bullock Mary Brown, *The Oil Prince's Legacy: Rockefeller Philanthropy in China*, Stanford, Stanford University Press, 2011.

Cayet Thomas, *Rationaliser le travail, organiser la production. Le Bureau international du travail et la modernisation économique durant l'entre-deux-guerres*, Rennes, Presses universitaires de Rennes, 2010.

Chamberlain Waldo, "Origins of the Kellog-Briand Pact," *The Historian*, 15, 1952, pp. 77–82.

Chatriot Alain, "Une véritable encyclopédie économique et sociale de la guerre," *L'Atelier du Centre de recherches historiques*, 2009, acrh.revues.org/413.

De Benedetti Charles, "James T. Shotwell and the Science of International Politics," *Political Science Quarterly*, 89–2, 1974, pp. 379–395.

De Benedetti Charles, *Origins of the Modern American Peace Movement, 1915–1929*, Millwood, KTO Press, 1978.

Ferrell Robert H., *Peace in their Time, the Origins of the Kellog-Briand Pact*, New Haven, Yale University Press, 1952.

Gelfand Lawrence, *The Inquiry, American Preparation for Peace 1917–1919*, New Haven, Yale University Press, 1963.
Howlett C. F., "Nicholas Murray Butler's Crusade for a Warless World," *The Wisconsin Magazine of History*, 67–2, 1983–1984, pp. 99–120.
Josephson Harold, *James T. Shotwell and the Rise of Internationalism in America*, London, Associated University Press, 1975.
Kuehl Warren F. & Dunn Lynn K., *Keeping the Covenant: American Internationalists and the League of Nations (1920–1939)*, Kent, Kent State University Press, 1997.
Link Edward S. (ed.), *The Papers of Woodrow Wilson*, vol. 53 (November 9, 1918–January 11, 1919), Princeton, Princeton University Press, 1986.
Murphy Kevin C., *Uphill All the Way: The Fortunes of Progressivism, 1919–1929*, PhD dissertation, Columbia University, 2013.
Ninkovich Frank A., *The Wilsonian century. U.S. Foreign Policy Since 1900*, Chicago & London, Chicago University Press, 1999.
Parmar Inderjeet, "The Carnegie Corporation and the Mobilisation of Opinion in the United States' Rise to Globalism, 1939–1945," *Minerva*, 37–4, 1999, pp. 355–378.
Parmar Inderjeet, "Engineering consent: The Carnegie Endowment for International Peace and the Mobilisation of American Public Opinion, 1939–1945," *Review of international Studies*, 26–1, 2000, pp. 35–48.
Parmar Inderjeet, *Foundations of the American Century. The Ford, Carnegie and Rockefeller Foundations in the Rise of American Power*, New York, Columbia University Press, 2012.
Ranshofen-Wertheimer Egon F., *The International Secretariat: A Great Experiment in International Administration*, Washington, Carnegie Endowment for International Peace, 1945.
Rosenthal Michael, *Nicholas Miraculous. The Amazing Career of the Redoubtable Dr. Nicholas Murray Butler*, New York, Columbia University Press, 2006.
Tournès Ludovic, "La fondation Rockefeller et la naissance de l'universalisme philanthropique américain," *Critique Internationale*, 35, avril-juin 2007, pp. 173–197.
Tournès Ludovic, "Comment devenir une superpuissance intellectuelle? La fondation Rockefeller et la documentation scientifique," in Hauser Claude, Loué Thomas, Mollier Jean-Yves & Vallotton François (eds.), *La diplomatie par le livre. Réseaux et circulation internationale de l'imprimé de 1880 à nos jours*, Paris, Nouveau monde éditions, 2011, pp. 165–180.
Tournès Ludovic, *Sciences de l'homme et politique. Les fondations philanthropiques américaines en France au XXe siècle*, Paris, Garnier, 2013 [2011].
Tournès Ludovic, "La Dotation Carnegie pour la paix internationale et l'invention de la diplomatie philanthropique," in Tournès Ludovic (ed.), *L'argent de l'influence. Les fondations américaines et leurs réseaux européens*, Paris, Autrement, 2010, pp. 25–44.
Tournès Ludovic, *Américanisation. Une histoire mondiale*, Paris, Fayard, 2020.
Webster Andrew, "The Transnational Dream: Politicians, Diplomats and Soldiers in the League of Nations' Pursuit of International Disarmament, 1920–1938," *Contemporary European History*, 14–4, 2005, pp. 493–518.
Susan Zeiger, "Finding a Cure for War: Women's Politics and the Peace Movement in the 1920s," *Journal of Social History*, 24–1, 1990, pp. 69–86.

3 A Global Health Policy
The Health Organization

Health was the leading area of League of Nations (LoN) activity in which US foundations were involved, notably through the Rockefeller Foundation's (RF) sustained funding for the Health Organization (HO) between 1922 and 1937. However, this contribution was not solely financial, as beginning in the 1910s the RF implemented an international public health policy and deployed its expertise across all five continents. It supported the HO's activities from the very beginnings of the organization and tried to comanage the implementation of an international health order based on developing and fostering communication between national health administrations in an effort to harmonize global standards. Through their respective activity and cooperation on certain subjects, the two organizations helped develop international networks of civil servants and health experts traveling from one country to another throughout the interwar period. This cooperation was not without rivalries, for beyond their shared objectives, the LoN and the RF had different conceptions of health. Their opposition in this regard cut across multiple fault lines: between Americans and Europeans, scientists and administrators, and private and intergovernmental organizations. In the space of about 20 years, their competitive synergy transformed the international health landscape by promoting the circulation of people, practices, and ideas and brought international legitimacy to public health—a notion that had haltingly emerged since the late nineteenth century—making it a natural area of intervention for international organizations. As part of this process, the RF contributed as much to the internationalization of US health practices as it did to making the LoN's work universal, a dynamic that paved the way for the World Health Organization (WHO) after 1945.

This chapter is divided into four sections. The first presents the RF's global project for medicine and public health, and how its support for the HO was in keeping with this project. The second and third analyze the two leading projects supported by the foundation: the Epidemiological Intelligence Service (EIS) and the collective study tour program for civil servants in the field of health. The final section examines the limits of cooperation between the RF and the HO by focusing on the functioning of the Malaria Commission.

DOI: 10.4324/9780429021213-4

The LoN in the RF's Global Medical Project

In 1913 the RF created the International Health Commission (IHC) to launch campaigns to eradicate diseases outside the US. Its objective was to promote public health and "spread knowledge of scientific medicine."[1] The IHC had a direct lineage to the numerous US organizations from reformist circles, which had expanded their activity outside the US since the late nineteenth century. They combined strict moral principles with pronounced US Messianism, in many respects making scientific philanthropy an heir to the missionary movement.[2] The novelty that distinguished the IHC was its intention to give this activity a scientific dimension: this would be the trademark of Rockefeller philanthropic activity during the ensuing decades, in both the US and abroad.

The IHC was the direct descendant of the Sanitary Commission for the Eradication of Hookworm Disease, created in 1909 at the initiative of John D. Rockefeller to promote health practices designed to eliminate endemic ankylostomiasis in the American South. Commission members arrived at two conclusions upon the completion of their work: (1) the activity had to be extended to all major diseases in order to create a public health system on the state level (there was no question of a federal system at the time); and (2) the activity had to be made international. This internationalization took the form of health campaigns organized in 1915 in the Caribbean and Latin America; support for the creation and development of public health administrations in Latin America, Europe, and Asia; and support for the creation of teaching curricula in the relatively new field of public health, modeled as much as possible on that of the Johns Hopkins School of Public Health, in which the RF invested massively from 1915 onward in an effort to make it the leading educational center for modern public health. To conduct this policy, the IHC became the International Health Board (IHB) in 1916, and in 1919 the foundation created a Division of Medical Education tasked with internationalizing medical instruction in accordance with US standards based on scientific medicine. As a result, after World War I the RF had a "unified program"[3] with a universalist inflection, one that would create institutions in key parts of the world (medical schools, public health administrations, epidemiological monitoring organizations) that would bring about, via a snowball effect, the modernization of public health on a planetary scale. Its work extended to nearly 40 countries on five continents. This strategy was based on the certainty that science could ensure human progress, which became a pillar of the philanthropic project in the 1920s. In February 1920, Edwin Embree urged the RF President, George E. Vincent, to help former belligerent countries rebuild, on the grounds that in the coming century Europe would be one of the areas on which "the progress of civilization"[4] depended. Medicine and public health were the central pillars of this project: a substantial part of the RF's international policy during the interwar period involved medical and health policy. Its investment in the LoN was in keeping with this logic, as it believed the LoN could help coordinate these institutions across the globe.

As the State Department was authorizing Hugh S. Cumming to attend the health conference in Brussels in the summer of 1922, the RF provided considerable funding for the Health Section (HS) and participated in its activities until the late 1930s. The foundation was not acting on the government's instructions, as the HS did not receive good press under the Harding administration, which made a clear difference between participating in the occasional conference organized by the Health Committee and collaborating with the HS, for the latter presented itself as a competitor to the International Office of Public Hygiene (IOPH). The IOPH, which was created in Paris in December 1907, was the first intergovernmental health organization. Its objective was to "gather and inform participating states regarding the facts and documents [...] of interest to public health, especially with regard to infectious diseases—cholera, the plague, and yellow fever in particular—and the measures taken to combat these diseases."[5] One could say it was the first permanent organization created to implement international coordination in the field of health. Nevertheless, its activity consisted essentially of gathering information rather than implementing preventative activities. In 1919 it had 37 members, including the US. However, the HO at the LoN had a more ambitious goal than the IOPH, for it aimed to combat epidemics and play an active role in regulating international public health through voluntarist measures going far beyond the gathering of statistics. It made no secret of its desire to absorb the IOPH, something that hardly pleased the US, which was not keen to submit itself to the decisions of an international organization of which it was not a member. For that matter, the LoN had many more member states than the IOPH, which over the long term could only translate into diluted US influence. When the IOPH met in April 1921 to explore the conditions for a *rapprochement* with the LoN, the US delegate refused any change that would place it under LoN authority. The government could not prevent the creation of the temporary Health Committee in August 1921 but did everything it could to keep the IOPH outside of its scope. In early 1923 when Ludwik Rajchman went to the US to discuss with the State Department regarding the implementation of a permanent Health Organization to succeed the temporary Committee, the IOPH's status was once again central to the discussions, with the State Department being opposed to placing it under the organization's management. While it could not prevent the partial integration of the IOPH in the HO, it tried to maintain its independence as long as possible, at one point even considering recruiting its director, Dr Pottevin, as a State Department consultant in order to thwart the HO's projects. This strategy ultimately failed, for the HS had many projects and was supported by an RF in favor of expanded international coordination in health, whereas the IOPH settled into semilethargy. The US government, clearly aware that it had lost, stopped supporting it in the late 1920s.

In this area the RF was clearly marching to the beat of a different drummer than its government; it showed a somewhat different conception of US national interest, seeking to integrate the US within international cooperation as much as possible so that the country could influence the development of health standards, at a time when the federal government had little interest in these matters. The funding provided to the HO in the summer of 1922 proceeded on the basis of a shared interest with the LoN. At the time the foundation was deploying a policy of building health administrations on the European scale and saw the Geneva-based organization as a partner it could rely on. The Director of the HS (the executive body of the HO), Ludwik Rajchman, also needed allies to complete his project. This Polish doctor, whose family had fled the repression of the Tsarist police in Russified Poland at the beginning of the century to settle in France, returned to his reconstructed country in 1918[6] and became involved in epidemiological matters, creating the country's first bacteriological laboratory in March 1919. The epidemics coming from Russia at the time were a serious threat to Poland, and Rajchman relied on multiple foreign organizations to combat them, especially the American Relief Administration, which in 1919 conducted a detailed study of the Polish health situation.[7] However, due to the gravity of the health situation in that part of Europe, in January 1920 the Polish government asked the brand new LoN to create an international organization to combat epidemics, a process that, as we saw earlier, resulted in the creation of the temporary Health Committee. Rajchman's legitimacy was fragile, for his election as the head of the HS and his dynamism sparked opposition not just from the US, but also—and more disconcertingly for him—from the two most important LoN countries, Great Britain and France. The latter also refused to have the Paris-based IOPH come under LoN authority. Rajchman began negotiations with the RF in the fall of 1921 to secure funding for his projects, but also to circumvent French and US support for the IOPH, and to shift the global health organization's center of gravity from Paris to Geneva. The substantial funding granted by the RF would provide him with the means to do so. If the HO secured a central role in the global health landscape in the matter of a few years, this was largely due to the RF, which acted against the immediate interests of its government, and at the same time helped place the HO outside of the French sphere of influence.

The foundation thus scored a double hit, as countering French influence was another objective of its project in medicine and public health. In the foundation's global medical project, the world was divided into two categories: the Latin world with Paris at its center and the Anglo-Saxon world with London as its capital. For the men of the RF, France was "a model in health throughout the Latin world,"[8] which is to say Mediterranean Europe, Latin America, and even areas under French colonial domination. The RF's objective of converting the entire Latin world to US medical standards—themselves a synthesis of the German and British systems—was inseparable from the goal of diminishing French influence, which was pursued throughout the interwar period. This is what emerged from a meeting in New York of the foundation's officers and trustees in February–March 1927, whose goal was to provide an update for on-going projects in the world: France was only one of 18 European countries where the foundation had initiated projects,[9] but was considered as a central one. Two months later, when they provided an outline of future projects, the trustees emphasized France's strategic nature in reforming global medical education due to its influence on "Latin countries," especially "Italy and South American countries, along with Belgium, Indochina, and Syria."[10] In 1929 when the RF was considering major investment to build a new medical school in Paris, the foundation saw the project as an opportunity to capture the "chief fortress of Latin medicine"[11]—the University of Paris—and convert it to Anglo-Saxon standards. As IHB directors wrote in November 1929, "Ever since exploratory studies in South America ten years ago, all of the activities conducted in Latin countries […] have had the ultimate goal of a major change […] in Paris."[12]

Consequently, analysis of RF investment in the LoN cannot be understood without taking into consideration its project to reform global medicine, with regard to education, research, and public health management. The foundation began to implement this project in the late 1910s, with its first health campaigns in Latin America and the construction of Peking Union Medical College in China, which was inaugurated in 1921. In 1917 it gained a foothold in Europe by launching a campaign against tuberculosis in France, and in 1919 it conducted exploratory studies in other countries, especially in Central Europe, which it did not know well, and which had enormous health problems. The geopolitical situation in that part of the continent was complex at the time, as the German, Austro-Hungarian, and Russian Empires had given way to nine states (Finland, Estonia, Latvia, Lithuania, Poland, Czechoslovakia, Hungary, Austria, and Yugoslavia), while previously existing countries (Bulgaria, Romania, Albania, Greece) saw major changes to their borders. There were considerable inequalities in development between an industrialized Czechoslovakia and Austria, a partially industrialized Poland and Hungary, and Balkan states that remained agricultural. Finally, demographic size varied considerably from one country to another, ranging from small Albania, with less than a million inhabitants, to large Poland, with 30 million.

Amid this kaleidoscope, the RF had its heart set in the spring of 1920 on Czechoslovakia, signing a cooperation agreement with the local government in May, which provided for one of its representatives, the former military doctor Frederick F. Russell, to travel to the new state in order to help establish a public health administration. Upon his arrival in Prague in August, Russell developed a project for a National Institute of Public Health,[13] and when he left the country in October, he was replaced by Selskar Gunn. This Harvard professor and public health administrator from Massachusetts had entered the Rockefeller orbit in 1917,[14] when he was hired as the Deputy Director and later Director of the Commission for the Prevention of Tuberculosis in France. In 1920 he became a technical advisor to the Czechoslovakian government, once again on behalf of the RF, a position he held until July 1922, and one that would serve as a forward base for extending Rockefeller policy in

Central Europe. In November 1920 Gunn organized a study tour for members of the Czechoslovakian Ministry of Health to the US and Canada to examine how public health was administered there.

It was also in the end of 1920 that initial contact between Gunn and Rajchman occurred. The latter, who was still in his position in Poland, was seeking funding to both expand the activity of his bacteriological laboratories and create a national health institute. After meeting in Prague, the two men entered into increasing contact with one another beginning in early 1921. When Rajchman was appointed Director of the HS, he continued negotiating a grant with Gunn for his Polish projects, but also began to discuss with him the possibility of establishing collaboration between the LoN and the RF. The foundation had signed an agreement with the Czechoslovakian government in July 1921 to provide 50% of the funding for a national health institute in Prague,[15] and planned to renew this experience in Poland and other Central European countries. As for the brand new HS, it expanded its projects, which included organizing the fight against epidemics, creating an epidemiological intelligence service, and organizing a conference on the standardization of serums in London in December 1921. In short, the HS was developing a genuine European policy, and Gunn, who was increasingly aware of the importance of health-related endeavors in Europe, also saw the RF's interest in relying on the young organization to carry out its projects on a European terrain it did not understand well. This was also the opinion of Wickliffe Rose, Director of the IHB, who believed that the new organization was in a good position to play the role of a "central authority"[16] in organizing public health in Europe. From early 1922 onward, a Yalta for Health began to implicitly take shape between the RF and the HS, with the former concentrating on establishing national health administrations, and the latter more on the fight against epidemics on the European scale. Relations intensified at the time between Rajchman and Gunn, who also exchanged a great deal of information and contacts.[17]

It was the European Health Conference held in Warsaw in March 1922 that convinced the RF to move beyond simple information exchange with the LoN, and provide funding for the organization. Rajchman had achieved the amazing feat of bringing almost all major European countries to the table, Russia included, despite tensions between the Bolshevik state and most of its neighbors. It is important to remember that the Treaty of Versailles did not define Poland's eastern border, nor that of the Baltic states or Finland, which had gained their independence from the Russian Empire thanks to the Bolshevik Revolution; and that there was a Polish-Soviet War in 1920–1921, following which the border was established by the Treaty of Riga in March 1921, to the advantage of the Poles. In the spring of 1922 the embers of this conflict were still warm, which is why the Warsaw conference was such a diplomatic feat. Gunn attended as a member of the Czechoslovakian delegation, and could see the concrete results; following the conference, immediate aid was provided to Russian authorities, and bilateral conventions were signed in which the various countries committed to keeping one another mutually informed in the event of an epidemic outbreak on their territory. This conference demonstrated the scope of possible activity in Europe, as well as Rajchman's talent as an organizer, two elements that prompted Rose to inform him, during a trip to Europe in April, of his wish to provide a grant to the HS.[18]

The foundation's Board of Trustees was yet to be convinced, something that Raymond Fosdick, a staunch supporter of developing technical activities, attended to in late May.[19] Several Trustees were reluctant to defy congressional disavowal of the Treaty of Versailles and thereby place the RF among the vanguard of pro-LoN movements in the US.[20] It took all of Fosdick's powers of persuasion—and the assent of George E. Vincent, who was also a fervent internationalist—to secure the proposal's acceptance. It was during the same Board of Trustees meeting that the decision was made to fund the National Health Institute in Warsaw, whose broad outlines Rajchman and Gunn had formalized when negotiating the nature of the Rockefeller grant to the LoN. In July 1922 the foundation signed an agreement with the Polish government based on the one signed a year earlier in Czechoslovakia, providing 50% of the funding to build a National Health Institute in Warsaw.[21] At the same time, the LoN Council officially accepted the Rockefeller gift to the HS, before the signing of an official agreement validated by the Council on September 2.[22] It was renewed regularly until 1937, when the funding came to an end: Rockefeller support was therefore constant and massive, as it amounted to nearly $2 million for the 1922–1937 period for the HS alone.

The scope and multiyear nature of this funding were in sharp contrast to the funds provided to the HS by national governments, which was paid on a yearly basis and was always subject to last-minute restrictions making it impossible to see beyond the current year. Rockefeller funding allowed the HS to develop medium-term projects. On a strictly accounting level, the funding represented a significant portion of the HO's resources: in 1924 its total budget was 1.18 million Swiss francs, of which 481,000, or 40% came from the RF.[23] Conversely, funds provided to the LoN also represented a considerable portion of the Rockefeller budget. In 1923 the foundation spent $142,000 worldwide in grants for public health administrations, of which $93,000 was just for the LoN, a portion that increased in 1924, with a relation of $150,000 for $113,000.[24] This brief accounting overview reveals a key fact, namely that Rockefeller funding was trivial neither for the foundation nor for the League: it was one of the major investments for the former, and vital operational support for the latter.

The Epidemiological Intelligence Service

The first destination of the Rockefeller grant was epidemiological intelligence and health documentation. In November 1921 the temporary Health Committee created an Epidemiological Intelligence Service (EIS) tasked with gathering information on the incidence of epidemics in Eastern Europe and circulating it with national health authorities. But it barely had any funding, and the Rockefeller grant, which was planned for 5 years, came at just the right moment, enabling it to launch its activities. The funding totaled $32,000 up through 1927, when the agreement was renewed until 1934 for an almost identical sum. In addition to this amount, there was $50,000 in 1925 to create a Singapore Bureau for the Service[25] to cover the Far East. In 1927 a project for a Health Documentation Centre expanded these measures, with part of the grant renewal being allocated for the salary of its director and two assistants until 1934.[26] Finally, in 1923 the foundation provided a grant to train statisticians in countries considered to be deficient in the field of health statistics, in an effort to promote the international harmonization of statistics. It would be renewed in 1925 in the amount of $63,000.

The Rockefeller contribution was crucial to implementing the EIS, as it represented 92% of its budget in 1924.[27] These funds allowed the Service to quickly supplant the IOPH and undermine the US government's strategy of maintaining that organization. In 1926 the Coolidge administration wanted to make the IOPH the primary center for collecting data on epidemics during negotiations of the International Sanitary Convention, a goal thwarted by the important work of the EIS.

The Service had multiple objectives: gathering intelligence on epidemics in Europe in terms of geographic distribution, periodicity, and diffusion processes; organizing studies of certain countries in collaboration with national health services; inviting "experts"[28] from the most affected countries to the HO to develop solutions with them; and organizing the exchange of epidemiological data between countries by publishing it in periodic bulletins distributed to health administrations. In short, the EIS was an "information service"[29] that centralized, processed, and redistributed health data on a European scale, in order to guide LoN policy for combatting epidemics. It had many points in common with similar bodies created in other European countries, bodies that the RF also often funded, such as the Office national d'hygiène sociale in France, which was created to guide nascent public health policy.[30] Foundation officers believed that these national services should be encouraged to cooperate, with the EIS in Geneva playing a role as an interface and centralizing office for information on a continental scale, and eventually on the global scale, as demonstrated by the creation of its Singapore Bureau.

This effort to collect information was inseparable from data harmonization, as EIS members realized that it was "impossible to compare information from countries with an adequate statistical service with that of countries where such an organization [is] insufficient or does not exist."[31] They therefore began a process to harmonize health statistics, with financial as well as technical and intellectual support from the RF. In July 1922 Rajchman asked Wickliffe Rose to suggest a health statistician to lead the Service, as he had not found a candidate in Europe for the position. After consulting with a number of specialists, Rose suggested he contact Edgar Sydenstricker, head of the Office of Statistics at the Public Health Service (PHS).[32] Sydenstricker was not unknown in the profession: born in China in 1881 to missionary parents, he studied economics at the University of Chicago, and then worked for the United States Immigration Commission and the United States Commission on Industrial Relations during the 1910s, conducting studies on the salaries, working conditions, and standard of living of workers employed by major industrial groups, immigrants in particular.[33]

His work was in keeping with the surveys typical of the 1900s, when social reform circles experimented with methods to solve the problems arising from the emergence of the US as a major industrial power. The survey was one of these methods and involved field study based on statistics. It was often funded by foundations, such as the Russell Sage Foundation (RSF), which funded surveys since its creation in 1907, the most emblematic one being the *Pittsburgh Survey*, which analyzed the living conditions of laborers in the industrial city. Everything was examined with a fine-tooth comb and backed up by statistics, including birth rate, death rate, housing size, salaries, household budgets, and the frequency of infectious diseases, among others. The survey published in 1909 had considerable impact, and in 1912 prompted the RSF to create a department of surveys that led to over 3,000 such efforts by the late 1920s.

These surveys were based on the social sciences (sociology, economics, statistics, etc.) and aimed to offer state and federal policymakers solutions for improving the social situation. This goal was partially met, for in 1912 the US Commission on Industrial Relations used this model to conduct a survey of the living and working conditions for workers throughout the country, whose report published in 1916 prompted the federal government to enact reforms. Sydenstricker participated in this commission by conducting statistical surveys of salaries and working conditions. In connection with expanded federal intervention, the PHS used statistical surveys to acquire an overall view of the problems. Sydenstricker became the first health statistician recruited by the federal government, and in the ensuing years conducted surveys of diseases common in working-class environments, notably pellagra and influenza. In 1920 he became the head of the Office of Statistics at the PHS, and the following year conducted the pioneering *Hagerstown Morbidity Survey*, which systematically analyzed the cause of death in the city and served as a model for similar surveys on the national scale.[34]

In the early 1920s Sydenstricker's work served as an authority in the field of statistics. When approached by Rajchman he accepted the offer and secured a one-year leave from his supervisor Hugh S. Cumming.[35] Now an LoN employee, he directed the EIS from January 1923 to March 1924. Shortly before his departure for Switzerland, Sydenstricker also recruited, on the RF's recommendation,[36] the statistician Thomas Duffield to assist in his work. Duffield had directed the statistics section of the Commission for the Prevention of Tuberculosis in France from 1917 to 1922, where he mapped out the disease's presence by region.[37] He worked for the EIS from April 1923 to December 1924 before returning to the US. The two men played a major role in organizing the Service and guiding its work.

In the fall of 1922, the EIS published its first *Epidemiological Intelligence* pamphlets, which focused on the state of epidemics in Central Europe and Russia, and were produced using statistics from national health administrations that were processed and harmonized by the EIS.[38] In 1923 under Sydenstricker's leadership, this pamphlet became thicker and more systematic; it was transformed into a monthly *Epidemiological Report* providing an update on the epidemic situation in 27 European countries, as well as the US, certain Latin American countries, colonial Africa, British India, a number of countries in Asia, Australia, and New Zealand. The following year these monthly reports were compiled into an *International Health Yearbook* numbering a few hundred pages and containing not only statistics but also public health synthesis reports for over 20 countries (including the US) and multiple organizations (HS, IOPH, RF, International Labour Office, League of Red Cross Societies). In the space of one year, the EIS had become a health monitoring body before its time, in which Sydenstricker applied the methods typical of US progressive movements on the international scale and began the international mapping of diseases. To do so he established cooperation with the statistical services of national public health administrations, especially in Europe, with these contacts no doubt facilitated by the fact that some of these services were also supported by the RF. During his term he also established cooperation with the statistics service of the LoN's Economic Committee, which conducted a survey of the global population at his request.[39]

He left for the US in 1924, as the PHS refused to extend his absence. Alongside his duties in the administration, he began to work for the Milbank Memorial Fund (MMF), initially as a consultant, then as Director of Research in 1929,[40] and finally as Scientific Director in 1935. He took Duffield with him. He maintained his relations with the LoN, attending meetings of the Health Committee in 1930 and 1934. His successor at the head of the EIS was also an American, Dr Otto R. Eichel, who was in charge of vital statistics at the New York Department of Health,[41] and remained in the position from March 1924 until his death in December.[42] The HS also hired an American Deputy Director to assist him in the person of Frank Boudreau. Born in Canada in 1886, he studied medicine at McGill University, and in 1912 became an epidemiologist at the Ohio Department of Health. He was recommended to Rajchman by the RF and Sydenstricker,[43] and assumed his duties in March 1925. In 1933 he was promoted to Director of the service, a position he held until his return to the US in 1937. He was also hired by Sydenstricker at the MMF in 1935, succeeding him as Scientific Director upon his death in 1936 and becoming its Executive Director in 1937. He made a brief return to the LoN in 1939 as a consultant, in connection with the reorganization of technical activities initiated by the Bruce Report. He left even more of a mark than Sydenstricker on the EIS, which had been directed by an American for practically its entire existence.

Upon his arrival, Boudreau focused on setting up the Singapore Bureau, whose origins went back to 1923 when, at Japan's request, the HO sent a representative to the Far East to conduct a health survey of the region's ports.[44] The representative returned convinced that the International Sanitary Convention of 1912, which governed the quarantine system, had to be revised in light of the knowledge produced by scientific research. He notably called for greater information exchange regarding infectious diseases, in order to lighten quarantine for ships free from disease and to promote international commerce. The development of epidemiological intelligence was not simply intended to improve the health of populations, it also occurred within a context of expanding economic exchange, which the LoN's technical bodies strove to simultaneously develop and regulate. It was also one of the objectives of the RF's health policy.

Informed of the contents of the report drafted by the LoN representative, the US expressed its interest in developing epidemiological intelligence in the ports of the Far East, which according to the State Department could only promote international commerce.[45] However, it was not the State Department that took the initiative of cooperating with the LoN, but the RF, which funded a conference in Singapore in February 1925 attended by regional governments (including that of the Philippines, under US administration), and quickly provided a grant to establish the Bureau. It included an Advisory Council consisting of representatives from the health administrations of the region's countries; while the US was not formally involved, it sent a member of the PHS[46] as an observer to represent the Philippines, and beginning in 1930 a second one for the Hawaiian Islands.

However, in this scenario as well, the RF, State Department, and PHS did not entirely share the same views. While the government supported the development of commerce, it believed the country was safe from the spread of infectious diseases due to the two oceans separating it from Europe and Asia. As for South America, an epidemiological monitoring system already existed in connection with the Pan-American Sanitary Bureau created in 1902. The federal government was thus more interested in maintaining the particularities of its existing regulation than in signing a global sanitary convention that would require revisions to its own commercial and migratory legislation (migrants were also affected by the quarantine system). Cumming defended this line at the Health Committee: the Director of the PHS did not try to promote the globalization of HO activity so much as to limit its impact—especially in Latin America—by trying to circumvent it in favor of the IOPH, which the US wanted to collect and process epidemiological data from ports as well as to conduct negotiations that would lead to the International Sanitary Convention of 1926. The latter supplemented and broadened the terms of the 1912 convention, which already recommended that states mutually communicate information relating to outbreaks within their borders. In 1912 it was the IOPH that was entrusted with gathering and redistributing information, although its logistical means were limited, for it transmitted information to states via mail, whereas diseases circulated more quickly than that. Thanks to the RF grant, the EIS's Singapore Bureau organized a competing and faster transmission system based on radio. However, under pressure from the US and the USSR, the 1926 convention maintained the IOPH in its role of coordinating and transmitting information.

According to the terms of the new convention, the LoN's Singapore Bureau was considered a regional office that had to send data to Paris, but it also sent it via radio to Geneva, where the EIS synthesized and diffused it much more quickly than the IOPH. The latter was in effect bypassed by the EIS in Geneva, to which countries increasingly sent their data rather than the IOPH. The Singapore Bureau provided health monitoring for all of Southeast Asia, receiving information via wireless telegraphy from ports each week, which it immediately redistributed to all other ports, before sending a copy of each report to Geneva for publication in the *Epidemiological Report*. The gathering of statistics was proceeding very well, as 62 local or governmental administrations provided statistics for the *Report* in 1924, with this number rising to 116 in 1926, covering two-thirds of the world's population.[47] In the late 1920s, it was the EIS and not the IOPH that served as an authority in health monitoring, with the Rockefeller initiative playing against the objectives of its own government.

Data collection and processing by the EIS was made possible by the LoN's documentary services, in which the US played a crucial role, for in 1927 the LoN built a new library to centralize its documentation and cataloging services thanks to the personal gift of $2 million from John D. Rockefeller, Jr mentioned in Chapter 2. The gift grew out of consultations between representatives from the RF and the LoN Secretariat (Raymond Fosdick, Abraham Flexner, Arthur Sweetser, and Eric Drummond).[48] Before making it official, Fosdick also consulted with the Under Secretary of State Robert Olds, in order to confirm that the gift would not pose a problem for the US government.[49] It was announced at the LoN General Assembly on September 12 in the presence of Aristide Briand, Gustav Stresemann, and Austen Chamberlain. The presence of the three signatories of the Locarno Treaties gave the Rockefeller gesture an internationalist symbolism that was immediately used by Sweetser, who ensured that the news was relayed by the press. The "galleries were full of journalists and spectators,"[50] including a group of 25 editorial writers that the CEIP had invited on a two-month trip to Europe to visit the institutions of international cooperation. As Geneva was one of the stops on their trip, Sweetser arranged for them to be present on the day of the General Assembly and distributed a press release to each of them announcing the gift, which was also on the front page of *The New York Times* on September 13.

This funding gave the library a new role, which now "had approximately ten times more space than currently," with its annual budget being twice that provided until present by the General Assembly.[51] Furthermore, the new building was not limited to the construction of a storage space, but also centralized the documentation generated by the technical sections since 1919, and inventoried them using an effective catalog and index system. The new building was thus a genuine place for research,[52] one that sought to provide documentation for the technical sections and to attract specialists from across the globe. An Organization Committee was created in late 1927 to lead the project, including multiple members from the LoN Council, librarians from the League and the International Labour Office, the administrator of the French National Library, Roland Manuel, Fosdick and Sweetser[53] (both of whom represented John D. Rockefeller, Jr.), and the University of Michigan librarian Warner Bishop, "whose opinions carried weight at the Carnegie Corporation and the Rockefeller Foundation,"[54] with the foundation paying for his trip to attend the meetings of the Organization Committee.[55] The architect chosen by the committee visited numerous libraries in Europe and the US in 1929. In the spring of 1935 with the building almost complete, Sweetser gave a tour to a Rockefeller delegation including David Rockefeller (son of John D., Jr.), and the officers John Van Sickle, Tracy Kittredge, and Sydnor Walker.

Equipped with its new space, the library could provide readers and researchers from technical sections with the governmental publications it housed. In 1934 Bishop observed that it had the world's largest collection of public documents for the previous decade, and that its impact was demonstrated by the 5,000 yearly requests it received to transmit documents. He also noted, with amusement, that it was easier for a US librarian to receive documents for South America by writing to Geneva than directly to the administrative services of Montevideo or La Paz. In 1934 the new LoN Secretary General, Joseph Avenol, planned to go further and merge the statistical services of the technical sections into a single organization that could provide the Secretariat and member states with information on economic, health, legal, and monetary issues. However, this would require staff that the Secretariat could not afford.[56] In December 1935 the RF provided a grant to pay the salary of an assistant librarian to launch the project, but it canceled its funding in July 1937 before anything had taken concrete form. Still, at that time the library was a major documentation center in Europe and the world.[57] It served, throughout the interwar period, as an essential medium for the expertise of the HO and other LoN technical organizations.

Study Tours by Health Experts

The second area benefiting from Rockefeller grants was collective study tours conducted by civil servants from national health administrations. The grant awarded by the foundation in 1922 provided for a payment of $60,000 per year for this activity, a sum that was increased to $100,000 in 1924 owing to the program's success.[58] This grant would be continued, on a decreasing

98 *A Global Health Policy*

basis, until 1937. The money was decisive for the Section, as $60,000—or 85%—of the $70,000 allocated for collective study tours by the LoN in 1923 and 1924 came from the RF.[59] From 1926 onward, the gradual decrease of Rockefeller funding and increase of LoN funding rebalanced the proportions. The US portion nevertheless remained substantial,[60] and Rockefeller money was instrumental to the HS establishing global channels for exchange and developing them over a number of years.

This travel program had its origins in both organizations. In 1917 the RF inaugurated a policy of scientific study tours by creating its first fellowships, and in 1922 organized collective study tours for health administrators and academics in the US and Great Britain. In January 1921 Rajchman sent a memorandum to the temporary Health Committee calling for a policy of exchange between LoN member countries. The origins of the project were also a matter of dispute between Rajchman and Gunn, judging from the unkind terms in a letter from the former to the latter in August 1922.[61] It is impossible to determine here who had the idea first, and this detail is hardly important: what is essential is that both organizations had, almost at the same time, identical projects in this area, and that it was these shared objectives and methods that convinced the foundation to fund the Section, although this incident shows that the two organizations were simultaneously and inextricably collaborating and competing.

The study tour program's goal was to help circulate working methods in public health, in an effort to improve the work of national administrations and promote international harmonization of their methods. Public health administrations were developed in numerous European countries in the years following World War I, but contact between them was rare. The LoN's objective was to expand contact in order to implement an international health policy. The tours included 20–30 civil servants who, over the course of 4–6 weeks, visited health institutions in one or more countries, including administrative services, hospitals, dispensaries, nursing schools, health managements schools, etc. Each tour involved a specific category and included civil servants from national public health services, dispensary doctors, malariologists, school hygiene specialists, tuberculosis specialists, staff assigned to disinfect high-risk areas, statisticians, staff from potable water supply services, and specialists in tropical diseases. Before returning to their countries, the participants visited the HS offices in Geneva to attend additional conferences and create comparative syntheses of policies from various countries in the sector. These logistics were costly and were only made possible by the Rockefeller grant.

The first exchange took place in the fall of 1922 in Belgium, and opened with conferences on international preventative medicine, a new concept that reflected the ambition of the HS. The program intensified the following year with four tours. The first took place in Great Britain from February 25 to April 11, with 23 civil servants from 16 countries (Austria, Belgium, Czechoslovakia, Denmark, Finland, France, Hungary, Italy, Japan, Norway, Poland, Romania, Yugoslavia, the USSR, Sweden, the US). The tour was planned by the HS in collaboration with the RF, the Society of Medical Officers of Health, and the British Ministry of Health. After a presentation of the health administration in Great Britain, the participants were divided into groups of four or five individuals, each of whom would visit a location such as a port, agricultural area, or mining zone. After multiple weeks in the field, the participants returned to London to share their results. The Rockefeller representative, Selskar Gunn, attended the closing conference.[62]

That same year, as part of the Europe-wide statistical harmonization process, a tour was organized for health statisticians from eight countries (Brazil, Bulgaria, Czechoslovakia, Hungary, Yugoslavia, Norway, Poland, the USSR) whose statistical services were deemed to be deficient by LoN and Rockefeller experts. The program included a one-month stay in Geneva for training in vital statistics; a visit to the health statistics offices in Bern, Paris, The Hague, London, and the LoN EIS; and a series of conferences in Geneva over a 10-day period to complete the synthesis effort. In total the tour lasted two and a half months, during which the civil servants worked on topics that were new to them, such as techniques for recording deaths and determining the cause of death, or the distinction between the stillbirth rate (stillborn babies) and infant mortality (death before the age of one) in health statistics.[63] In total 78 civil servants of 18 nationalities participated in tours in 1923, a number that rose to 99 and 20 nationalities in 1924. That year saw another tour of statisticians in October-November,[64] while in the spring a group of malariologists visited Italy to study the country's efforts to combat the disease. Given the success of these tours, as well as the persistent lack of funding from LoN member states, Rajchman asked the RF to extend the grant, which was scheduled to end in 1925. The grant extension allowed the program to intensify and diversify destinations and areas of study.

Seven tours took place in 1925. From February to April, civil servants from 13 countries (Canada, Denmark, Estonia, France, Germany, Greece, Italy, Holland, Norway, Poland, the US, the USSR, and Yugoslavia) visited London to study urban and rural public health administration in the city and its surrounding area. All aspects were studied including housing, sanitation, nutrition, school hygiene, industrial hygiene, the screening and identification of diseases, maternity, child welfare, nursing care, and vital statistics. The tour ended in Geneva with conferences by the HO. In March there was the first tour on industrial hygiene attended by a dozen health and safety inspectors, and organized in cooperation with the Division of Industrial Hygiene of the International Labour Office. There were two other tours later in the spring, to Belgium and Yugoslavia, while in October and December a tour to Japan was organized for doctors in the Pacific region,[65] which brought together 17 individuals from Australia, China, the Federated Malay States, Hong Kong, British India, the Dutch East Indies, French Indochina, New Zealand, Siam, the USSR, and the US Territory of Philippines. Meanwhile in Europe, the year's seventh tour was devoted to health problems in Mediterranean ports, bringing together 12 specialists from neighboring countries (Algeria,

Egypt, Spain, France, Great Britain, Greece, Italy, Yugoslavia, Syria). The group visited the ports of Barcelona, Marseille, Algiers, Genoa, Naples, Haifa, Alexandria, Piraeus, Trieste, Suez, and El Tor in the South Sinai. The participants compared methods for port health administration, quarantine, and the collection of epidemiological data. As usual, the tour ended at HO headquarters in Geneva. In total between 1922 and the end of the program in 1935, nearly 50 tours took place, including 24 between 1922 and 1926; 600 public health specialists participated between 1922 and 1930, and most likely close to 1,000 for the entire period. The participants came from over 40 countries, a sign of the genuinely international nature of the undertaking, and the number of countries visited rose to 23. While France, Great Britain, Belgium, Switzerland, and the Netherlands were the most frequently visited destinations, tours were also made to Eastern Europe—notably Czechoslovakia, Poland, and Yugoslavia—and Northern Europe, as well as outside of Europe in North Africa, Sub-Saharan Africa, the Far East, and the US.

In keeping with the Secretariat's general strategy, Rajchman ensured that the US was involved in the program from the beginning. In 1923, the US sent one or more representatives on each tour, with the nomination process being handled for the time being by Cumming, who chose the participants from the PHS and the health departments of numerous states including New York, Arkansas, and Georgia.[66] In early 1925 Drummond tried to give the affair a more official turn by directly informing the State Department regarding upcoming tours, albeit in vain, as the Secretary of State verbally informed Cumming that he would not follow up on any official request made by the LoN. It was thus the Surgeon General who continued, as a member of the Health Committee, to serve as the intermediary between the US and the LoN.[67] This would be the case until the early 1930s, when the Secretary of State began to personally examine invitations from the technical sections.

Four tours took place in the US during the period. The first, in the fall of 1923, was for statisticians.[68] The second occurred in the spring of 1925 for civil servants from ten countries in Central and South America including Argentina, Brazil, Mexico, Costa Rica, El Salvador, Uruguay, Peru, and Venezuela. The US was only one destination in a long journey that took participants to Cuba and Canada to study the work of public health services. It then shifted to Europe with stops in Great Britain and the Netherlands to become acquainted with vital and housing statistics; Belgium to examine the dispensary system; Switzerland and France to visit antituberculosis dispensaries and child health centers; and Italy to observe the fight against malaria, before ending the tour in Geneva with the ritual conferences at the HO.[69] On April 24 during their stop in Washington, the participants were hosted by the White House, although the evening's social event was somewhat spoiled by the confusion of President Calvin Coolidge, who thought he was before a health mission organized by the Pan-American Union—the rival of the HS in Latin America—to the great fury of Rajchman, who wanted to use the tour to present the LoN's health activities to the US![70] As an anecdote, Louis Ferdinand Destouches (who did not yet have his pen name of Céline) was also present during the tour. He was recruited the previous year by the HS on Gunn's recommendation and attended to the tour's logistical aspects. He would work at the HS until 1927, and this stay in the US provided him with material for multiple chapters of *Journey to the End of the Night* a few years later.[71]

The third tour, in 1927, was led by two members of the LoN's Malaria Commission, Colonel James and Dr Swellengrebel. The objective was to observe efforts to combat malaria in the Southern US, where the disease was long endemic and where the RF implemented programs in the 1910s that it wanted to publicize, especially with regard to mosquito larvae destruction. Finally, the fourth tour took place in November and December 1935 and was devoted to housing, food, and physical education. Frank Boudreau made special preparations in advance, conducting an exploratory visit funded by the MMF.[72] The tour was not intended for health civil servants but for members of the Health Committee, who held senior positions in their respective health administrations. The participants visited all of the federal administrations in charge of health (the Departments of Labor, Treasury, the Interior, and Agriculture). After Washington they made a detour to Baltimore to visit Johns Hopkins University, to Nashville to see the social and medical programs of the Tennessee Valley Authority, and then to Chicago, Cincinnati, St. Louis, Boston, New Haven, and New York, where they met representatives from major associations, such as the American Public Health Association and the National Tuberculosis Association, as well as actors in philanthropy such as the RF, the MMF, and the Commonwealth Fund.[73] They were accompanied for part of the tour by a civil servant from the PHS made available by Cumming. After the tour they published a long report in the *Quarterly Bulletin of the Health Organisation*. One of the elements that left the greatest impression was the extensive measures put in place by authorities on all levels (federal government, states, cities, rural areas) to "coordinate all activities promoting hygiene and protecting health."[74] The US struck the visitors as a place where this coordination, which the HO was trying to promote in all countries, was the most developed. Committee members also noted the systematic connection between "efforts to protect health" and "the simultaneous and general improvement of social welfare"; in other words, hygiene and health issues were considered in conjunction with economic, agricultural, and industrial problems. This connection was the most striking at the New Deal's most prominent experiment, the Tennessee Valley Authority: "that is where the coordination of multiple efforts is the most visible […] for the revival of this vast area." The experiment was carefully scrutinized by the visitors.

The system of collective study tours was accompanied by a program of individual fellowships. The HS took direct inspiration from the fellowships created by the RF in 1917, which served as a model for the major fellowship programs of the twentieth century.[75] In 1923 at the request of the health services of multiple countries, the HS granted 16 of them to civil servants with specific projects: an Italian visited school hygiene services in France, the Netherlands, and Belgium; two Australian bacteriologists took a tour of European laboratories, as did a Swiss parasitologist. There were many others, as between 1922 and 1935, 175 civil servants received individual fellowships funded by the Rockefeller grant.[76]

The documentation gathered during these tours expanded the library's collections made available to governments, such as in 1928 when the Greek government called on the LoN to help organize its public health system. The HO sent a group of experts on-site to assess needs and develop a multiyear plan of action, which was adopted by the Greek government in 1929. Through 1935 the HS trained at least 60 health civil servants from Greece, either via individual fellowships or by participation in collective tours. HS activity was, like in other countries, supplemented by that of the RF, which implemented a campaign to combat malaria in the 1930s.[77] This activity included technical assistance for the Greek government to create a malariology section within the Ministry of Public Health; 22 fellowships for doctors and nurses to receive training in public health in US universities (especially Johns Hopkins University); and backing to develop the School of Hygiene in Athens.

In 1930 China also sought out the LoN to improve certain deficient sectors, especially the quarantine system in ports, hospital organization, and the effort to combat certain diseases such as cholera and smallpox. Employees from the Chinese quarantine service were invited to Geneva to examine the available documentation, and traveled for a number of months in European ports with LoN assistance. The LoN also sent a representative to China, who spent 3 years in Nanjing overseeing the creation of an Institute of Public Health. In the space of a few years, spectacular progress was made in quarantine and the fight against cholera. LoN activity was once again supplemented by that of the RF, which had been highly present in China since 1914, as well as the MMF, which initiated activity in the country starting in 1930.[78]

The synergy between the HS and the RF was also present in the systematic exchange of information and best practices. The two organizations exchanged their lists of fellows[79] and consulted regularly when they received applications for individual fellowships. They also served as representatives for one another, as in August 1923 when Thomas Duffield, the EIS statistician, visited Spain to study health statistics, where he was hosted by Manuel Tapia, the Director of the Instituto nacional de higiene de Alfonso XIII, who informed Duffield he wanted to study in the US. Duffield inquired with the RF, where he had contacts, and provided him with instructions on how to prepare the application.[80] With his recommendation from the HS, Tapia was awarded a one-year fellowship to study in the US in 1926.

The two organizations mutually relied on one another where they needed to. The RF, which still did not have deep knowledge of Europe, relied on the network of the HS. For instance, in the spring of 1925, when it granted a fellowship to F.J. Netusil, the Director of Vital Statistics for the Czechoslovakian government, it asked Rajchman to facilitate his visits with European health administrations by drafting letters of introduction.[81] The following year, when the foundation granted a fellowship to a Turkish doctor to study how public health was organized in Germany, Gunn wrote to Rajchman: "As I have never worked in this country, my knowledge of institutions is fragmentary: could you suggest a German institution where he could receive the appropriate training in public health?"[82]

In the early 1920s, the RF habitually offered some fellows a stop in Geneva for a few days upon the completion of their tour, as it did in July 1923 for Otto Studenhy, a member of the Austrian health administration; it did the same for other fellows from Czechoslovakia, Bulgaria, Poland, Hungary, Yugoslavia, and even India, with at least 16 occurring between June 1925 and August 1927.[83] They were taken care of during this tour by the HS, which sometimes would pay for a tour instead of the foundation. This was the case for Antonin Kolinski, a civil servant in the Czechoslovakian Health Ministry, whom the foundation had already awarded a fellowship that it could not renew for administrative reasons. It was therefore the HS that paid for his tour to Yugoslavia in April 1925.

The HS also took advantage of the RF's contacts. When Rajchman organized the Section's collective tours, he often consulted Gunn for the addresses of institutions to visit, such that tour programs were regularly conceived jointly between the HS and the RF, especially when they took place outside of Europe. For instance, for the tour organized to the US in October 1923, the program was largely conceived by the foundation, which after the journey organized and funded a dinner in New York for all participants.[84] Another example was the aforementioned dinner in April 1925 at the White House, when Coolidge confused the HS and the Pan-American Union. For the tour to Japan in the fall of 1925, the RF provided the names of Chinese doctors that could be invited.[85] Four years later in 1929, when the Deputy Director of the Institut Pasteur in Tunis went to study leprosy in Latin American for the HS, the RF provided him with letters of introduction to doctors in Brazil and Columbia.[86] When Rajchman went to China in 1929, the RF put him in contact with doctors at the Peking Union Medical College, the "model" medical school built in 1921 with foundation money.

The HS also relied on institutions supported by the RF in Europe. As stated earlier, in 1921 and 1922 the RF signed agreements with the Czechoslovakian and Polish governments to establish national health institutes. In late 1924 the Warsaw Institute opened its doors even though its offices were not yet complete, followed in November 1925 by that of Prague.[87] In the meantime, the foundation launched studies in Bulgaria (1922), Yugoslavia (1924), and Romania (1925)[88] in an effort to extend its activities there, leading to funding for similar institutes in Zagreb and Budapest, which opened in 1926, as well as in London in 1929. The foundation tried to do the same in Paris, but got bogged down in mandarin rivalries and ministerial instability.[89] In 1924 when the HS expanded its activities to include the teaching of hygiene by creating an

104   *A Global Health Policy*

ad hoc commission, it relied on RF achievements. In 1925 Warsaw and Prague were among the destinations for the first collective study tour it organized with Rockefeller funding to visit European schools of hygiene. In 1926 the Director of the commission, Léon Bernard of France, visited Warsaw for the Institute's official inauguration.[90] The following year, in September–October 1927, the commission organized a tour for the directors of European schools of hygiene to Budapest and Zagreb in order to develop methods to harmonize studies on the European level.[91] The activities of the two institutions were therefore interconnected and represented the concrete manifestation in the field of the common project of the RF and the LoN, namely a government through science and expertise.

The Limits of International Cooperation

Another major aspect of HS and technical sections activity was the work of commissions and subcommissions of experts, and the conferences that grew out of their meetings. This is where the process for producing international standards unfolded, which was highly important during the interwar period. The number of these commissions rose as the HS expanded its activity, and they almost always included Americans from universities, philanthropic organizations, the federal government, and state administrations, such as the Commissions for mortality statistics, serum standardization, nutrition, housing, leprosy, opium, syphilis,[92] and malaria.[93] Americans also participated in the work surrounding the use of leisure time, which was conducted by the International Labour Office in relation with the HS. Finally, they attended the conferences organized by the HO from the very outset: in November 1922, Dr A.B. Wadsworth from the Rockefeller Institute for Medical Research attended the Second International Conference on the Standardization of Serums and Serological Tests; in 1924, the Committee of Statistical Experts working to harmonize international statistics invited W.H. Davis of the Federal Census Bureau to take part in the effort; and in 1927 the International Rabies Conference was attended by a Department of Agriculture representative, while the International Conference on Vitamin Standardization was attended by the Director of the National Institute of Hygiene, G.W. McCoy. The same was true for the successive Conferences on Rural Hygiene held between 1931 and 1936, or those organized by Directors of Schools of Hygiene held in 1935 and 1936.

The work of the commissions gives another view of the relationship between the RF and the LoN, and also reflects its limits, which were established from the very beginning by the RF. One example of this came in the spring of 1922, when the foundation created a permanent bureau to coordinate its developing European activities and chose to locate it in Paris rather than Geneva as Rajchman had hoped.[94] At the same time, Wickliffe Rose declined Rajchman's proposal to join the temporary Health Committee.[95] Rajchman tried again in 1931 with George E. Vincent, who had recently retired as foundation president, but once again met with refusal.[96] A close look at the work of the Malaria Commission sheds lights on the distance maintained between the two organizations despite their cooperation.

A joint effort took form in connection with this commission, although it never led to any real synergy. In the late 1910s, the RF gained experience in the fight against malaria, one that was based on the scientific research of the Rockefeller Institute for Medical Research, as well as the foundation's activity in the Southern US and Latin America. However, the HS was unfamiliar with this field, even as malaria was resurging in numerous regions in Europe in the aftermath of the war, especially in Albania, Italy, Yugoslavia, Greece, Bulgaria, Turkey, and Corsica. This called for a vast health undertaking, with Rajchman planning to rely on RF experience: in 1923 the first discussions on the topic were held with Frederick F. Russell, Rose's successor as Director of the IHB. In February 1924 the LoN's Health Committee created a Malaria Commission,[97] with Rajchman inviting Lewis Hackett, one of the RF's specialists, to take part.[98] He declined the proposal, for the foundation was initiating activities in Europe, and he preferred to maintain his independence. This was especially true in Italy, where Hackett conducted a survey at the fascist government's request, upon whose completion he established an experimental malaria research station in Rome in 1924. His recommended strategy was the same as the one deployed by the foundation in the US, namely eradicating the disease through scientific research and antilarval efforts in infected areas to eliminate mosquitos, the primary vectors of propagation. This position was not the one held by the majority of the doctors and public health administrators on the Malaria Commission, who believed it was impossible to completely get rid of mosquitos, and instead supported social hygiene measures to reduce its impact, including hygiene education, improved housing, and the draining and cultivation of wetlands.[99]

In the spring of 1924, the Malaria Commission (MC) organized the first collective study tour for malariologists to the infested areas listed above, as well as to the Institute of Tropical Medicine in London and Emile Brumpt's Parasitology Laboratory at the University of Paris. In its first report published at the end of the year, the MC expressed its skepticism regarding the US strategy, which was deemed to be unsuitable for the European situation. In 1925 one of the RF's malariologists, Dr Darling, nevertheless joined the MC, and conducted a tour to Syria and Palestine with its members over the summer, after which Rajchman proposed to the Americans that the two institutions expand cooperation,[100] and Rajchman planned to organize a tour to the US by the MC to study the efforts of the PHS, local health services, and the RF in the South.[101]

The program for this tour in June and July 1927 was developed, as always, in agreement with the RF, which conceived the itinerary based on sites where it had conducted activities. It included a visit to the laboratories at Johns Hopkins University, and then a big tour of Southern states (Maryland, Tennessee, Mississippi, Alabama, North and South Carolina, Virginia) to study local policies and pilot experiments, such as the aerial spraying of insecticide.[102] Owing to the RF's role in the organization, the two LoN experts spent a great deal of time at sites where the RF had conducted experiments with its methods, to the detriment of those where other strategies for combatting malaria had been tested. This itinerary irritated Cumming, the Director of the PHS, who was also skeptical of the radical nature of the Rockefeller method, and would have preferred that the work presented to European experts not be reduced to that of the foundation.[103]

It was after this tour that the conflict between Americans and Europeans crystallized, as the report drafted by Dr Swellengrebel concluded that it was impossible to apply the eradication methods used on the American continent in Europe.[104] The Rockefeller method, which was almost entirely based on efforts to combat larvae, was criticized in particular, and also deemed to be too costly. Rajchman, who seemed more favorable toward the Rockefeller approach, proposed to the Americans that they become more involved in the MC's work. They attended the June 25, 1928 MC meeting in large numbers[105] to defend their point of view. The meeting brought together 34 malariologists from across the world, with the US being the most represented country with seven experts, all of whom were RF members or advisors. The discussion turned to strategies for combatting the disease, and there was a sharp division between the Americans and other members of the Commission, the majority of whom once again expressed their disagreement with US practices. The final report concluded that

> in Europe, taking the current state of the science into account, the only goal that can be proposed in the fight against malaria is to decrease the disease's frequency and seriousness. Measures seeking to accomplish more (especially those aiming to radically extirpate the disease) are not part of a prudently conceived program, and can be justified only under exceptional circumstances. [...] It is not always essential, in combatting malaria, to base preventative methods on biological knowledge of the mosquitos that transmit the disease.[106]

It is abundantly clear that the MC opposed the Rockefeller's scientific approach based on eradication with a more social approach based on reducing the disease's scope, especially through collective hygienic measures. This fundamental divergence explains why in the following years the envisioned collaboration never materialized, despite what Lewis Hackett's promotion as Vice President of the Commission upon its reappointment in 1935 might suggest. He actually had little regard for the work conducted by his European colleagues[107] and preferred conducting his own policy. In fact, during the spring of 1935, when Rajchman proposed that the RF and HS coordinate epidemiological studies on malaria in Europe, he indicated he was not interested,[108] subsequently bringing the matter to an end.

Conclusion

As a sponsor as well as an intellectual and technical partner, the RF clearly played a central role in implementing and developing two major HO programs, namely in epidemiological intelligence and the circulation of health experts. It did so from the beginning by taking positions contrary to those of the US government, as shown by its early and continued support for the HO against the IOPH. The HO greatly benefited from its partnership with the RF, not only because Rockefeller support allowed it to develop an essential statistical working tool for collecting and processing data on an international scale—thereby acquiring a global view of health issues—but also because funding for exchange among health experts enabled it to build a network and be recognized as a major player in the international health landscape. While the RF benefited symbolically[109] from the assistance it provided, which helped improve its reputation, the HS did not represent the European foothold it hoped to facilitate its policy. This was due to the strong personality of Rajchman, who systematically sought out US assistance all while preventing the foundation from appropriating its projects, as well as the structural opposition between "American" scientific medicine and "European" social medicine, as noted with regard to malaria. The latter dominated at the HS, and most probably curbed greater investment by the foundation, and perhaps even explains its 1937 withdrawal, thereby showing the limits of health internationalism and the RF's attempts to establish global health government led by US experts.

Notes

1. Rockefeller foundation, *Annual Report*, 1913, p. 37.
2. Tournès Ludovic, *Américanisation. Une histoire mondiale*, Paris, Fayard, 2020, ch. 6.
3. Rockefeller Foundation, *Annual Report*, 1918, p. 35.
4. Embree to Vincent, February 2, 1920, RF 3/900/21/159.
5. Prophylaxie internationale. Résumé des conférences données par O. Velghe, directeur général de l'administration d'hygiène de Belgique, octobre 1922, SDN 12B/R848/25605/25605.
6. On Rajchman, see Balinska Marta Aleksandra, *Une vie pour l'humanitaire. Ludwik Rajchmann, 1881–1965*, Paris, La découverte, 1995.
7. American Relief Administration European Children's Fund Mission to Poland, 1919–1922, RAJ-IP C1.
8. IHB Minutes, November 6, 1924, RF 1.1/500L/13/151.
9. Conference on European policies and programs, February 28–March 3, 1927, RF 3/900/22/166.
10. RF Minutes, May 25, 1927, RF 1.1/500A/3/23, for this and the following quotation.
11. IHB Minutes, November 13, 1929, RF 1.1/500A/5/53.
12. IHB Minutes, November 13, 1929, RF 1.1/500A/5/53. On the project of the Faculty of Medicine in Paris, see Tournès Ludovic, *Sciences de l'homme et politique. Les fondations philanthropiques en France au XXe siècle*, Paris, Garnier, 2013 [2011], pp. 155–163.

13　RF Minutes, May 1920, RF 1.1/712/1/3.
14　Litsios Socrates, "Selskar 'Mike' Gunn and Public Health Reform in Europe," in Borowy Iris & Hardy Anne (eds.), *Of Medicine and Men. Biographies and Ideas in European Social Medicine between the World Wars,* Bern, Peter Lang, 2008, pp. 23–44.
15　Memorandum of agreement, July 1921, SDN 12B/R839/21836/26222.
16　Gunn to Rose, January 3 and 5, 1922, RF 1.1/712/2/13.
17　Gunn to Rajchman, February 22, 1922, SDN 12B/R839/26222/21836.
18　Rajchman to Gunn, April 14, 1922, SDN 12B/R839/26222/21836.
19　Weindling Paul, "Philanthropy and World Health: The Rockefeller Foundation and the League of Nations Health Organisation," *Minerva,* 35-3, 1997, pp. 269–281.
20　Fosdick to Sweetser, July 26, 1922, SDN 12B/R839/26117/21836.
21　Memorandum of agreement between Republic of Poland and the Rockefeller foundation, July 1922, SDN 12B/R839/21836/26222.
22　George E. Vincent (Rockefeller Foundation President) to Drummond, September 18, 1922; Frederick F. Russell (IHB Director) to Drummond, September 18, 1922, SDN 12B/R839/21836/21836.
23　Budget for 1924, SDN 12B/R866/26652/26652.
24　IHB Minutes, October 24, 1922 and October 23, 1923, RF 1.1/100/20/164.
25　RF Minutes, May 1925, SDN 12B/R868/33269/27184.
26　IHB Minutes, May 25, 1927 and March 15, 1928, RF 1.1/100/20/164.
27　Budget for 1924, SDN 12B/R866/26652/26652.
28　SDN. Comité d'hygiène. Service auxiliaire de renseignements médicaux de la fondation Rockefeller, appendice au projet d'accord, 17 août 1922, SDN 12B/R839/21836/21836.
29　Prophylaxie internationale, *doc. cit.*
30　Tournès, *Sciences de l'homme…, op. cit.*, ch. 3.
31　Blayac Pierre, *L'Organisation d'hygiène de la Société des Nations,* thèse pour le doctorat en médecine, Université de Toulouse, 1932, p. 37.
32　Rose to Rajchman, July 21, 1922, SDN 12B/R839/26117/21836.
33　King Wilford I., "Edgar Sydenstricker," *Journal of The American Statistical Association,* 31–194, 1936, pp. 411–414.
34　Sydenstricker Edgar, "The Incidence of Illness in a General Population Group: Results of a Morbidity Study from December 1, 1921 through March 31, 1924 in Hagerstown, Md.," *Public Health Reports (1896–1970),* 40–7, February 13, 1925, pp. 279–291.
35　Hubbard Ursula, *La collaboration des Etats-Unis avec la Société des Nations et l'Organisation internationale du travail, des origines à 1936,* Paris, Centre européen de la dotation Carnegie, 1937, p. 795.
36　Duffield to Sydenstricker, December 9, 1922, SDN 33/S760bis/26379/26379.
37　Tournès, *Sciences de l'homme…, op. cit.*, ch. 2.
38　Gunn to Russell, August 24, 1926, RF 1.1/100/20/170.
39　Sydenstricker Edgar, "Population Statistics in Foreign Countries," *Journal of the American Statistical Association,* 20–149, 1925, pp. 80–89.
40　"The Fourth New York Health Conference", *Milbank Memorial Fund Quarterly Bulletin,* 7–2, 1929, p. 36.
41　"The League of Nations Health Service," *Journal of the American Statistical Association,* 19–146, 1924, pp. 243–236.

42 Otto Eichel, League of Nations Search Engine, www.lonsea.de/pub/person/5461, accessed August 19, 2021.
43 Sydenstricker to Gilchrist (Treasury Department), December 6, 1924, Frank Boudreau personal file, SDN 18/S725bis.
44 Sealey Anne, "Globalizing the 1926 International Sanitary Convention," *Journal of Global History*, 6–3, 2011, pp. 431–455.
45 Showan Daniel P., *United States Policy Regarding League of Nations Social and Humanitarian Activities*, PhD dissertation, Pennsylvania State University, 1969, p. 69.
46 Minutes of the Third Session of the Advisory Committee of the Eastern Bureau, held in New Delhi from December 26–29, 1927, SDN 8D/R5980/435/435.
47 Rockefeller Foundation, *Annual Report*, 1926, p. 249.
48 Flexner to Sweetser, September 28, 1927; Drummond to Rockefeller, Jr., October 4, 1927, SDN 18/R1269/61838/62113.
49 Lavelle Kathryn, "Exit, Voice and Loyalty in International Organizations: US Involvement in the League of Nations," *International Organization*, 2, 2007, p. 377.
50 Sweetser to Fosdick, September 13, 1927, SDN 18/R1269/61838/62113.
51 *Journal de Genève*, 11 septembre 1927, SDN 18/R1269/61838/62113.
52 William Warner Bishop, Trip to Rome, Geneva and London, January–February 1934, RF 1.1/100/90/831.
53 Note pour le Secrétaire général, 15 mars 1937, SDN 16/R5264/8294/28352.
54 Note du 29 décembre 1934, SDN 16/R5264/8294/9018.
55 RF Minutes, January 5, 1934, RF 1.1/100/90/831.
56 John Marshall (Assistant Director of the RFs' Humanities Division) interview with Sevensma (LoN Librarian), June 4, 1934, RF 1.1/100/90/831.
57 David H. Stevens, Notes on the Library of the League of Nations, July 1, 1937, RF 1.1/100/90/833.
58 Rajchman to Gunn, September 25, 1924, SDN 12B/R848/39376/25635; Budget for 1924 interchange, SDN 12B/R868/33269/27184.
59 Interchange for public health personnel, 1923, SDN 12B/R848/26485/25635; Budget for 1924, SDN 12B/R866/26652/26652.
60 Interchange for public health personnel, October 1925–April 1926, SDN 12B/R848/50857/25635.
61 Rajchman to Gunn, August 7, 1922, SDN 12B/R839/21836/26222. I was unable to locate the January 1921 memorandum that Rajchman mentions in this letter.
62 Report on the second international interchange for public health personnel, 1923, SDN 12B/R847/25292/28490.
63 The Health section of the League of Nations, "Work Being Done by the Service of Epidemiological Intelligence and Public Health Statistics," *Public Health Report (1896–1970)*, 39–9, 1924, pp. 414–419.
64 Gunn to Russell, August 24, 1926, RF 1.1/100/20/170.
65 Interchange for public health personnel, October 1925–April 1926, SDN 12B/R848/50857/25635.
66 Rajchman to Manley O. Hudson, March 23, 1925, SDN 12B/R935/38455/35816.
67 Drummond to Charles Evans Hughes, January 15, 1925; Cumming to Rajchman, February 16, 1925; Rajchman to Cumming, March 23, 1925, SDN 12B/R935/38455/35816.

68. Rockefeller Foundation, *Annual Report*, 1923, p. 121. I didn't find any information on this tour in LoN archives.
69. World Peace Foundation, *Sixth Yearbook of the League of Nations. Record of 1925*, Boston, 1926, p. 259 sq; see also Rockefeller foundation, *Annual Report*, 1925, p. 263. I didn't find any information on this tour in LoN archives.
70. Gunn to Russell, April 29, 1925, RF 1.1/100/20/169.
71. Roussin Philippe, "Destouches avant Céline: le taylorisme et le sort de l'utopie hygiéniste (une lecture des écrits médicaux des années vingt)," *Sciences Sociales et Santé*, 6–3/4, 1988, p. 9; and Balinska, *Une vie…, op. cit.*, pp. 175–180.
72. Ludwik Rajchman au Trésorier de la SdN, 6 septembre 1934, SDN 8A/R6114/13266/13266.
73. Voyage d'études collectif de fonctionnaires d'hygiène publique aux Etats-Unis, 4 novembre-6 décembre 1935, SDN 12B/R6118/16649/16649.
74. "Hygiène publique et problèmes sociaux aux Etats-Unis d'Amérique," *Bulletin Trimestriel de l'Organisation d'Hygiène*, 5–4, 1936, p. 984 and p. 988 for the following quotation.
75. Tournès Ludovic & Scott-Smith Giles, "A World of Exchanges: Conceptualizing the History of International Scholarship Programs (Nineteenth to Twenty-First Centuries)," in Tournès Ludovic & Scott-Smith Giles (eds.), *Global Exchanges: Scholarship Programs and Transnational Circulations in the Modern World*, New York, Berghahn Books, 2017, pp. 1–29.
76. Boudreau Frank G., "Health Work of the League of Nations," *The Milbank Memorial Fund Quarterly*, 13–1, 1935, pp. 3–22.
77. Gardikas Katerina, "Relief Work and Malaria in Greece 1943–1947," *Journal of Contemporary History*, 43–3, 2008, pp. 493–508.
78. "A Rural Health Experiment in China", *Milbank Memorial Fund Quarterly Bulletin*, 8–4, 1930, pp. 97–108.
79. For the year 1927, see SDN 12B/R982/50232/50232.
80. Duffield to Tapia, January 25, 1924, SDN 12B/R865/5448/28478.
81. Bevier (Rockefeller Foundation) to Rajchman, May 12, 1925; Rajchman to Ney (Director of the Federal Bureau of Statistics at Bern), May 16, 1925, SDN 12B/R865/5448/28478.
82. Gunn to Rajchman, September 22, 1926, SDN 12B/R865/5448/28478.
83. Letters from Gunn to Rajchman, SDN 12B/R965/44954/44954. See other examples in SDN 12B/R865.
84. Florence M. Reard (IHB) to Norman V. Lothian (State Board of Health, Boston, MA), November 8, 1923, RF 1.1/100/20/166.
85. Gunn to Rajchmann, August 24, 1924, RF 1.1/100/20/169; Russell to Gunn, May 21, 1925, RF 1/.1/100/20/169.
86. Strode to Russell, February 16, 1929, RF 1.1/100/21/174.
87. IHB Minutes, November 5, 1925, RF 1.1/712/1/3.
88. Weindling Paul, "Public Health and Political Stabilisation: The Rockefeller Foundation in Central and Eastern Europe between the Two World Wars," *Minerva*, 31–3, 1993, p. 256 sq; Page Benjamin B., "The Rockefeller Foundation and Central Europe: A Reconsideration," *Minerva*, 40–3, 2002, pp. 265–287.
89. Tournès, *Sciences de l'homme…, op. cit.*, ch. 4.
90. Bernard Léon, "L'école d'hygiène de Varsovie," *La presse médicale*, 22 mai 1926.
91. SDN. Organisation d'hygiène. *Rapport sur les travaux des conférences de directeurs d'écoles d'hygiène (Paris, 20–23 mai 1930, et Dresde 14–17 juillet 1930)*, Genève, 1930.

92 Gilbert to Hull, March 20, 1937, NARA RG 84/496.
93 SDN. Organisation d'hygiène. Composition de la commission du paludisme, 15 juin 1938, BPT-IP G3.
94 Rajchman to Gunn, April 14, 1922, SDN 12B/R839/26222/21836.
95 Rose to Rajchman, June 6, 1922, SDN 12B/R839/21836/21836.
96 Gunn to Vincent, April 21, 1931; cable from Vincent to RF Paris Office, May 1, 1931, RF 1.1/100/21/176.
97 SDN. Organisation d'hygiène. Commission du paludisme, *Rapport sur son voyage d'études dans certains pays d'Europe en 1924*, Genève, 1925, BPT-IP G1.
98 Gunn to Russell, February 11, 1924; Gunn to Russell, February 15, 1924, RF 1.1/100/20/167.
99 On this debate, see Evans Hughes, "European Malaria Policy in the 1920s and 1930s. The Epidemiology of Minutiae," *Isis*, 80, 1989, p. 45 sq.
100 Rajchman to Gunn, April 23, 1927, RF 1.1/100/20/171.
101 Rajchman to Cumming, March 8, 1926, SDN 12B/R981/50105/50105.
102 Programme, League of Nations interchange, July 4, 1927, SDN 12B R981/50105/50105.
103 Cumming to White, July 15, 1927, SDN 12B/R981/50105/50105.
104 Rapport préliminaire sur un voyage d'études aux Etats-Unis en 1927, 28 février 1928, SDN 12B/R982/61783/50105.
105 Gunn to Vincent, April 27, 1928, RF 1.1/100/20/172.
106 SDN. Organisation d'hygiène. Commission du paludisme. Session des 25–29 juin 1928, rapport destiné à la presse médicale, BPT-IP G2.
107 Hackett to Strode, April 2, 1935, RF 6.1/1.1/38/467.
108 Rajchman to Hackett, March 29, 1935; Hackett to Rajchman, April 2, 1935, RF 6.1/1.1/38/467.
109 Gunn to Russell, April 1, 1924, RF 1.1/100/20/167.

References

Balinska Marta Aleksandra, *For the Good of Humanity. Ludwik Rajchman, Medical Statesman*, Budapest, Central European University Press, 1998.

Evans Hughes, "European Malaria Policy in the 1920s and 1930s. The Epidemiology of Minutiae," *Isis*, 80, 1989, pp. 40–59.

Gardikas Katerina, "Relief Work and Malaria in Greece 1943–1947," *Journal of Contemporary History*, 43–3, 2008, pp. 493–508.

Lavelle Kathryn, "Exit, Voice and Loyalty in International Organizations: US Involvement in the League of Nations," *International Organization*, 2, 2007, pp. 371–393.

Litsios Socrates, "Selskar 'Mike' Gunn and Public Health Reform in Europe," in Borowy Iris & Hardy Anne (eds.), *Of Medicine and Men. Biographies and Ideas in European Social Medicine between the World Wars*, Bern, Peter Lang, 2008, pp. 23–44.

Page Benjamin B., "The Rockefeller Foundation and Central Europe: A Reconsideration," *Minerva*, 40–3, 2002, pp. 265–287.

Roussin Philippe, "Destouches avant Céline: le taylorisme et le sort de l'utopie hygiéniste (une lecture des écrits médicaux des années vingt)," *Sciences Sociales et Santé*, 6–3/4, 1988, pp. 5–48.

Sealey Anne, "Globalizing the 1926 International Sanitary Convention," *Journal of Global History*, 6-3, 2011, pp. 431–455.

Showan Daniel P., *United States Policy Regarding League of Nations Social and Humanitarian Activities*, PhD dissertation, Pennsylvania State University, 1969.

Tournès Ludovic, *Sciences de l'homme et politique. Les fondations philanthropiques en France au XXe siècle*, Paris, Garnier, 2013 [2011].

Tournès Ludovic & Scott-Smith Giles, "A World of Exchanges: Conceptualizing the History of International Scholarship Programs (Nineteenth to Twenty-First Centuries)," in Tournès Ludovic & Scott-Smith Giles (eds.), *Global Exchanges: Scholarship Programs and Transnational Circulations in the Modern World*, New York, Berghahn Books, 2017, pp. 1–29.

Tournès Ludovic, *Américanisation. Une histoire mondiale*, Paris, Fayard, 2020.

Weindling Paul, "Public Health and Political Stabilisation: The Rockefeller Foundation in Central and Eastern Europe between the Two World Wars," *Minerva*, 31-3, 1993, pp. 253–267.

Weindling Paul, "Philanthropy and World Health: The Rockefeller Foundation and the League of Nations Health Organisation," *Minerva*, 35-3, 1997, pp. 269–281.

4 The International Commission on Intellectual Cooperation and New International Power Relations

What was referred to as intellectual cooperation during the interwar period offers another example of US participation in LoN activities. In this case, the US presence was both early and sustained. The period following World War I was marked by heightened US presence in all international scientific institutions. The International Commission on Intellectual Cooperation (ICIC) of the LoN was just one of them, and the relations that the US maintained with it during the 1920s reflected the developing intellectual and scientific confrontation. When the ICIC was created in 1922, internationalist circles in the US initially joined in but did not so much seek to cooperate with it than to neutralize or short-circuit it, for two reasons. The first was that it was acting in the name of a universalism that they did not subscribe to and that it aimed to coordinate international cultural and scientific life according to principles they deemed unsuitable. The second reason was that the ICIC—and its soon-to-emerge armed wing, the International Institute of Intellectual Cooperation (IIIC)—were under French influence and were a way for France to preserve some of the power it had lost in 1918. US internationalists largely mobilized against French-style universalism by seeking to neutralize ICIC activities as much as possible. In this process, philanthropic foundations served as an instrument for the international projection of US scientific circles, and their activity broadly contributed to preventing the ICIC and IIIC from taking hold in the global scientific landscape.

This chapter is divided into four sections. The first presents the new international scientific configuration that emerged after World War I and the context in which the ICIC was born. The second examines the strong US presence at the ICIC and the role played by the Carnegie Endowment for International Peace (CEIP) in this representation. The third shows how the ICIC faced stiff competition in the organization of international intellectual and scientific life from projects led by US scientists with foundation support. Finally, the fourth section explores the crisis that rocked the IIIC in the late 1920s, which led to expanded investment by foundations in its activities.

DOI: 10.4324/9780429021213-5

The New International Scientific Configuration after 1918

International cooperation in the scientific field developed before World War I in the form of increased international congresses, as well as international associations for the circulation of knowledge and the development of new research fields. The creation of the International Association of Academies in 1899 was an important date in this process. It grew out of a German initiative to organize meetings between science academies. Its first general assembly was held in Paris in 1901 and brought together 18 academies of science and letters, all of them European; the US delegate, who was the only non-European representative, had to cancel at the last moment for health reasons and was not replaced,[1] a sign that the US still had a marginal role within the system of scientific cooperation. The Association barely had time to develop its activities before 1914 and stopped meeting when war broke out. It was reborn in a completely different context in 1918, with altered power relations: in October, a few weeks before the armistice, an Interallied Conference of Scientific Academies was held in London with the participation of France, Great Britain, Belgium, Italy, Serbia, and two non-European countries, the US and Brazil. The goal was to pursue the endeavor that had begun before 1914, but this time without the Central Powers. The participants believed that the recently ended war—contrary to earlier wars that "had not destroyed the mutual esteem of scientists from belligerent countries"—was marked by an unprecedented escalation of violence, particularly by the Central Powers, who had "broken the laws of civilization" and perpetrated "atrocities that had made the entire world indignant."[2] The result of this irrevocable judgment was the banning of the Central Powers from international scientific life. The participants in the Interallied Conference of Scientific Academies created new international associations from which they would be excluded, but in which the US would have a much more important role than before 1914. Power relations in international science had therefore fundamentally changed after World War I and were marked by a number of institutional novelties.

The first of these was the creation of the International Research Council (IRC). It was initiated during the meeting of the academies in October 1918 and made official in the spring of 1919 when political leaders met in Versailles for the Peace Conference. The three powers driving the creation of the IRC were France, the US, and Great Britain, who were joined at the outset by nine other academies from Belgium, Canada, Italy, Japan, New Zealand, Poland, Portugal, Romania, and Serbia.[3] The new institution had three objectives: to promote the creation of international associations in different disciplines; to discuss with states in order to identify new areas of research; and to develop scientific cooperation by initiating international projects.[4] The first objective was quickly met, for in 1919 a number of unions were created across various disciplines, such as the International Astronomical Union, the International Union of Geodesy and Geophysics, the International Association for the Physical Sciences of the Ocean, and the International Mathematical

ICIC and New International Power Relations 115

Union. In 1926 following the Locarno Treaties, the IRC invited German, Austrian, Hungarian, and Bulgarian scientists to take part in the work but was flatly turned down by the Germans, who boycotted international scientific institutions.[5] In 1931 when the IRC transformed into the International Council of Scientific Unions (ICSU) following the merger of the IRC and the International Association of Academies, which had been dormant since 1914, the Germans once again refused to take part.

The second novelty in the scientific landscape after 1918 was the creation of the International Academic Union (IAU), which had the same goal as the IRC but in the human and social sciences (philology, archeology, history, ethics, political science, and sociology). The initiative came from the Académie des inscriptions et belles lettres in Paris, which in March 1919 sent invitations to scientists from victor countries, taking advantage of their presence in Paris as members of their national delegations to the Peace Conference.[6] The founding meeting took place from May 15–17 in the National Library in Paris. Eleven countries were represented: France, Belgium, Denmark, Great Britain, the US, Russia, Japan, Greece, Italy, Poland, and the Netherlands. Another meeting was held in October, also in Paris, before the first general assembly held in Brussels in 1920, at which four additional members joined, namely Romania, Serbia, Portugal, and Norway. It was during this assembly that the decisions were made to locate the organization in Brussels, make French the official language, and initiate its first collective research projects.[7] However, as with the IRC, the Central Powers were excluded. Curiously, Germany would be reintegrated in 1935,[8] even though it had not been a part of the LoN for two years.

The third novelty of the post-1918 period was the institutionalization of intellectual cooperation in connection with the LoN, which resulted from activity by certain European intellectual circles and the French government. While technical activities had a marginal role in article 23 of the LoN Covenant, scientific cooperation was not even mentioned, despite the insistence of certain internationalist circles revolving around the Union of International Associations (UIA) created in 1910, especially those in Belgium. In February 1919 the UIA proposed a project during the Peace Conference to coordinate the work of these associations and to inscribe the objective of international cooperation in the LoN Covenant. The proposal was not adopted, but after the signing of the Treaty of Versailles, the Union continued its lobbying efforts with associations supporting the LoN. These efforts led, during their 3rd conference in December 1919, to the adoption of a resolution calling on the LoN to take an interest in educational and scientific matters. Its goal was to create an "international mentality,"[9] particularly among intellectual, academic, and administrative elites. One of the debates that occurred between 1919 and 1922 was whether to rely on an existing organization or to create a new one. Belgian internationalist circles were in favor of the former, seeing the UIA in this role and making Brussels the center of intellectual cooperation. But the French had a different take and argued for the creation of a new organization that would help establish French influence, which was experiencing difficulty due to the government's maximalist positions toward Germany during the Peace Conference. The *Président du Conseil* (Prime Minister), Aristide Briand, supported this idea in late 1921, and was joined by Léon Bourgeois in January 1922. The Belgian solution would subsequently be abandoned. The ICIC held its first session in Geneva in August and appointed as its president the French philosopher Henri Bergson, who was at the peak of his international reputation.

A complex, multilevel system was gradually put in place. The first was that of the ICIC itself, which included twelve members appointed for their international reputation, but was also based on a subtle balance between nations. Its original composition included two individuals from France (Henri Bergson and Marie Sklodowska-Curie, who also represented Poland), two from Switzerland, and one representative each from India, Norway, Brazil, Belgium, the US, South Africa, Italy, and Spain.[10] The year 1924 saw the addition of a representative from the Netherlands and Argentina and the replacement of the Indian representative by a Briton. While the traditional great powers were well represented (France and the British Empire), the ICIC was seen as a space where small countries could express themselves, as demonstrated from the outset in the active participation in debates by the Norwegian delegate Kristine Bonnevie. While Germany was excluded from the LoN, its considerable influence in the intellectual and scientific world made it difficult to sideline it from the newly-formed ICIC, which was supposed to promote reconciliation among former enemies. The dilemma was resolved through the nomination of Albert Einstein, who was a Swiss national but a professor of physics at the Universities of Berlin and Leiden, and a member of the Academy of Sciences in Berlin. The artificial nature of this nomination fooled nobody, but it was a symbol[11] that made it possible to assert that Germany was present in the ICIC.

The second level of the apparatus for intellectual cooperation consisted of national commissions for intellectual cooperation, which were created from 1923 onward to help the ICIC strengthen its international duties by creating ties with national intellectual circles, which would help make its decisions more representative of the international intellectual community. Eleven commissions were created in 1923, a number that rose to 19 the following year[12] and 25 in 1929. In 1924 the representatives of national commissions took part in ICIC meetings; from 1923 onward they held meetings among themselves, albeit at fairly spaced-out intervals, with four meetings being held during the interwar period in 1923, 1926, 1929, and 1937.

The third level was the IIIC, which was created in 1926 by the French government. The initiative had a dual origin. First, it was intended to pull France out of the diplomatic isolation that the 1923 military intervention in the Ruhr had placed it, following which it was "dropped" by the US and Great Britain and had to face its international demotion. The creation of the IIIC was a way of reaffirming French influence in a field in which it was practically unchallenged, namely culture. The other underlying goal of the IIIC's creation was to "counter British opposition to French policy within the ICIC,"[13] especially with regard to the role of Germany, which Great Britain wanted to add to the ICIC against France's objections. Preempting intellectual cooperation was therefore a way for France to preserve its international status and to bolster its positions in Europe. The IIIC would become the ICIC's executive body and would be recognized as a fully-fledged technical organization with respect to the LoN in 1931. It was not an international institution, but an organization under French law financed by the French government rather than the LoN; while it was tasked with implementing the policy decided on by the ICIC, which only met a few days per year, it was also a competing institution designed to make intellectual cooperation a French rather than a League affair. What's more, it was located in Paris, whereas the ICIC met in Geneva. Thanks to the creation of state delegates representing the governments of LoN member countries (with the notable exception of the US and Great Britain, which did not have any), the IIIC could bypass the ICIC. This arrangement was validated by the LoN General Assembly in September 1926.

Despite the consensual appearance of its name, intellectual cooperation was marked by great tension. It primarily opposed a group of countries gathered behind France and another in which Great Britain and the US were the primary representatives. The first group was in favor of greater institutionalization of intellectual cooperation, especially through the creation of the permanent body of the IIIC. This group of "French-speaking and Francophile countries"[14] included Latin America, Italy, Switzerland, and Belgium, in addition to Poland, Czechoslovakia, Romania, and Yugoslavia—in other words countries of the "Little Entente" created by France to surround Germany. For these countries, the IIIC was a way to counter British and German influence. However, the group was far from homogenous. The first reason for this was the French government hardly supported its own creation: intellectual cooperation was a potential "diplomatic weapon in its own right,"[15] but one that the government rarely used. The second reason was France's preemption of intellectual cooperation was not to the taste of all partners, especially Belgium, as it had opposed the creation of the ICIC and was hardly favorable to the IIIC, which partly took up a Belgian initiative. It ultimately rallied behind the project, but primarily because it wanted to stand with France against the Anglo-Saxon bloc.

The second group of countries included Great Britain, its dominions (Canada, Australia, New Zealand, South Africa), and the US, along with Scandinavian countries; all of these countries were hostile to centralized organization because they believed that the initiative should be left to private actors rather than an international bureaucracy, and because they were concerned the IIIC would become a "center for French propaganda and a representative for French cultural imperialism";[16] and finally because a new organization would swell the already considerable LoN machinery, meaning additional costs. This opposition between two conceptions of intellectual cooperation was present from the beginning in IIIC policy during the 1920s, in the confrontation between its Director Julien Luchaire—"a pure product of French high administration"[17]—and its Deputy Director Alfred Zimmern of Great Britain. The former "counted on state activity coordinated by an intergovernmental international organization"[18] and wanted to expand the IIIC's centralized initiatives, while the latter wanted it to remain a small organization helping to drive international projects forward by putting participants in touch with one another, but leaving them independent.

US Representation at the ICIC

The speed with which the US became a central actor in international intellectual and scientific life immediately after World War I has not been sufficiently emphasized, nor has how its relation with the apparatus of intellectual cooperation reflected the fact that its arrival thoroughly reshuffled the deck in international scientific relations. The US rise in international scientific life would be difficult to grasp without taking into account the transformations in US scientific life, which in the space of a few years propelled the country to the rank of a scientific superpower. The most visible manifestation of these transformations was the growth of universities beginning in the final decades of the nineteenth century,[19] fostered by significant funding from the world of industry, either in the form of individual donations or through the establishment of foundations that played a decisive role in creating an ecosystem for higher education and research. Among these, the Rockefeller and Carnegie networks played a major role throughout the first half of the twentieth century by funding chairs and research laboratories, constructing university buildings, supporting organizations awarding grants for individual and collective research—such as the Social Science Research Council (1923)—and opening up the US university system to international life, as with the Institute of International Education created in 1919 at the initiative of Elihu Root and Nicholas Murray Butler. This final creation was intended, in the minds of the CEIP leadership, to counteract the strong isolationist tendency in the US by developing intellectual exchange with the rest of the world, in order to train an internationalist elite and ensure US presence in the international academic market, which was controlled by major European powers at the time (Germany, France, Great Britain).[20] The Institute of International Education, which was funded by the Carnegie Corporation of New York, would help organize hundreds of exchange programs created by universities and philanthropic institutions, contribute to the internationalization of the student population, and make US universities a destination preferred by students from the rest of the world in the 1920s.

The rise of US academia was also visible with the creation, at the turn of the twentieth century, of professional associations, which attests to the growing importance of researcher communities with major scientific ambitions. This was true for the natural sciences, with the creation of the

American Physiological Society in 1887, the American Mathematical Society in 1888, and the American Physical Society in 1899. This was also true in the human and social sciences, with the creation of the most senior of associations, the American Historical Association in 1884, followed by many others such as the American Philosophical Association in 1900, the American Anthropological Association in 1902, the American Political Science Association in 1903, and the American Sociological Association in 1905.

Finally, it is important to note the creation of organizations that would enable the US to secure a central role in international scientific life. This was especially true of the National Research Council (NRC), which was created in 1916 in connection with the war, and made permanent in 1918 to establish a federation of the country's scientific organizations under the leadership of the National Academy of Science. When it stopped receiving government funding in 1919, foundations such as the Carnegie Corporation of New York took the reins,[21] although governmental representatives continued to sit on its leadership board. One of the NRC's missions was to ensure the international impact of US science, which it did in partnering with the State Department[22] and the IRC. The NRC's articles of organization were adopted in February 1919, just as the talks that would lead to the creation of the IRC were being held in Paris. The goal behind making the NRC permanent was to create an institution that would allow US scientists to speak in one voice, in an effort to wield greater influence in the creation of the IRC, whose objective was to become the LoN of scientists. Americans attended the IRC's first meeting held in Brussels in July 1919 in significant numbers, with 21 representatives,[23] whose stated goal was to make the organization an international extension of the NRC.[24] The central figure of the delegation was the astronomer George Ellery Hale, who was the Director of the Mount Wilson Observatory, and a member of the NRC's Executive Board.[25]

This effort to form groups based on scientific activity was also underway in the human and social sciences, as demonstrated by the creation of the American Council of Learned Societies (ACLS), which followed the same logic as the NRC, even though the connection with the federal government was less clear. The ACLS was also created to represent the US at the IAU, whose founding meeting in Paris in May 1919 crafted the IAU's articles of organization, which stipulated that each country had to send two representatives from its learned societies. While major scientific powers such as France and Great Britain had national academies that represented learned societies in the humanities, this was not the case in the US. At the meeting, the US was represented by two medieval historians, the Harvard Professor Charles H. Haskins, and James T. Shotwell. They were both also members of the Peace Conference delegation, but in this case were there as representatives of the American Historical Association and the American Academy of Arts and Science,[26] and not in the name of the US scholarly world taken as a whole. In September 1919 learned societies and professional associations met to create a federating organization—in order for the US voice to be heard at the IAU[27]—and to designate the representatives for the inaugural conference to be held the following month. A few months later, in the spring of 1920 the composition of the ACLS was finalized, and its articles of organization approved. It would quickly play an important role within the IAU. Shotwell was its representative until 1924. In 1927 thanks to financial support from the Laura Spelman Rockefeller Memorial (LSRM), the ACLS created a permanent secretariat to develop its international activities, with the historian Waldo Leland appointed to lead it; in 1938 he also became the president of the IAU.

These elements show that the interwar period was when the US acquired a central role in the international intellectual and scientific world. Its relations with the LoN's institutions of intellectual cooperation should be analyzed in light of this. When the creation of the ICIC under French initiative was taking shape, the US seized the opportunity to strengthen its international presence. In March 1922 Hale and his colleague, the physicist Robert A. Millikan, sent a letter to British authorities asking for the IRC and IAU to be represented within the ICIC.[28] When the latter's composition was discussed among stakeholder countries, Hale represented both the US and the IRC; but it was his deputy Millikan who was elected as the US representative to the ICIC, a position he held until 1932, when he was officially replaced by Shotwell, who was reappointed until 1938.[29] The US thus had a representative at the ICIC throughout the interwar period.

Americans were also present in almost all of the subcommissions gradually created by the ICIC and played an active role in them. As in the LoN's other technical activities, the Americans were often respected figures in their field of activity, signaling the importance that the US attached to their presence. This was the case for the Sub-Commission on Bibliography created in 1923, which in addition to two permanent members from the ICIC, included outside experts such as the botanist J.R. Schramm, who was a professor of botany at the University of Pennsylvania, and the Executive Secretary of the Division of Biology and Agriculture at the NRC. Schramm would occasionally be replaced during meetings by William Dawson Johnston,[30] the Director of the American Library in Paris, and more often by Warner Bishop, who was the Director of the University of Michigan Library, and one of the best-known figures in the US library landscape, as he had served as President of the American Library Association and the Bibliographical Society of America before becoming the President of the International Federation of Library Associations in 1931. In 1927 Bishop was also a member of the pilot committee for the LoN library project, which was created after the personal gift by John D. Rockefeller, Jr. In 1924 the ICIC also created a committee of experts for the international exchange of publications; its American member was H.W. Dorsey, who headed the International Exchange Service of the Smithsonian, which had extensive experience in the field since its creation in 1849 to ensure the international diffusion of US scientific publications and to provide US public and university libraries with scientific publications from other countries.

The US was also well represented in the commissions relating to schools and universities. The Sub-Committee for University Relations created in 1923 had Stephen Duggan as a member,[31] who was the Director of the Institute of International Education. Also sitting on the subcommittee in 1929 was Paul Van Dyke, the representative of the American University Union in Europe, an organization that planned trips to European universities for US students. For that matter, when an International Office of University Information was created at the ICIC's initiative in 1924, the representative from the American University Union in Europe at the time, Algernon Coleman, was a member from the very outset. Americans were also present in the two other committees created by the ICIC in the field of education: the Committee of Experts for the Coordination of Higher International Studies, created in 1928; and the Permanent Sub-Committee for Teaching Youth the Goals of the League of Nations, created in 1930, of which Duggan was a member, as was Helen Clarkson Miller Davis, the Director of the Spence School in New York, one of the pioneering high schools with respect to international engagement, especially in the teaching of foreign languages.

Americans also sat on the Sub-Commission on Intellectual Property created in 1923, of which Robert A. Millikan was a member; on the Committee of Arts and Letters, created in 1927; on the Steering Committee of the International Office of Museums, created in 1932, of which the Egyptologist Herbert E. Winlock, who was the Director of the Metropolitan Museum of New York, was a member; and in the ICIC's satellite institutions such as the International Educational Cinematographic Institute in Rome, whose board of directors included the entomologist Vernon Kellogg, a professor at Stanford University and the General Secretary of the NRC, as well as Carl E. Millikan, who was the Executive Secretary of the Motion Picture Producers and Distributors of America (MPPDA), which was created in 1922 to support the internationalization process for the Hollywood film industry. In short, there was no sector of intellectual cooperation that Americans were not involved in: their presence was massive, as it was in all of the other technical sections.

They put in place a strategy, unique among ICIC members, of replacing the official representative with someone more qualified depending on the subject debated at each meeting and of having multiple attendees under various pretexts, as was the case with the LoN's other technical sections. In total at least 24 US representatives sat at least once at the ICIC or its subcommissions between 1922 and 1931, no doubt making the US the best-represented nation, even ahead of France. Robert A. Millikan is a case in point: he attended the ICIC's founding meeting in 1922 but practically did not return, for with his colleague Hale he had ensured that matters relating to the natural sciences would remain largely within the IRC's remit. The ICIC thus concentrated on the human and social sciences, cultural heritage, and university exchange, with Millikan being replaced at almost every session by one or more of his colleagues. In 1923 three individuals sat at the ICIC: the jurist John

H. Wigmore from Northwestern Law School, the economist Paul Perigord from the California Institute of Technology, and the French literature specialist Algernon Coleman.[32] In the following years, Millikan was almost systematically replaced. In 1932 Shotwell succeeded him as the American representative to the ICIC. While the historian was initially active, he also had himself replaced, with the Americans once again taking advantage of this to attend in numbers. For instance, in 1935 Shotwell designated two replacements in the persons of Malcolm W. Davis, the new Director of the European Center of the CEIP (CEIP-CE), and Waldo Leland, the Secretary-General of the ACLS. Davis used the pretext that given his recent nomination to lead the European Center, he was unfamiliar with the mechanics of Geneva and the issues in question and succeeded in having himself assisted by Carol Riegelman Lubin, who was the former Secretary of the American National Committee on Intellectual Cooperation and was hired at the ILO in the spring of 1935. All in all the US was the most represented country at the meeting, with three people![33] In 1937 Malcolm W. Davis joined the Executive Committee of the Organization for Intellectual Cooperation.[34] Not only was the US the most present country at the ICIC, but the number of institutions from which they came attests to the diversity and rising power of the US academic system.

Finally, the last component of the US strategy was the CEIP's creation of an American National Committee on Intellectual Cooperation. Among the national committees created beginning in 1923, it was "one of the best organized"[35] and certainly the one with the most substantial financial resources. Elihu Root was behind it, and its founding meeting took place in January 1926 in the CEIP's offices in New York. Until the late 1930s, it was largely if not entirely funded by the CEIP.[36] Its date of creation was not an accident, as in 1924 France had announced the creation of the IIIC, and the American National Committee was clearly the instrument of a US counter-offensive to prevent French control over intellectual cooperation. It is significant that during the ICIC's fourth session in 1924, at which the French proposal was discussed, Millikan proposed creating national correspondents for the ICIC to present its work outside of Geneva, with the goal of avoiding Parisian centralization in intellectual cooperation. His proposal was adopted,[37] but it did not prevent the creation of the IIIC. During the fifth session in 1925, at which the new institute's organization was discussed, Millikan did not travel to Geneva, instead sending a letter to the ICIC announcing the imminent creation of the American National Committee,[38] which was officially created a few weeks before the IIIC. Its director was Millikan himself,[39] assisted by Vernon Kellogg, with Root and Hale as members as well.[40] Millikan directed it until 1932, when he was replaced by Shotwell, who fulfilled this duty at the same time as that of US representative to the ICIC. The central fact that emerges from these elements is that while it was not a member of the LoN, the US had a key role in the apparatus of intellectual cooperation, one that was less visible than France but potentially just as important, and perhaps even more so, as the ensuing events will show.

The Marginalization of the ICIC

Like the LoN's other technical activities, intellectual cooperation had to face the regularity of funding, which was a recurring topic of discussion during ICIC and IIIC meetings.[41] The members of the two institutions cast a jealous eye at the HS, which had "considerable funding provided by the Rockefeller Foundation. The Commission on Intellectual Cooperation or the national commissions cooperating with it could also receive more substantial funding,"[42] which would allow them to organize exchange programs and other initiatives. In 1925 talks were held between the LoN Secretariat and the CEIP regarding financial support. The foundation's interest in intellectual cooperation was clear. In 1922 Nicholas Murray Butler had been a candidate as the American representative to the ICIC, but he was not chosen, most probably due to the personal intervention of Fosdick, who was not on good terms with him and considered him an adversary of the LoN, a judgment most likely echoed at the ICIC by Sweetser before the election of representatives.[43] In May 1925 when he had just succeeded Root as CEIP President, Butler informed Eric Drummond that his organization was ready to collaborate with the League, in a form that remained to be determined, in order to "help promote international understanding and develop international cooperation in all things connected to the advance of civilization."[44] The Secretary-General responded that there were many ways to collaborate, especially in the field of intellectual cooperation.[45] In July 1925 during his many trips to Europe,[46] Butler stopped in Geneva and visited LoN headquarters.[47] In September the new Director of the CEIP-CE, the Romance language specialist Earle Babcock, made a visit to attend the General Assembly; in December Julien Luchaire, the Director of the nascent IIIC, contacted the CEIP-CE,[48] while his Deputy Director Alfred Zimmern traveled to the US to officially request funding from the CEIP. The foundation responded favorably to this contact, declaring its association with the IIIC's work, which in its opinion represented the intellectual side of the *rapprochement* initiated by the Locarno Treaties.[49] It is therefore clear that the participation envisioned by the CEIP was in keeping with the broader strategy of a global Locarno that Shotwell was trying to put in place at the same moment, as mentioned in Chapter 2. During 1926, contacts continued with Luchaire,[50] but the CEIP did not take the leap and provide direct funding for the institution, with Butler's prudence most likely being explained by domestic political considerations, as he was aspiring to the Republican Party nomination for the 1928 elections, and the LoN remained a sensitive subject within the Grand Old Party.

April 1926 saw initial contact with Rockefeller philanthropy, when Abraham Flexner, a Trustee of the General Education Board, suggested that the IIIC create a system for the exchange of scientific publications between European scholars, one that also included German scholars.[51] Luchaire saw this as a sign of the good disposition of philanthropic circles toward the IIIC. Poorly informed regarding the specializations of the various Rockefeller boards,[52] Luchaire sent a letter to Alan Gregg, Deputy Director of the Rockefeller Foundation's (RF) Division of Medical Education, who responded that his organization was solely concerned with medical education, and could not fund the IIIC.[53] A second attempt made with the foundation's President a few weeks later did not succeed either,[54] which is not surprising given that the RF's programs for 1926 were not connected to intellectual cooperation. Zimmern returned empty-handed from a second trip to the US in 1927. ICIC members bitterly complained that from a financial point of view, intellectual cooperation was "one of the LoN's most sacrificed organizations."[55]

The lack of a response on the part of foundations to the IIIC's requests can be interpreted in a number of ways. It can of course be seen as the result of a series of circumstantial causes, especially the fact that intellectual cooperation was not among the RF's areas of activity in 1926 (the Division of Social Sciences and the Humanities Division would not be created until 1929), in addition to the CEIP's prudence due to the proximity of the presidential elections. However, the true reason was most likely deeper, namely the suspicion that academic and philanthropic circles had toward the IIIC, which they believed to be exclusively in the service of French interests, and the *de facto* competition that took hold between the ICIC and IIIC on the one hand, and the US academic and philanthropic world on the other, which clearly wanted to make the US central to international intellectual and scientific life. In this struggle for influence that began in the 1920s, US scientific circles supported by philanthropy secured decisive gains, gradually marginalizing the League system. The field of bibliographical coordination was just one characteristic example of this process.

There were a number of organizations that had already conducted significant work in this field in the early 1920s, such as the International Institute of Bibliography in Brussels (created in 1895), the Concilium Bibliographicum in Zurich (1896), the International Catalogue of Scientific Literature in London (1902), and the UIA. All of these institutions were mistrustful of the ICIC's intrusion in this domain. The latter also had to contend with the IRC, in which the US wielded great influence. In fact, the US was intent on marking out its territory, for at the ICIC's first session in August 1922, Millikan asked for the LoN to abstain from giving instructions to the IRC and intervening in international scientific cooperation, contradicting the Swiss delegate Reynold, who supported the opposite position. The President of the Commission, Henri Bergson, found a compromise after an animated discussion, by proposing that the ICIC inform the IRC that it was at its disposal and ready to work with it.[56] The resolution stipulated that the ICIC

> supports the development [of cooperation in the field of scientific research], but as a principle believes it should be the work of scientific

societies themselves. Consequently, the Commission, mindful not to interfere with their organization or its work, nevertheless wishes to practically provide them with its full support.[57]

Despite this declaration of principle, collaboration between the two institutions proved difficult, as demonstrated by bibliography projects in various scientific fields. Since the early twentieth century, the proliferation of knowledge became a major problem in scientific research, with the increase of publications making it impossible for a single person to master a particular field of research, subsequently requiring new tools to help scientists inform one another, present their research, and exchange information. The number of publications increased enormously, with there being over 1,500 journals publishing 100,000 articles per year in the field of medicine alone.[58]

Two new tools were developed in this context: thematic bibliographies and compilations of abstracts. Both of these areas required international harmonization, and there was an intense struggle for influence between countries and organizations seeking to impose their standards. The ICIC envisioned ambitious projects from its very first session, contemplating the creation of a universal bibliography in all fields of knowledge. Some ICIC members, especially the Swiss delegate Reynold, spoke in favor of ICIC support for existing European institutions. Marie Curie called for the creation of a "unified international abstracts service,"[59] in other words a publication including abstracts for all scientific articles.

Hale and Millikan had a different point of view, as they wanted bibliographies and abstracts to be coordinated by the IRC rather than the ICIC. They had two arguments: scientific unions were more capable and had to have control over the classification of disciplines and publications; and most especially, they had already begun work to this effect, particularly physics and chemistry unions, which had developed a standard form for abstracts that the IRC planned to propose "for adoption by European journals."[60] Hale concluded that in this field, "the matter should be left to scientists rather than librarians," and that the ICIC had to "simply approve the work completed by the IRC regarding abstracts, and avoid intervening in this effort."[61] This point of view won out in the end, with Hale securing the agreement of other ICIC scientists, especially Marie Curie and Kristine Bonnevie of Norway, who was a professor of zoology at the University of Oslo. Commission members agreed that a universal bibliography was too ambitious a project and that it was important to proceed sector by sector. The decision was therefore made to create a Sub-Commission for Bibliography that would present the results of its reflections at the next session of the ICIC in 1923. The subcommission concluded that it was possible to proceed with international bibliographical coordination in three fields: philology, the physical sciences, and the social sciences and that it would be advisable to develop the abstracts system. While we do not know what came of efforts in philology, it is possible to reconstruct what happened in physics and the social sciences. In both cases, the international position of the US increased beginning in the early 1920s.

With regard to physics, in December 1923 the ICIC decided to organize a conference on the coordination of bibliographical work.[62] It was held in Brussels in 1924 and brought together members of the ICIC, the International Union of Pure and Applied Physics, the NRC, and members from the editorial boards of multiple French, British, and American scientific journals. The US imposed its standard, for after discussion it was decided that research published in the field of physics would henceforth include an abstract, and it was recommended that the rules for the presentation of these abstracts be those applied by the *Physical Review* in the US and that every body publishing analytical bibliographies henceforth include a table of contents by alphabetic order (by subject) based on analysis of essay contents or excerpts, following the example of *Chemical Abstracts* or *Physical Review*.[63] In the mid-1920s, the US bibliographical standard had thus become the international standard.

In the social sciences, the ICIC also began a project in international bibliography in 1923, doing so in association with the American Sociological Association.[64] For practical reasons, it was initially decided to limit the effort to the economic sciences. In 1925 a group of experts was appointed to complete the project and included representatives from the US, Great Britain, Belgium, Brazil, France, Italy, Poland, and Switzerland. The Columbia University professor William Ogburn represented the American Sociological Association and the Social Science Research Council.[65] The overall project aimed to create an annual register of published works, as well as a selection of abstracts for articles published in scientific journals, for which the experts had to prepare a selective analysis.

At this stage of the discussions, Ogburn declared he was unable to make decisions on behalf of the American Sociological Association and the Social Science Research Council.[66] This wait-and-see attitude was hardly by chance, as the ICIC project was competing with a similar one initiated at the same time under the coordination of the Social Science Research Council. The two projects were not strictly identical, as that of the ICIC was solely on economics and sought to exhaustively cover all of the world's publications, whereas the US project covered all of the social sciences and consisted of a selective bibliography in English. However, ICIC members were aware of the rivalry between the two projects, with the second one aiming to "render independent the intense scientific activity of a single, rich, and powerful country."[67] Still, ICIC representatives avoided pouring fuel on the fire, for they knew that their own project was not feasible without US collaboration, both intellectual and financial, and that the ICIC did not have the funding to complete it, hoping for help from foundations:

> We know that it is from America that we hope to receive the required grant. We expect the influential support of the League of Nations will prompt major American philanthropic foundations to add this undertaking to those they have already developed.[68]

The ICIC did not have the financial means to complete such a project, no more so than the IIIC. The Americans soon decided to go it alone. In 1927 the Social Science Research Council was provided a budget by the RF to produce *Social Science Abstracts*, an annual publication providing an overview of publications in economics, anthropology, sociology, political science, geography, statistics, and history.[69] When the sociologist Stuart Chapin, who was the project coordinator, presented it before the ICIC in July 1928, the latter had not made progress and could only note with elegance its inability to pursue its own project: "the grants that have already been received, however encouraging they may be, do not allow for [...] proceeding any further than following, with sympathy, the development of the work."[70] In March 1929 the monthly periodical *Social Science Abstracts* published its first issue: in one year it presented 11,000 abstracts from 3,000 journals in 24 languages, with 1,400 collaborators from over 20 countries reading articles and drafting abstracts.[71] From its very first year, the periodical had 2,000 subscribers, of which 1,500 were in the US and 500 in Great Britain. It also had its own network of collaborators, making it entirely independent of the LoN. The undertaking continued until 1933, when publication was interrupted due to its high cost.[72]

This episode clearly shows the rivalries involving the ICIC and its activities and the scientific and intellectual rise of the US—which tended to impose its standards in the production of scientific knowledge—along with Europe's decline due to a lack of funding for its own projects. While the IIIC created a Section for Scientific Relations in 1927, published the *Bulletin des Relations Scientifiques*, sent observers to congresses of scientific associations and held meetings in Paris with representatives of associations, its chronic lack of funding condemned it to a passive role, whereas US organizations were much more dynamic due to foundation support. In the domain of scientific bibliography, the track record of the ICIC and IIIC in the late 1920s was meager: the two organizations were neither able to complete their projects for lack of funding nor to impose themselves as intermediaries with scientific unions, where US influence was strong, and whose projects in many respects bypassed those of the LoN.

This competition between Europe and the US was even more present in the late 1920s. In 1928, the 16th International Conference of American States was held in Havana, at which an Inter-American Institute of Intellectual Cooperation was created in connection with the Pan-American Union. In September 1929 during the ICIC's session in Geneva, the US representative Mann presented his colleagues with a *fait accompli* by announcing the institute's imminent creation. This was bad news for the ICIC, as it challenged the monopoly in intellectual cooperation by creating a competing institution centered on the American continent, one that would bypass the ICIC. Despite the bad mood of his colleagues, who considered the initiative "inadmissible,"[73] Mann presented his own projects, notably the creation of exchange programs between the US and certain Latin American countries. This once again amounted to pulling the rug out from under the ICIC, for it had recently recommended the creation of exchange programs but did not have the first penny to finance them. Aside from the obvious challenge to ICIC authority represented by the new institute, its creation raised highly concrete problems, for the ICIC was in the midst of talks with philanthropic foundations for funding, and it was obvious that the creation of an inter-American institute ran the "risk of preventing the ICIC or IIIC from receiving American donations, should that occur."[74] The Inter-American Institute was officially created in 1930.[75] The Seventh International Conference of American States held in Montevideo three years later went further by organizing programs of cooperation as part of the Good Neighbor policy that the US was trying to promote with South America since the election of Franklin D. Roosevelt. For example, partner states signed a convention on the teaching of history and the revising of school textbooks, adopted recommendations regarding the exchange of artwork between the continent's museums, developed cooperation in the field of scientific bibliography, addressed the protection of monuments, especially those of Pre-Columbian civilizations, and finally drove the development of exchange programs for teachers and students. Some of these projects were simply the American version of the projects that the ICIC and IIIC had been trying to put in place since 1922. In this respect, it is clear that during the early 1930s, the IIIC had a competitor in Latin America, one with strong American influence as well as more substantial financial means.

The Crisis of Intellectual Cooperation and the Rise of the US

The rise of the US was fostered by the crisis that rocked the intellectual cooperation apparatus in the late 1920s. The creation of the IIIC shifted the center of gravity for intellectual cooperation from Geneva to Paris. This geographical shift was accompanied by the Jacobin style of government adopted by the institute's first director, Julien Luchaire, whose goal was to make the IIIC a kind of global ministry of culture coordinating projects in all fields of intellectual, scientific, and artistic life. Luchaire's activism and centralizing tendencies quickly prompted protest among other ICIC members, such that by the late 1920s anger was rising in many countries, Francophilic ones included. In 1926 the Swiss delegate Reynold criticized Luchaire's strategy of increasing projects and asserting independence from the ICIC, which was supposed to supervise its activity. The ICIC's natural sciences representatives, Albert Einstein and Marie Curie, were hardly favorable to the IIIC's preemption of the coordination of scientific relations, as it would encroach on the prerogatives of the IRC. The IIIC Deputy Director Alfred Zimmern also criticized Luchaire's vision and expressed his support for an IIIC whose function would essentially be that of encouraging projects subsequently implemented locally by dedicated institutions. Drummond was, on principle, opposed to the IIIC's wishes for autonomy but was also concerned by the rising costs of Luchaire's projects. He had the approval of the British government, which wanted to limit the LoN's activities, deeming them to be too expensive. Finally, other ICIC members criticized the organization's lack of control over the IIIC, stemming from the fact that it only met once per year; indeed it was more a case of the IIIC controlling the ICIC, or at least imposing its policy.[76]

All of these criticisms coalesced in 1928 when the project for intellectual cooperation reform, initiated by the South African Gilbert Murray, who had succeeded Henri Bergson as ICIC President, came up for discussion. The project's goal was to weaken the IIIC and French influence by shifting the management of intellectual cooperation to Geneva, with the IIIC abandoning its ambition of involving all fields of international intellectual and cultural life and instead concentrating on specific projects. The matter was debated during the ICIC's 1928 and 1929 sessions, at which the IIIC was sharply criticized, and a restructuring project giving greater authority to the ICIC was sketched out. Despite the support of multiple countries (Spain, Czechoslovakia, Belgium, Brazil), France remained in the minority but nevertheless succeeded in countering the situation at the last moment thanks to the skill of Paul Painlevé, the President of the IIIC Board of Directors, who had most of the project's provisions canceled.[77] The reform would not translate into a diminished remit for the IIIC or an increased one for the ICIC; its primary manifestation was the official creation of an Intellectual Cooperation Organisation (ICO) by the LoN General Assembly, in addition to the bolstering of national commissions. These commissions initiated the reform process and were included in the decision-making process in 1931. As their number had increased (rising from 12 in 1923 to 38 in 1930), there was a change in the power relations within the IIIC—albeit not as important as at the outset—in which French influence remained prominent. Moreover, while Luchaire's successor Henri Bonnet was French, he had spent most of his career in the LoN apparatus and was not seen by other countries as a representative of Paris, which facilitated consensus regarding his name. Murray was confirmed as the President of the ICIC, thereby ensuring the balance that did not exist during Bergson's presidency, when the ICIC and IIIC were in French hands. While France had limited the damage, its authoritative position at the ICIC was nevertheless diminished by the crisis. In addition, the bolstering of national commissions could only favor the US, whose commission funded by the CEIP was both the best endowed and the largest.

Americans remained discreet during this episode, all while attentively following how the discussions unfolded. One of the RF's correspondents in Europe, the British journalist and alpinist Geoffrey Winthrop Young, sent a report in 1929 to the foundation to provide an update regarding the full-blown crisis. He emphasized the general discontent at the ICIC toward the IIIC, which was deemed to be overly centralizing and Parisian. The Briton was not gentle toward a "French culture"[78] imbued with its superiority and was quick to give lessons to the rest of the world. He believed that the RF should promote cooperation between European countries along other lines and that it could promote the development of activities in Geneva in an effort to counter Paris. This is apparently also what philanthropic officers believed, for in 1928 the LSRM planned to fund an academic exchange project at the ICIC on the condition that it be managed from Geneva rather than Paris. While this funding never materialized, it shows that foundations were lying in ambush and were following the evolution of power relations within the ICIC, ready to tip them in the direction that suited their projects. It was therefore in the ICO, where French influence was diminishing, that Americans would expand their presence, a dynamic that was most visible in the International Studies Conference (ISC).

This organization grew out the objective to study international relations in a scientific manner. In the aftermath of World War I, the complexity of international problems required the development of expertise in the new problems faced by the contemporary world, in order to prevent future wars. It was in this context that multiple institutes emerged in Europe and the US to study international issues, either within an academic setting or as private or governmental institutes. The first chair in international relations in the strict sense of the term was created in Great Britain in 1919, at Aberystwyth University, and was first held by Alfred Zimmern. When he became Deputy Director of the IIIC, he was particularly aware of this matter. As for philanthropic foundations, they played a major role in the emergence of this new field of study by funding numerous institutions dedicated to its analysis in the early 1920s, in both the US and Europe.[79] In 1926, the LSRM provided support for the Institute of Pacific Relations (IPR) at the University of Hawaii, which was created the previous year to coordinate research on the Pacific region, a strategic issue for the US in the aftermath of World War I.[80] After the LSRM was integrated into the RF in 1929, the latter continued to fund the IPR, which was also supported by the CEIP.[81] In the mid-1920s, the CEIP and LSRM also funded the development of international law and international relations in US universities, notably Harvard and Yale. The RF also provided support for the Council on Foreign Relations (CFR) beginning in 1929 and for the Foreign Policy Association (FPA) beginning in 1933.

Rockefeller philanthropy also supported institutions outside the US. This was especially true in Great Britain, where beginning in 1923 it provided funding for the London School of Economics (LSE), part of which would be devoted to international relations. In 1924 the institution created a chair in international relations, and the following year a chair in international law and international history, ultimately creating a department of international relations in 1927.[82] There were many other institutes funded outside the US, including the Graduate Institute of International Studies (GIIS), which was created in Geneva in 1927, and supported for 10 years; the Deutsche Hochschule für Politik of Berlin (funded from 1929 to 1933); the international section of the Institute for Economics and History in Copenhagen; the Institute for Constitutional and International Law at the University of Lviv in Poland; the Royal Institute of International Affairs in London; the Canadian Institute of International Affairs; and the Centre d'étude de politique étrangère in Paris, which was created in 1935, and almost entirely funded by the foundation until 1940.[83]

The mid-1920s saw attempts to coordinate the international studies being conducted in various countries. The IPR showed the way by institutionalizing cooperation among specialists from neighboring Pacific countries through its biennial conferences. In 1928 the IIIC followed suit by creating the permanent ISC, which was the first step in crystallizing a European circle of specialists in international relations. During a meeting of IIIC members in Berlin, it was decided to coordinate the research conducted in various countries by creating national committees managed by the IIIC.[84] Eight countries were represented at the meeting, with the British dominating: the delegation included four members from the LSE, including its Director William Beveridge, along with three from the Royal Institute of International Affairs. The objective formulated during this meeting was to build a new science at the intersection of multiple disciplines, especially law, economics, geography, and history. Participants would henceforth meet each year and structure their collective reflection through the study of topics determined by the Conference's Executive Committee.

As part of its funding strategy for expertise on international issues, US philanthropy took an interest in the ISC from the very beginning. The CEIP-CE was among the founding institutions during the conference held in Berlin in 1928;[85] its Director, Earle Babcock, was a member of the ISC's Executive Committee from the beginning,[86] a position he held until his death in 1935 when he was succeeded by Malcolm W. Davis,[87] who stayed in the position until the late 1930s. The RF joined the ISC in 1932; in May of that year, Selskar Gunn, the foundation's Vice President in charge of Europe, attended the meeting in Milan,[88] with Babcock and Shotwell also present.[89] Gunn left with a favorable impression of the IIIC's new director, Henri Bonnet, who struck him as being independent of the French Ministry for Foreign Affairs, as well as of the work conducted by participants,[90] with the project for "coordinating research in the field of international issues"[91] being in sync with the foundation's objectives.

But it was Shotwell who played the central role in the philanthropic foundations' engagement in the ISC's work. In July 1931 he attended an ICIC meeting for the first time as Millikan's replacement, before officially succeeding him the following year. From the very beginning of his participation, he expressed his total agreement with the new philosophy resulting from the creation of the ICO: "the Intellectual Cooperation Organization should not present itself as a dictatorship over intellectual and artistic life, but on the contrary should collaborate with existing national and international organizations,"[92] implicitly referring to France.

Shotwell expressed his support for developing the study of international issues. He observed that the ICIC "had devoted itself during its early years to the almost exclusive study of intellectual forms entirely devoid of any political aspects."[93] He believed it was important to

> examine the application of scientific disciplines in the fields of economics and politics, in the same manner as the natural sciences, letters, and arts [sic]. If the Commission does not consider this new form of its activity, it runs the risk of failing to attract the attention of those leading the life of nations, thereby courting failure.[94]

Shotwell recommended a study "on the possibility of extending [its] activity to politics and social issues,"[95] believing that "if the Commission expects to one day fulfill its mandate of promoting international *rapprochement*, it should pursue this new path."

The project sketched out by Shotwell was quite similar to that of the ISC, but since it was an IIIC initiative, the ICIC had little control over its activity. Given these conditions, the apparent goal of Shotwell's proposal was to directly involve the ICIC in ISC activity, in order for the American National Committee on Intellectual Cooperation to assert its point of view. At the same time, Millikan, whose term was about to end, made no secret of his lack of consideration for the activity conducted up to that point by the ICIC, which he considered "the most ineffective [...] portion of the League," its work amounting to "a mere gesture of good will."[96] From his perspective, Shotwell's nomination—and the proposal for development he supported—would, on the contrary, transform the ICIC into an "active working body,"[97] which is to say an organization with expertise in international issues able to develop concrete solutions to international problems, and one that simultaneously would expand US influence over intellectual cooperation.

But Murray was also reluctant regarding this change in power relations within the ICIC, which, if successful in countering French influence, could also eventually threaten British influence. Faced with his hesitation, Shotwell raised the possibility of his resignation as the American representative to the ICIC, while Millikan also suggested, in veiled words, the withdrawal of the American National Committee on Intellectual Cooperation, which was by far the most important organization, and would further weaken an ICIC that was barely pulling out of the crisis.[98] US pressure proved effective, as Shotwell's proposal was accepted in August 1932, especially his idea of

> encouraging the social and political sciences to do for the community of nations what they had heretofore done for the national state, namely to conduct studies of the major international problems handled in Geneva by the League of Nations, and to ultimately secure the direct collaboration of science in this effort.[99]

In the ensuing years it would conduct considerable activity to complete its project, with the logistical and financial support of the CEIP and the RF.

During the ICIC meeting in July 1933, he provided a more specific argument. He believed that "since the war, the number and importance of political and social problems had broadened the field of these sciences, and given them particular topicality." He proposed that the ICIC add to its program "this entire group of sciences"[100] so useful for moral disarmament, namely by organizing conferences of experts. This proposal was firmly in line with those he had formulated since the Peace Conference in 1919 and would take concrete form at the ISC. In the meantime, foundations' interest in the ISC translated into funding in 1932. It was initially marginal, as that year a first CEIP grant represented 0.7% of the IIIC's total budget,[101] while that same year the RF provided the ISC with a grant of $1,500, which was renewed in 1933 and 1934.

Conclusion

While intellectual cooperation was often seen as a strictly European affair, and even a French one, it is actually quite clear that during the interwar period the US played an important role from the very beginning, doing so with the support of philanthropic foundations. As with health-related topics, intellectual and cultural issues were not exempt from geopolitical rivalries and power relations between states, which changed fundamentally after 1918, with repercussions in intellectual cooperation just as in other fields. This process became even more evident in the 1930s in the evolution of the ISC, which I will now examine.

Notes

1 Association internationale des académies, Première assemblée générale tenue à Paris du 16 au 20 avril 1901, Paris, 1901.
2 Institut de France. Académie des sciences. Conférence interalliée des académies scientifiques tenue à Londres les 9, 10, 11 octobre 1918, Paris, 1918.
3 Baker F.W.G., *Le Conseil international des unions scientifiques*, Paris, Secrétariat du CIUS, 1981, p. 11.
4 Greenaway Frank, *Science International. A History of the International Council of Scientific Unions*, Cambridge, Cambridge University Press, 1996, p. 23. See also Statut du Conseil international de recherches, in Union géodésique et géophysique internationale, première assemblée générale, Rome, mai 1922, *Bulletin Géodésique*, 1, 1922.
5 Schroeder-Gudehus Brigitte, *Les scientifiques et la paix. La communauté scientifique internationale au cours des années 1920*, Montréal, Presses Universitaires de Montréal, 1978, p. 298.
6 *American Council of Learned Societies Bulletin*, 1, 1920, p. 1.
7 Tournès Ludovic, "Jalons pour une histoire de l'internationalisme scientifique: le Conseil international des unions scientifiques et l'Union académique internationale," in Defrance Corine et Kwaschik Anne (eds.), *Science et guerre froide*, Paris, CNRS éditions, 2015, pp. 51–68.

8 Reinbothe Roswitha, *Deutsch als internationale Wissenschaftsprache und der Boycott nach dem Ersten Weltkrieg*, Frankfurt am Main, Peter Lang, 2006, p. 196.
9 Renoliet Jean-Jacques, *L'UNESCO oubliée: la Société des Nations et la coopération intellectuelle, 1919–1946*, Paris, Publications de la Sorbonne, 1999, p. 13.
10 SDN. Commission internationale de coopération intellectuelle. Procès-verbaux de la première session. Première séance, 1er août 1922.
11 Schroeder-Gudehus, *Les scientifiques…, op. cit.*, p. 193.
12 Renoliet, *L'UNESCO…, op. cit.*, pp. 32–33.
13 *Ibid.*, p. 40.
14 *Ibid.*, p. 21.
15 *Ibid.*, p. 30.
16 Renoliet Jean-Jacques, "La genèse de l'Institut international de coopération intellectuelle," *Relations Internationales*, 72, 1992, p. 395.
17 Renoliet, *L'UNESCO…, op. cit.*, p. 110.
18 *Ibid.*, p. 80.
19 Thelin John R., *A History of American Higher Education*, Baltimore, Johns Hopkins University Press, 2004, chs. 4 and 5.
20 Tournès Ludovic & Scott-Smith Giles, "A World of Exchanges: Conceptualizing the History of International Scholarship Programs (Nineteenth to Twenty-First Centuries)," in Tournès Ludovic & Scott-Smith Giles (eds.), *Global Exchanges: Scholarship Programs and Transnational Circulations in the Modern World*, New York, Berghahn Books, 2017, pp. 1–29.
21 *Report of the National Academy of Science for the Year 1919*, p. 12.
22 *Ibid.*, p. 76.
23 *Report of the National Academy of Science for the Year 1919*, p. 77.
24 Kevles Daniel J., "George Ellery Hale, the First World War, and the Advancement of Science in America," *Isis*, 59–4, 1968, pp. 427–437.
25 SDN. CICI. Procès-verbaux de la première session. Première séance, 1er août 1922.
26 *American Council of Learned Societies Bulletin*, 1, 1920, p. 2.
27 Shotwell James T., "La coopération intellectuelle entre les sociétés savantes des Etats-Unis et de la France," *Cahiers de politique étrangère*, 65, 1938, p. 4; *American Council of Learned Societies Bulletin*, 1, 1920, p. 13.
28 SDN. CICI. Procès-verbaux de la première session, annexe III, août 1922.
29 Gilbert to Stimson, September 30, 1932, NARA RG 84/415; Bukknell to Hull, January 26, 1938, NARA RG 84/503.
30 SDN. CICI. Deuxième session. 26 juillet-2 août 1923. Rapport de la commission.
31 SDN. CICI. Procès-verbal de la treizième session, Genève, 20–25 juillet 1931.
32 SDN. CICI. Deuxième session. juillet 26–août 2, 1923. Rapport de la commission.
33 Waldo Leland, *Report to the American National Committee on Intellectual Cooperation*, July 31, 1935, CEIP-CE I/31/3.
34 SDN. CICI. Rapport de la commission sur les travaux de sa dix-neuvième session plénière, août 1937; SDN. OCI. Comité exécutif. Vingt-quatrième session, première séance, 25 avril 1938; SDN. OCI. Comité exécutif. Vingt-sixième session, première séance, 19 décembre 1938.
35 *Ibid.*, Onzième session, Genève, 14 septembre 1929.
36 *Report for the Commission of Intellectual Cooperation*, n.d. (January 1926), CEIP-CE I/28/2; *Report on the Work of the American National Committee on Intellectual Cooperation*, September 30, 1935, CEIP-CE I/31/5.
37 SDN. CICI. Procès-verbaux de la quatrième session, juillet 25–29, 1924, p. 38.

38 *Ibid.*, Cinquième session, 11–14 mai 1925.
39 Luchaire to Babcock, December 10, 1925, CEIP-CE I/28/2.
40 *Bulletin of the American Council of Learned Societies*, 5, 1926, p. 11.
41 Renoliet, *L'UNESCO...*, *op. cit.*, p. 202 sq.
42 SDN. CICI. Procès-verbaux de la troisième session, annexe 1, p. 39, 3–8 décembre 1923.
43 Fosdick to Sweetser, May 16, 1922, AS-LOC 14.
44 Butler to Drummond, May 20, 1925, AS-LOC 14.
45 Drummond to Sweetser, June 2, 1925, AS-LOC 14; Sweetser to Butler, n.d (September 1925), AS-LOC 31.
46 Butler was in Europe between the months of June and September almost every year. While there he met with members of the European Centre of the CEIP as well as numerous politicians and intellectuals, and also took part in many social events. This was the case in 1921, 1923, 1925, 1926, 1927, 1929, 1930, 1931, 1932, 1934, and 1937 (CEIP-CE VII/217 to 224).
47 The Secretary General of the European Centre to Manley O. Hudson, July 25, 1925, CEIP-CE VIII/219/2.
48 Le Secrétaire général du Centre Européen à Luchaire, 8 décembre 1925, CEIP-CE I/28/1.
49 Cited in Renoliet, *L'UNESCO...*, *op. cit.*, p. 245.
50 Réunion du conseil d'administration du Centre européen, 25 octobre 1926, CEIP III/105/3.
51 Note du Chef-adjoint de la Section scientifique, 20 avril 1926, UNESCO-IICI D/XI/16.
52 In the 1920s Europeans frequently mixed up John D. Rockefeller, Sr., his son John D. Rockefeller Jr., the Rockefeller Foundation, the General Education Board, the Laura Spelman Rockefeller Memorial, and the Rockefeller Institute for Medical Research. They were often indiscriminately referred to as the "Rockefeller Foundation" or "Rockefeller Institute."
53 Gregg to Luchaire, April 21, 1926, UNESCO-IICI D/XI/16.
54 Vincent to Luchaire, May 12, 1926, UNESCO-IICI B/IV/23.
55 SDN. CICI. Procès-verbal de la treizième session, Genève, 20–25 juillet 1931, p. 16.
56 SDN. CICI. Procès-verbaux de la première session, cinquième séance, 3 août 1922.
57 *Ibid.*, Huitième séance, 4 août 1922 après–midi.
58 Rockefeller Foundation, *Annual Report*, 1924, p. 12.
59 SDN. CICI. Procès-verbaux de la première session, troisième séance, 2 août 1922 matin.
60 *Ibid.*
61 *Ibid.*, Quatrième séance, 2 août 1922 après–midi.
62 *Ibid.*, Procès-verbaux de la troisième session, 3–8 décembre 1923.
63 *Ibid.*, Procès-verbaux de la quatrième session, 25–29 juillet 1924, p. 30.
64 *Ibid.*, Procès-verbaux de la troisième session, annexe 19, 3–8 décembre 1923, p. 60.
65 *Ibid.*, Procès-verbaux de la sixième session, 27–30 juillet 1925, annexe 11, p. 46.
66 CICI. Sous-commission de bibliographie. Ordre du jour de la neuvième session (Genève, 11–13 juillet 1927), Rapport du professeur Von Gottl-Ottlilienfeld sur la réunion d'experts pour la coordination de la bibliographie des sciences économiques, tenue à Paris en janvier 1927, p. 2.
67 *Ibid.*, pp. 18–19, this and the following quotation.
68 *Ibid.*, p. 17.

136 *ICIC and New International Power Relations*

69 SDN. IICI. Rapport de l'Institut à la sous-commission des sciences et de bibliographie, 1929.
70 SDN. CICI. Sous-commission des sciences et de bibliographie, dixième session, 23 juillet 1928, p. 8.
71 Rockefeller Foundation, *Annual Report*, 1930, p. 241.
72 Rockefeller Foundation, *Annual Report*, 1933, p. 250; *Ibid.*, 1935, p. 209.
73 SDN. CICI. Procès-verbal de la onzième session, Genève, 14 septembre 1929.
74 *Ibid.*
75 SDN. Actes de la deuxième Conférence générale des commissions nationales de coopération intellectuelle, Paris, 5–9 juillet 1937, p. 21 sq.
76 SDN. CICI. Procès-verbal de la onzième session, Genève, 14 septembre 1929.
77 See the details of the episode in Renoliet, *L'UNESCO...*, *op. cit.*, pp. 77–118.
78 G. Winthrop Young, Intellectual cooperation, June 1929, RF 1.1/100/105/952.
79 Mosely Philip E., "International Affairs," in Weaver Warren (ed.), *US Philanthropic Foundations. Their History, Structure, Management and Record*, New York, Harper & Row, 1967, pp. 375–394; Parmar Inderjeet, "The Carnegie Corporation and the Mobilisation of Opinion in the United States' Rise to Globalism, 1939–1945," *Minerva*, 37-4, 1999, p. 363; Riemens Michael, "International Academic Cooperation on International Relations in the Interwar Period: the International Studies Conference," *Review of International Studies*, 37-2, 2011, pp. 911–928; Pemberton Jo-Anne, *The Story of International Relations, Part One: Cold-Blooded Idealists*, Palgrave MacMillan, 2020.
80 Roberts Priscilla, "The Institute of Pacific Relations: Pan-Pacific and Pan-Asian Visions of International Order," *International Politics*, 55, 2018, pp. 836–851; Akami Tomoko, "Missed Opportunities to be Global: Conversion and Diversion of the Scientific Field of Knowledge of International Relations of the International Studies Conference and the Institute of Pacific Relations," *Monde(s). Histoires, Espaces, Relations*, 19–1, 2021, pp. 183–202.
81 Rockefeller Foundation, *Annual Report*, 1931, p. 247.
82 Scot Marie, *La London school of economics and political science. Internationalisation universitaire et circulation des savoirs en sciences sociales 1895–2000*, Paris, PUF, 2011, p. 127 sq.
83 Tournès Ludovic, *Sciences de l'homme et politique. Les fondations philanthropiques américaines en France au XXe siècle*, Paris, Garnier, 2013 (2011), ch. 6.
84 League of Nations. International Studies Conference, *Collective Security. A Record of the Seventh and the Eighth International Studies Conferences*, Paris 1934–London 1935, edited by Maurice Bourquin, Paris, 1936, p. ix; see also *L'Europe Nouvelle*, 4 juin 1932.
85 Institut international de coopération intellectuelle. Recommandations de la réunion des experts pour la coordination des hautes études internationales, Berlin, 22–24 mars 1928, CEIP-CE I/28/2. The original name was "Conférence des institutions pour l'étude scientifique des relations internationales" (Conference of Institutions for the Scientific Study of International Relations). The name was changed in "International Studies Conference" in 1934.
86 Séance du 9 décembre 1929 tenue à l'IICI, CEIP-CE I/28/5; le Secrétaire de l'IICI à Babcock, 12 mai 1934, CEIP-CE/I/30/5.
87 Chalmers Wright (IICI Secretary) to Walter H. Mallory (Council on Foreign Relations Executive Director), October 28, 1935, CEIP-CE I/31/4; Chalmers Wright to Davis, January 8, 1936, CEIP-CE I/32/2; Bonnet to Davis, May 25, 1937, CEIP-CE I/32/5.

88 Séance solennelle d'ouverture de la conférence, 23 mai 1932, UNESCO-IICI K/VII/I.
89 *L'Europe Nouvelle*, 4 juin 1932.
90 Gunn to Max Mason (Rockefeller Foundation President), May 31, 1932, RF 1.1/100/105/952.
91 Gunn to Day, June 22, 1932, RF 1.1/100/105/952.
92 SDN. CICI. Procès-verbal de la treizième session, Genève, 20–25 juillet 1931, p. 16.
93 *Ibid.*
94 *Ibid.*
95 *Ibid.*
96 Millikan to Murray, January 7, 1932; Shotwell to Thompson (Executive Secretary of the American Committee on Intellectual Cooperation), January 5, 1932, JTS-CU 134 and 135.
97 Millikan to Murray, January 7, 1932, JTS-CU 134 and 135.
98 Josephson Harold, *James T. Shotwell and the Rise of Internationalism in America*, London, Associated University Press, 1975, pp. 190–192.
99 SDN. CICI. Rapport de la commission sur les travaux de sa quatorzième session plénière, août 1932, p. 16.
100 SDN. CICI. Quinzième session, Genève, 17–22 juillet 1933. Rapport de la commission.
101 Renoliet, *L'UNESCO...*, *op. cit.*, p. 206.

References

Akami Tomoko, "Missed Opportunities to be Global: Conversion and Diversion of the Scientific Field of Knowledge of International Relations of the International Studies Conference and the Institute of Pacific Relations," *Monde(s). Histoires, Espaces, Relations*, 19–1, 2021, pp. 183–202.

Baker F.W.G., *Le Conseil international des unions scientifiques,* Paris, Secrétariat du CIUS, 1981.

Greenaway Frank, *Science International. A History of the International Council of Scientific Unions,* Cambridge, Cambridge University Press, 1996.

Josephson Harold, *James T. Shotwell and the Rise of Internationalism in America,* London, Associated University Press, 1975.

Kevles Daniel J., "George Ellery Hale, the First World War, and the Advancement of Science in America," *Isis*, 59–4, 1968, pp. 427–437.

Mosely Philip E., "International Affairs," in Weaver Warren (ed.), *US Philanthropic Foundations. Their History, Structure, Management and Record,* New York, Harper & Row, 1967, pp. 375–394.

Parmar Inderjeet, "The Carnegie Corporation and the Mobilisation of Opinion in the United States' Rise to Globalism, 1939–1945," *Minerva*, 37–4, 1999, pp. 355–378.

Pemberton Jo-Anne, *The Story of International Relations, Part One: Cold-Blooded Idealists,* London, Palgrave MacMillan, 2020.

Schroeder-Gudehus Brigitte, *Les scientifiques et la paix. La communauté scientifique internationale au cours des années 1920,* Montréal, Presses Universitaires de Montréal, 1978.

Reinbothe Roswitha, *Deutsch als internationale Wissenschaftsprache und der Boycott nach dem Ersten Weltkrieg,* Frankfurt am Main, Peter Lang, 2006.

Renoliet Jean-Jacques, "La genèse de l'Institut international de coopération intellectuelle," *Relations Internationales,* 72, 1992, pp. 387–398.

Renoliet Jean-Jacques, *L'UNESCO oubliée: la Société des Nations et la coopération intellectuelle, 1919–1946,* Paris, Publications de la Sorbonne, 1999.

Riemens, Michael, "International Academic Cooperation on International Relations in the Interwar Period: The International Studies Conference," *Review of International Studies,* 37–2, 2011, pp. 911–928.

Roberts Priscilla, "The Institute of Pacific Relations: Pan-Pacific and Pan-Asian Visions of International Order," *International Politics,* 55, 2018, pp. 836–851.

Scot Marie, *La London school of economics and political science. Internationalisation universitaire et circulation des savoirs en sciences sociales 1895–2000,* Paris, PUF, 2011.

Thelin John R., *A history of American Higher Education,* Baltimore, Johns Hopkins University Press, 2004.

Tournès Ludovic, *Sciences de l'homme et politique. Les fondations philanthropiques américaines en France au XXe siècle,* Paris, Garnier, 2013 [2011].

Tournès Ludovic, "Jalons pour une histoire de l'internationalisme scientifique: le Conseil international des unions scientifiques et l'Union académique internationale," in Defrance Corine et Kwaschik Anne (eds.), *Science et guerre froide,* Paris, CNRS éditions, 2015, pp. 51–68.

Tournès Ludovic & Scott-Smith Giles, "A World of Exchanges: Conceptualizing the History of International Scholarship Programs (Nineteenth to Twenty-First Centuries)," in Tournès Ludovic & Scott-Smith Giles (eds.), *Global Exchanges: Scholarship Programs and Transnational Circulations in the Modern World,* New York, Berghahn Books, 2017, pp. 1–29.

5 From Intellectual Cooperation to Economic Expertise

Beginning with the Great Depression, the Rockefeller Foundation (RF) and the Carnegie Endowment for International Peace (CEIP) deepened their commitment to technical activities, especially through their increasing interest in economic issues in an effort to find solutions to the Great Depression. The two organizations they invested in were the Economic and Financial Organization (EFO) and then the International Studies Conference (ISC). This support was characteristic of their project of government through science, in the sense that it aimed to mobilize the intellectual resources of economists from all countries (in reality only Western countries) to analyze the mechanisms of the world economy and to simultaneously reconfigure the social sciences on a national level with a view to carrying out this project. It was therefore an ambitious program. The League of Nations (LoN) had a clear role in this project, as the foundations sought to make it a platform for coordinating the expertise activities conducted in different countries. In doing so, the RF and the CEIP contributed to the expansion of the LoN's technical activities during the 1930s, as well as to the legitimacy of its expertise work. As the LoN was increasingly discredited from the political standpoint, the EFO established genuine legitimacy with economic experts across the western world, thereby strengthening its position at the intersection of multiple networks, a process partly due to philanthropic support. This intellectual dynamism supported by US philanthropy explains why the EFO continued its activity when the system of collective security built by the LoN collapsed in the late 1930s. This chapter subsequently explores a paradox: while the US increasingly distanced itself from the LoN with regard to politics by passing neutrality laws, it increased investment in technical activities, not only through its membership in the International Labour Organization (ILO) as mentioned earlier but also through its growing investment in the activities of the EFO and the ISC. However, this investment had other major consequences for the LoN, which were more visible in the field of economics than health. By funding the technical sections, foundations helped autonomize them with regard to the League system, thereby eroding its coherence and the central organization's authority over its technical sections, and in particular over the EFO and the

DOI: 10.4324/9780429021213-6

ISC, which in the 1930s *de facto* became quasiindependent organs of the LoN, paving the way for the explosion of the League system in 1940.

This process will be analyzed in the two sections of this chapter, the first focusing on the EFO and the second on the ISC.

The Economic and Financial Organization

Analysis of the World Economy

By creating the EFO in 1927, the LoN established itself as one of the major centers for economic analysis and an important crossroads in the international circulation of experts. Its objective was to conduct scientific research on international economic issues in order to solve the problems that emerged from World War I and later from the Great Depression. The LoN was not the only organization to address international economic issues in the aftermath of World War I. This was also the case for a number of private organizations in the US, the CEIP in particular, which, as we saw above, initiated the enormous editorial undertaking of the *Economic and Social History of the World War*. This was also true of the Laura Spelman Rockefeller Memorial (LSRM), which played an important role in this field during the 1920s, before being absorbed by the RF in 1929. Beginning in 1922, the LSRM launched an ambitious project to develop international economic expertise by funding institutes located in key countries in an effort to create a global network of specialists working on contemporary problems, notably those coming in the wake of World War I. It provided grants to numerous US institutes, especially the National Bureau of Economic Research (NBER) and the Brookings Institution, in addition to European institutions such as the London School of Economics (LSE), starting in 1924. These grants were not exclusively awarded for international economic issues, although from 1924 onward the latter became a central concern of the leaders of Rockefeller philanthropy, as demonstrated by another project from the General Education Board (GEB) to create an institute to guide the LoN's global policy.[1] Raymond Fosdick was once again central to the process. The idea took shape following his discussions with Abraham Flexner and GEB trustees: it would be an organization of expertise conducting scientific studies on the issues, economic ones in particular, falling under the LoN's remit. While the LoN's economic and financial committees had neither the money nor the staff to conduct such studies,[2] they believed that an independent institution well-endowed by foundations could perform this function. It would simultaneously represent a place for documentation, reflection, centralization, and redistribution of information and would work with the LoN, national governments, and private expertise institutions. In late 1926, Fosdick and Flexner submitted the project to John D. Rockefeller, Jr.,[3] and sent a memorandum to Eric Drummond.[4] The project was not carried out for two reasons: the reluctance it generated at the LoN, based on the notion that an institute supported by US funds would be a think tank *avant la lettre* guiding the organization's policy[5]; and the fact that the LSRM was in the process, at the very same moment, of providing a grant to the new Graduate Institute of International Studies (GIIS) created at the University of Geneva, whose areas of activity partly overlapped with those of Fosdick's project, even though there was no organic link with the LoN.[6] The institute, which was created in 1927, would be almost exclusively funded by the RF during its first ten years of existence. The aforementioned funding provided for the new LoN library by John D. Rockefeller, Jr. in 1927 was also in keeping with this global project, in that the gathering of documentation involved not just international health issues but economic ones as well.

With the Great Depression, understanding the mechanisms of the world economy became a crucial subject. During the reorganization of Rockefeller philanthropy, which culminated in 1929 with the integration of the LSRM in the RF, the Board of Trustees made economic issues the leading agenda item for the foundation for the coming years. It had two objectives: understanding the logic of the international economy and especially of the economic crisis, in order to identify solutions, and working to prevent conflicts by studying relations between states, economic ones in particular. With this in mind, the Rockefeller intensified its contacts with American and European academic circles in order to help create or develop institutes to study the economic situation and to establish a division of labor among them in order to obtain a panoramic view of the economic issues affecting the contemporary world. From 1930 onward, the foundation's Division of Social Science increased contact with European study institutes, a number of which had existed since the preceding decade, such as the Romanian Institute of Social Sciences in Bucharest (founded in 1921), the Austrian Institute for Business Cycle Research (AIBCR) in Vienna (1927), along with its counterpart in Sofia (probably 1929). In total, between 1930 and 1940[7] the Rockefeller provided grants to 46 institutions working on international economic issues, half of which were located outside the US, mostly in Western Europe (Germany, Austria, Belgium, France, Great Britain, the Netherlands, Switzerland), but also in Northern Europe (Sweden, Norway, Denmark), Central and Eastern Europe (Poland, Romania, Bulgaria), and a few other countries (Canada, China, Mandatory Lebanon). While the institutions that received the most foundation funding were in the US (NBER, Harvard University, Chicago University, the Social Science Research Council), the LSE and the League of Nations came right behind, followed by Charles Rist's Scientific Institute for Economic and Social Research (ISRES), which received grants from 1933 onward. The foundation provided more modest grants to other institutes, which were sometimes in the tens of thousands of dollars and covered periods between five and ten years, thereby enabling them to develop multiyear research projects, whereas in most countries both private and public financing was granted annually, as was the case for the LoN's technical sections. Philanthropic funding was thus an important vector for the development of scientific policies during the interwar period, as clearly shown by the RF's role

142   *From Cooperation to Expertise*

in the organization of research in France. The amount of these grants bears witness to the importance of economic issues among Rockefeller concerns, for between 1930 and 1940 the 46 institutes it funded worldwide received $10 million in total, which allowed them to launch research on business cycles in order to understand the logic behind crises. A few examples suffice to show the diverse efforts led with Rockefeller grants.

The AIBCR in Vienna, which was created in 1927 by Ludwig von Mises and Friedrich A. Hayek, was one of the primary organizations that the foundation planned to endow. Its goal was to help steer a crippled Austrian economy in the early 1920s, as well as to further the theoretical understanding of economic phenomena. The LSRM and later the RF granted multiple fellowships to Austrian economists beginning in the middle of the decade: Ludwig Fritscher left for the US in 1924 to study the relations between agriculture and industry; Oskar Morgenstern spent three years in the US between 1925 and 1928 to work on theoretical questions; Gottfried von Haberler did the same in 1927; and Paul N. Rosenstein-Rodan also crossed the Atlantic in 1930. The institute in Vienna, which was led by Friedrich Hayek, who already enjoyed an international reputation, was an incubator of talented economists, and quickly drew the Rockefeller's attention by way of Arthur Sweetser, one of whose many roles was to provide the foundation information on Europe. A Rockefeller grant to a few European institutes, including the one in Vienna—as Sweetser suggested to Fosdick—could open a new field of activity for the foundation and simultaneously help the LoN, whose budget for the study of business cycles was limited. The AIBCR received its first five-year grant in 1930, which was renewed in 1935 and again in 1937, before being interrupted in the aftermath of the Anschluss when the institute was absorbed by its counterpart in Berlin. In parallel to this general grant, the Rockefeller also provided other fellowships beginning in 1930, notably for Ernst John, a young doctor recently recruited by the institute, who left in 1936 for the US to study business cycle fluctuations. He worked at Harvard University with Joseph Schumpeter, and later in Chicago and at the NBER, before a stay in France at Charles Rist's ISRES. His path clearly shows the RF's objective of creating an international network of organizations working on subjects that would provide a better grasp of the logic behind the international economy. Another fellow was Gerhardt Tintner, who also conducted a Grand Tour of economic study institutes at Rockefeller expense between 1934 and 1936, which took him to Harvard, Cambridge, Paris, and Geneva to study the monetary aspects of business cycles and statistics for cyclical fluctuations. He later settled in the US to pursue his career. Finally, there was Fritz Machlup, who between 1933 and 1936 worked on the topic of prices in the US and Great Britain.

While the AIBCR was one of the better-endowed institutes, it was not the only one. There was also the Institute of Economic Studies at the University of Oslo, with the RF being deeply involved in its creation. In 1927 it granted a fellowship to the young economist Ragnar Frisch to study in the US. Upon his return, and after discussions with Rockefeller officers, who saw him as a promising researcher, he drafted a project for the institute's creation, which he submitted to the foundation in 1930. There was no institute of this kind in Norway at the time,[8] and after a first on-site visit in the spring of 1931, the foundation accepted to fund it on the condition it would be led by Frisch. He had just obtained a position as a professor at the University of Oslo and also had an offer from Yale University. His choice to remain in his country immediately resulted in a grant from the RF; the well-endowed institute began to operate on January 1, 1932, and the foundation renewed its funding in 1936.

The list of institutes funded does not end there, as it also included the Institute of Economics and History in Copenhagen, which was also founded in 1927. One of its members, Enevold Sorensen, received a fellowship in 1928 to study business cycles in the US, while the institute received four successive grants to continue its research on this subject in 1930, 1933, 1936, and 1938. This was also the case for the Institute for Economic Studies in Rotterdam, whose scientific management was entrusted in 1930 to Willem Valk, a former Rockefeller fellow who had just returned from the US, where he had gone to study economic theory in 1928. The institute, which cooperated with the Central Agency for Statistics in The Hague, received its first Rockefeller grant in 1931, which was renewed in 1936 and 1939. There was also the Institute for Social Science in Stockholm, to which the foundation awarded a grant in 1930. The foundation was, once again, familiar with the local landscape, as it had granted a fellowship in 1929 to a young PhD in economics, Gunnar Myrdal, to go work in Great Britain. The list continues, as beneficiaries of Rockefeller grants included the Kiel Institute for Maritime Transport and World Economics (from 1931 to 1933), the Romanian Institute of Social Sciences in Bucharest (beginning in 1931), the Institute of Economic Research at the University of Leuven (from 1933 to 1938), and the Institute of Economic Research in Sofia, whose development the Rockefeller supported from 1934 onward, and whose director was former fellow Oskar Anderson. In Great Britain the LSE had received funding since 1924, with the foundation also supporting the Institute for Statistics at Oxford University from 1934 onward and the London and Cambridge Economic Service in 1937. Finally, the ISRES, founded in Paris in 1933 by Charles Rist, also bears mention. That same year, the foundation awarded it one of the largest grants it had given to a non-US organization and funded it entirely until 1940, enabling it to conduct substantial research on the French, European, and international economic situation. The institute was home to numerous young economists, some of whom were former fellows of the foundation, such as Philippe Schwob, who received a fellowship in 1930 to travel to the US for his dissertation on investment trusts, or Robert Marjolin, who conducted research on the New Deal during a stay in the US in 1932–1933. Finally, there was Henry Laufenburger, who obtained a fellowship in 1935, allowing him to visit economic study institutes in a number of European countries (Great Britain, Germany, Italy, Austria, Denmark, Sweden, Norway).[9]

In short, it is difficult to find an institute in Europe that did not, at one point or another, receive Rockefeller funding. The process was the same everywhere: after exploratory phases that translated into a few fellowships for young and promising economists, the foundation helped create or develop an institute for which the study of business cycles was an important area of focus, with the grant continuing in the form of new fellowships to hand-picked researchers, most of whom traveled to the US, as well as Europe. There were, however, a few instances where it did not come to a successful conclusion, as in Finland and Hungary. The overall picture that emerges is nevertheless clear, as beginning in the late 1920s, the Rockefeller philanthropies represented one of the major sources of support for expanding the discipline of economics, and from the 1930s onward more specifically for the development of studies on business cycles and international matters. Between 1925 and 1935, a European network of economic expertise was established, with the foundation playing a major role in its organization.

The Coordination of Research

The RF trustees quickly grasped that the research conducted in these national institutes needed coordination that the foundation could not provide, for it lacked the necessary intellectual capital. Despite being made up of officers with academic backgrounds, the foundation was first and foremost an institute for the management of science and was not equipped to carry out scientific coordination work, especially on such a scale. This is why it turned to the League of Nations. This element is often neglected in the history of philanthropy, which focuses on the financial power of foundations; it is nonetheless important to remember that these organizations were not designed to create knowledge, like universities, but to provide the conditions for making this production possible and for promoting its circulation. In other words, philanthropists do not know how to create ideas, but they know very well how to highlight them and make them circulate. In this respect, the fact that many LoN projects were conducted largely thanks to Rockefeller support is not necessarily a sign of US hegemony over the LoN, for it can even be seen as a sign of the dominated position of the US philanthropy in the field of science.[10] In any event, there is no unequivocal answer to this complex question.

The first manifestation of the Rockefeller's interest in the LoN's economic and financial research materialized in the late 1920s through a grant of 200,000 Swiss francs awarded to the Gold Delegation of the Financial Committee to conduct a study of gold legislation in the world.[11] It continued in 1930 with a grant to the Fiscal Committee to conduct a study on double taxation, which was completed under the direction of Mitchell Carroll, who, as we saw in Chapter 1, was sent on a temporary assignment by the Department of Commerce to devote himself to this endeavor on a full-time basis, becoming an employee of the Secretariat for the duration. The committee had been working on this topic since 1920, and the substantial funding of $140,000 it received from the foundation between 1930 and 1936 allowed it to develop a multilateral convention standardizing tax regulation and avoiding double taxation for certain income categories (salaries, life annuities, royalties and patent income, compensation for border workers, etc.). After drafting the convention[12] and publishing a lengthy report in five volumes,[13] the working group oriented its research toward adapting national tax systems to international economic fluctuations[14] in an effort to guide governments in the development of their tax policy. It produced a series of 14 national monographs[15] published in another substantial report in 1939.[16]

Beyond these sector-based efforts, what interested the Rockefeller was the EFO's overall project, for it was on the whole similar to its own, namely setting up the management of the world economy. At that time, the EFO had already acquired legitimacy with regard to expertise, with its meetings being a required forum for experts working on international economic issues. From 1930 onward, the Great Depression represented the greatest challenge it had yet to face. In September, the Eleventh General Assembly of the LoN called for greater information exchange between experts as well as international coordination for the research conducted in various countries and approved a budget designed to finance research on world economic cycles. It was to achieve this objective that the Economic Intelligence Service (EIS)[17] was created within the EFO and placed under the direction of Alexander Loveday, a British economist who had been working for the LoN since 1919.

Following this decision, the LoN organized two conferences in March and July 1931, which were held on the banks of Lake Geneva at the luxurious hôtel des Bergues. They were attended by members of national economic councils and private institutes studying the economic situation from 15 countries. The central issue was how to coordinate the research being conducted by these institutions, and hence the assignments that could be assumed by the EIS. The US was represented by Edward Eyre Hunt, who was sent by the Department of Commerce and submitted a detailed summary after the first meeting to his administration and the RF. The foundation was aware of the creation of the EIS, as Sweetser had informed Gunn and Fosdick of the LoN General Assembly's decision in December 1930.[18] The foundation worked to support its development.

It initially played an important role in the New Zealander economist, John Bell Condliffe, joining the EIS to supervise work on international issues. Condliffe was born in 1891 and worked for a time as a statistician for the New Zealand government before starting an academic career in Australia at Canterbury College until 1927, when he became the secretary of the Institute of Pacific Relations (IPR). In 1926 the LSRM provided him with funding to create a permanent scientific secretariat to coordinate its research. The position was given to Condliffe, who moved to Honolulu, where he remained until 1929. His work was sufficiently appreciated that the following year Edmund Day, director of the RF's Social Science Division, provided a recommendation

146   *From Cooperation to Expertise*

to help him secure a position at the University of Michigan. The same was most likely also true in September 1931[19] at the EIS, where he would remain until 1937 and where he performed the same work as at the IPR. In any event, his presence was crucial to the foundation awarding financial support to the EIS in the spring of 1933.[20]

The interest of the RF and the US federal government in the EFO's work reveals the converging economic objectives of the LoN and the US from the early 1930s onward. At the beginning of the preceding decade, the federal government had adopted a protectionist logic that took the concrete form of the Fordney McCumber Act of 1922, which substantially raised tariffs for products entering the US. The crisis reinforced this logic by passing the Hawley-Smoot Act of 1930, which established the highest tariffs in US history. Roosevelt did not challenge this protectionist logic when he was elected and concentrated his energy on the first measures of the New Deal, as he believed that restarting the US economy would first and foremost be achieved through domestic measures rather than a revival of foreign trade. It was this lack of interest in international matters that prompted him to torpedo the London Economic Conference in June 1933 by refusing lower trade barriers. However, the US position changed the following year under the impetus of Cordell Hull, who wanted to revive foreign trade, which had fallen by 76% since 1929 due to the Great Depression and retaliation on the part of European countries following implementation of the Hawley-Smoot tariff. This process led to the enactment of the Reciprocal Trade Agreement Act in June 1934, a law that marked a break in US trade policy, as for the first time in the country's history, Congress delegated to the president and his administration its prerogative of determining the amount of tariffs, as well as the ability to negotiate bilateral agreements without previous approval from Congress. Between 1934 and 1945, this policy led to 32 agreements involving 65% of foreign trade, including 22 that were signed between 1934 and 1939.[21] Hull was aware that it was in the US interest to establish international economic collaboration, especially to promote trade. The 1930s were a pivotal moment in the conversion of the US to free trade; it was at this time that the country more or less adopted the position that the EFO had defended since its creation, namely promoting lower international trade barriers in an effort to revive global commerce and emerge from the depression.[22] This convergence only increased during the 1930s, while the ties between the EFO and the LoN's major powers, Great Britain and France, frayed, with the two countries opting for a withdrawal into the protected markets of their colonial empires to emerge from the crisis rather than the globalization of commerce. While Germany and Italy launched policies of autarky and the USSR was on the margins of international trade, the US henceforth served as a key ally in the EFO's strategy of fully opening up international trade. EFO experts were henceforth sharper in their criticism of the international economic policy of major European powers and expanded their contacts with US experts in committee meetings, conferences, and other occasions, such as Loveday's trip to the US in October 1934.[23] The RF's investment in the EFO should be understood in light of this *rapprochement*, with this funding enabling it to develop its expertise activities.

Projects Funded by the RF

The funding of the EIS bears witness to expanding Rockefeller investment in the LoN's economic activities. In April 1933 the foundation awarded the EIS a grant of $125,000 over five years,[24] with the objective of making it a "global center"[25] for gathering and synthesizing the research conducted in other places, as well as working on the international economy, notably on the causes of depressions. Through this funding, the Rockefeller sought to further autonomize the EFO with respect to the LoN—and hence from governments—in order to expand the room for maneuver available to experts. The funding provided to the EFO, like that of the other technical sections, was thus in firm keeping with the Rockefeller strategy of creating a global government of experts working in parallel to political bodies. This is essentially what Edmund Day wrote to Fosdick in December 1933. The director of the Social Science Division believed that the LoN had originally been poorly conceived and entrusted with a mission—the implementation of peace treaties—that it was unable to enforce. He believed it would have been better for it to concentrate its efforts on two areas: organizing conferences in advance of major actions and strengthening scientific expertise. It was based on this observation that Day believed that the RF could, through its funding, help develop a partially autonomous body, one that was free to work on the subjects of its choice, whereas the EFO was not free to conduct studies on subjects deemed sensitive by the governments of major powers. The situation thus seemed favorable for the implementation of such a project, for at the same moment the Italian government was campaigning for a change to the LoN's structure. Day believed this provided a window of opportunity to reconsider the League's overall aims, an opportunity the foundation could use to transform the LoN into a body of expertise on international economic issues.[26] In the summer of 1933, a Rockefeller officer visited Geneva and met with Drummond just before his departure from the Secretariat; the two men agreed that Rockefeller funding should not only continue but increase. They also discussed the possibility of creating a system of fellowships allowing young economists from various countries to work for two years at the EIS, thereby strengthening its position as an international crossroads.[27]

The first goal that the LoN General Assembly set for the EIS was to create a synthesis of the studies conducted throughout the world on business cycles, in order to better understand the mechanisms governing the alternation between phases of growth and depression. This was a new undertaking for the EFO, due to the work of the Swedish economist Bertil Ohlin, who submitted a report to the Assembly in 1931 on economic depressions, which marked a major epistemological break in relation to the research undertaken by LoN economists in the 1920s, who were more focused on monetary aspects. Ohlin conducted an empirical study of the depression on an international scale, which broadened the spectrum of analysis through its interest in currency and other factors, including changes in demand for raw materials, agricultural production, capital flows, increased customs duties on the part of states. The report paved the way for the LoN's major research on business cycles in the following years,[28] which would be largely funded by the RF.

As the foundation's grant was partly intended to pay the salary for a researcher and three assistant statisticians to conduct this effort, a team had to be formed. Loveday, Condliffe, and the Rockefeller officers Van Sickle and Kittredge agreed in the fall of 1933 to hire the former Austrian fellow Gottfried von Haberler as the coordinator. Haberler, who was born in 1900, studied at the University of Vienna, where he was a student of Ludwig von Mises. After completing his doctorate in 1925, the LSRM provided funding for a two-year visit to the US, Great Britain, and France in 1927–1929, after which Harvard University hired him for one year. In 1932 he continued his research on international commerce with a supplemental grant from the RF,[29] which considered him one of the best economists of his generation. In 1933 he was hired by the Vienna Chamber of Commerce. From March 1934 to the summer of 1936, he was hired by the EIS to complete a comparative analysis of business cycle theories and to draft a synthesis identifying the smallest possible number of explanations for the causes of depressions. Published in the fall of 1936, *Prosperity and Depression*[30] immediately drew an important audience in the world of economists and quickly became a widely used university textbook.[31] In 1939 Haberler produced a revised version integrating the contributions of the *General Theory of Employment, Interest, and Money* by Keynes, which had been published after his manuscript had gone to press. In the meantime, Haberler had left the EIS in the summer of 1936 to teach at Harvard University, where he would continue his career, notably working with Joseph Schumpeter.

Haberler's work was only the first part of a vast project undertaken by the EIS with the Rockefeller grant. The second part consisted of scrutinizing the theoretical explanations assembled by Haberler with statistical analysis in order to confront them with the reality of economic phenomena, in an attempt to identify strategies for preventing crises. To carry out the second part, Condliffe and Loveday agreed to hire the Danish economist Jan Tinbergen,[32] whose work in applying mathematical models to the economy had a growing audience. Sent on a temporary assignment to the EIS between the summer of 1936 and the summer of 1938, his time at the LoN allowed him to apply a method tested on the Danish economy to the international economy,[33] thereby giving his work a considerable sounding board. His study was undertaken in collaboration with numerous European economists including Dennis H. Robertson from Cambridge University,[34] Ragnar Frisch of Norway, Erik Lundberg of Sweden, Charles Koopmans of Denmark, and Haberler, who remained involved in the project from the US. Tinbergen's work was largely based on public statistics from the US, Great Britain, and France, in addition to the considerable material amassed by the EIS and the research conducted in the various European and US institutes studying the economic situation.[35] In 1939 he published the results in two large volumes that immediately became reference works on business cycles.[36]

The grant awarded by the RF to the EIS allowed it to gather international economic, financial, and commercial statistics. This endeavor began in 1920 with the creation of the *Monthly Bulletin of Statistics*, whose data was gathered annually beginning in 1926 in the weighty *Statistical Yearbook*. In 1932 Condliffe produced a *World Economic Survey* each year until his departure, which consisted of a synthesis of the EIS's work. In their activity of gathering and analyzing statistics, members of the EIS came up against the same problem faced by their colleagues in the Health Section's Epidemiological Intelligence Service, namely the lack of harmonization between countries. The LoN had of course encouraged the signing of an international convention on economic statistics in 1928, but it was not widely implemented. As a result, in 1936 the EIS planned to organize study tours for economic statisticians in an effort to strengthen harmonization between national statistics organizations and the LoN. When solicited once more, the RF accepted to support the project,[37] granting short-term fellowships. The organization used the money to plan study tours for civil servants from national statistics services, in the same spirit as the study tours for health civil servants organized by the Health Organization. This funding came from the RF's fellowship program rather than a specific budgetary line, which is significant, for it meant that the foundation rather than the LoN Secretariat was directly administering the project, even though it was in constant consultation with Loveday.[38] It played a decisive role in selecting fellows and identifying the locations they would visit. This detail not only attests to the RF's growing role in EFO decisions but also to its autonomy with respect to the Secretariat.

The EIS director and Rockefeller officers began by jointly establishing a list of "model countries"[39] with centralized and well-organized statistics services,[40] including Canada, Norway, Great Britain, Denmark, Germany, Poland, Italy, Czechoslovakia, the Netherlands, and especially the US.[41] They then created a list of countries whose administrations were deemed to be deficient, and therefore likely to send statisticians to study what was being done in the first group of countries. France, which the two men believed had a national statistics service that did not perform as well as those of its neighbors, could be a part of the second group. However, the Statistique générale de la France (SGF) was in the midst of a full-blown internal crisis, and the RF's attempt to develop an economic documentation center at the Ministry of Finance was largely blocked by confrontations between ministerial services.[42] In the spring of 1938, Loveday and Kittredge reviewed the French situation with the foundation's French advisor Charles Rist, concluding that the situation was too sensitive and that it was better not to include France in the project.[43]

150 *From Cooperation to Expertise*

The first tour took place between May and December 1938, when the Director of the Statistics Service of Yugoslavia traveled to Great Britain, the Netherlands, Belgium, and Geneva to study population censuses. Between September 1938 and March 1939, Swiss statisticians visited the US and Canada to study statistics for industrial production and balance of payments; in the summer of 1939, a group of their colleagues visited Great Britain to study the same data in order to compare them with US methods, while a member of the Swiss customs administration visited Great Britain, the Netherlands, and Belgium to work on commercial statistics. In total, between the fall of 1938 and the summer of 1939, at least eight tours lasting multiple months were made—in addition to the Swiss and Yugoslavians—by Belgians, Danes, an Indian,[44] and two Romanians, who made a long journey in the first quarter of 1939 taking them to Geneva, Denmark, Sweden, Norway, the Netherlands, and Belgium, before crossing the Atlantic to the US and Canada. Upon completing these tours, the fellows drafted reports that were forwarded to the RF and the LoN, with all of the research being compiled by the Committee of Statistical Experts (created in 1931), which used them to supplement its reflections on the comparability of global statistics. This was the beginning of the process that would lead to the establishment of national accounts, which crystallized during World War II but did so largely outside of the Committee of Statistical Experts, whose work was interrupted by the outbreak of war.[45]

The International Studies Conference

The Assumption of Control by Foundations

Alongside its investment in the EFO, the RF bolstered its presence in the ISC created by the IIIC in 1928. As mentioned above, the foundation first provided modest funding in 1932, which increased substantially when the RF granted nearly $30,000 in September 1935[46] and then $112,000 in October 1937.[47] In total, it gave approximately $140,000 to the IIIC between 1932 and 1939; in this final year, its grant represented 2.9 million francs, "or more than the total of all governmental grants"[48] from the states in the IIIC, which made the foundation the largest contributor to the Intellectual Cooperation Organization (ICO), far ahead of the French government. In 1935 the foundation provided over half of the ISC's resources and practically 100% in 1939. The share of Rockefeller funding in the IIIC's total budget also speaks for itself, rising from 0.7% of the total in 1932 to 2.9% in 1935, 25.2% in 1937, and 46.4% in 1939. In addition to this funding, there were the more modest sums provided by the CEIP, which represented 1.4% of the IIIC's total budget in 1936 and 2.8% in 1939. The institute's funding thus changed completely in the space of a few years. The portion of the budget from governmental grants fell from 90% in 1926 to 42.4% in 1939, with the portion of private funding rising symmetrically from 1.75% of the budget in 1926, with a sharp rise in

1935 to reach 50% of the institute's resources in 1939 due to the presence of the US. As a result, France, which provided 78% of the institute's budget in 1926, fell to 35% in 1939. The economic crisis explains this decrease, but it is not the only reason. France, which had sponsored the creation of the IIIC and insisted that it be based in Paris, quickly lost interest in its baby, which it saw as "costly and cumbersome,"[49] with the civil servants of the French Ministry of Foreign Affairs considering the issues connected to intellectual cooperation to be of secondary importance. France's disengagement from the IIIC left a vacuum that would be filled by philanthropic foundations.

The central purpose of RF investment in the ISC was to make it a complementary organization to the EIS, especially for the international aspects of economic depressions. In July 1936 the foundation organized a meeting of economists in Annecy (France) to discuss the continuation of the work initiated by Haberler.[50] The Rockefeller invested as much money as it did in the ISC in order to expand the study of the international aspects of depressions. It did not pursue this effort at the EIS because at the time it was busy producing the second part of the program under Jan Tinbergen's direction, but also because it was under the permanent gaze of governments, which considerably hindered Loveday's initiatives. The ISC was seen by the foundation as a place where it would have a free hand to develop its projects and complement the studies conducted by the EFO. The goal of Rockefeller funding was thus to make the ISC an extension of sorts of the EFO, and the massive presence of the RF and the CEIP would have immediate and important consequences from an organizational standpoint as well as that of research topics.

First, with regard to organization and governance, Rockefeller officers set up at ISC headquarters as soon as the first grant was awarded: John Van Sickle, the Deputy Director of the Social Science Division, attended as a guest to the 1933 and 1934 sessions of the Conference,[51] although at his request his name was not included in the list of attendees.[52] The officers maintained a discreet but powerful presence, and henceforth also participated in the ISC's Executive Committee, which met a number of times per year, even though they were not official members: Van Sickle attended starting in January 1934, and beginning in the fall of 1935, when the RF increased its grant, Tracy Kittredge also attended almost systematically,[53] taking part in developing the program and recruiting researchers. The CEIP was also present, as Malcolm W. Davis became a member of the IIIC's Executive Committee in 1936[54] and that of the ICO in 1938.[55] Americans were therefore present at all decision-making levels, and this was true up through the invasion of Europe in the spring of 1940.

However, this presence was only the tip of the iceberg, for over half of the Rockefeller grant for 1935 was intended for organizational expenses, especially to pay the salaries of a full-time Secretariat consisting of two people. Fortified by its financial commitment, the Rockefeller was henceforth in a position to give its opinion on the ISC's activities and did not refrain from doing so. This was firstly true with respect to the selection of the two secretaries, Leo

Gross of Austria and Jiri Vranek of Czechoslovakia, who until 1939 would be paid with Rockefeller funds. Gross was a former fellow of the foundation. After earning a doctorate in political science at the University of Vienna, he traveled to the US in 1929 on a fellowship, and in 1931 was awarded another doctorate in political science from Harvard University. He returned to practice at the University of Cologne and went into exile in Switzerland in 1933 with Hitler's rise to power.

Rockefeller influence was also present with regard to the ISC's leadership. In early 1937, Kittredge was concerned that it did not have an economist on its Executive Committee and asked Condliffe to become the General Rapporteur to coordinate research for the 1938 and 1939 sessions. The initiative was made in consultation with Loveday, with whom Condliffe had collaborated closely at the EFO since 1931. However, it irritated Henri Bonnet, who was not consulted and accused the foundation of wanting to take control of the ISC,[56] to which Kittredge responded that the importance of the foundation's investment gave it a right to oversee the management of projects.[57] Bonnet had to yield, and in July he officially offered Condliffe to assume these duties.[58] The New Zealander was appointed General Rapporteur in September 1937 for the two coming years. At the same time, the foundation renewed and considerably increased its grant, which rose to $112,000 for two years[59] in large part to provide greater means for the permanent Secretariat. At this point the foundation was providing almost 100% of the ISC's funds.

During their discussions, Kittredge and Condliffe briefly considered creating an organization separate from the ISC but concluded that it would be preferable to use the existing structure. While they kept the framework, they profoundly changed how it functioned. Condliffe's arrival was accompanied by a revamped organizational chart, with the consent of Kittredge and Malcolm W. Davis.[60] This concentrated the administrative and scientific responsibility for the ISC in the hands of the General Rapporteur.[61] The permanent Secretariat, whose two members were paid by the foundation, transitioned from being under the administrative supervision of the IIIC Director to being under the authority of the General Rapporteur. Finally, the use of the Rockefeller grant would henceforth be managed by the General Rapporteur. This reorganization stripped the IIIC Director of any authority—intellectual, administrative, or financial—over the ISC, which for all practical purposes became *de facto* independent. Bonnet's fury with regard to the foundation's initiative thus becomes clear, but he did not have the cards to oppose the process, as the Rockefeller grant for 1937 was essentially the ISC's only source of funding. The new organization was supplemented with the creation of an Executive Committee consisting of three individuals: Condliffe, Bonnet, and Davis. Bonnet no longer had authority over the ISC, and Condliffe informed him that the allocation of funds would henceforth be decided by the Executive Committee rather than IIIC management.[62]

When it awarded its third grant in October 1937, the Rockefeller also provided another one to fund the Geneva Research Centre (GRC), which had an identical field of study. It was created in 1930 by a group of Americans living in Geneva to ensure the transmission of information from the LoN to the US. Initially named the Geneva Research Information Committee, it received funding from the CEIP and the RF.[63] It became the Geneva Research Centre in 1932 and founded two publications: *Geneva: A Monthly Review of International Affairs*, which provided an overview of the LoN's activities, and *Geneva Special Studies*, which contained studies of certain international issues. The director of the GRC was the editor Malcolm W. Davis, who did not have any duties at the European Center of the Carnegie Endowment (CEIP-CE), which he joined only in 1935. The Steering Committee of the GRC included two US members from the LoN's Information Section, Sweetser and Benjamin Gerig. Also present were academics such as the economist Jacob Viner, who taught at the GIIS at the time. In 1933 the RF awarded the GRC a grant of $24,000[64] to develop its activities. Its publications were sent to US universities and the CEIP's network of International Relations Clubs,[65] in addition to over 200 newspapers in 12 countries, for which it was a substantial source of information on international questions.[66] It was therefore an important part of the transatlantic networks connecting the LoN and the US, and its function would be to strengthen RF control over the ISC.

In the fall of 1936, the GRC was reorganized as a research institute specializing in international issues, with joint support from the CEIP and the RF,[67] which henceforth provided its entire budget. The composition of its team reflected a desire to establish relations with other research institutes: Davis was succeeded by the economist John Whitton, a professor at Princeton University and the GIIS. He was supported by a Steering Committee that included the director of the Foreign Policy Association, along with a member of Chatham House and a representative from the Centre d'étude de politique étrangère in Paris.[68] Bonnet and Norwegian and German members of the ISC were also present. Finally, Sweetser and Gerig were reappointed. The GRC aimed to be a place of research and exchange,[69] hence the creation of a system of fellowships enabling young researchers to spend a few months in residence at the center. In 1936 six fellows went to Geneva, a number that rose to twelve in 1937, when the RF increased its funding to $43,000 yearly.[70] In late 1937, the RF asked Condliffe to serve as the Chairman of the Steering Committee. This promotion came a few weeks after he became the ISC's General Rapporteur, subsequently putting two institutions in his hands. The GRC's Steering Committee met in January 1938,[71] with Kittredge presenting the RF's objectives, which was involved in 14 research programs on international economic issues,[72] and wanted to enhance coordination between them. The decision was made to give this task to the GRC and to establish a pool of economists from key institutions in order to develop a research program. Included were Condliffe and EIS Director Loveday, along with numerous directors of European institutes. The Rockefeller immediately awarded a new grant to establish a program with three focuses: the structuring of monetary markets, industrial protectionism, and the regulation of international trade.[73]

154   *From Cooperation to Expertise*

The latter was directed by Condliffe and would be implemented via the ISC's research. The work conducted over the next two years was based on this new organization and took the concrete form of plenary sessions held in Prague in May 1938 and in Bergen in August 1939.

National Committees and Fellows

When the foundation increased its grant to the ISC in the fall of 1935, part of the money was intended to create national committees whose mission would be to conduct research for the ISC's plenary sessions. In all, foundation funding helped create at least twenty ISC national committees, mostly in Europe, and to fill them with former or future Rockefeller fellows. Other committees were created in Japan, Australia, Mexico, and Brazil, although they were less active. The foundation's role in creating committees was decisive, not only because it provided money that allowed them to operate, but also because a significant number of their members were from its own scientific network, a result of its policy of granting fellowships, which it had developed since the late 1910s.[74]

The first committees were created in major European countries, especially Great Britain, France, and Germany. In Great Britain the study of international relations was institutionalized early on with the creation in 1919 of the Royal Institute of International Affairs, also known as Chatham House. An ISC national committee was established in 1935, which received Rockefeller funding in the spring of 1936 to recruit a young economist to perform scientific secretariat duties for two working groups, one on colonial problems and the other on the strategic question of access to raw materials.[75] Upon Kittredge's recommendation, Bonnet hired the former Norwegian fellow Halfdans Olans Christophersen to lead this effort.

Germany also had a tradition of international relations studies, notably at the Deutsche Hochschule für Politik in Berlin, where an informal ISC committee was apparently created in 1932. Germany suspended its participation in the ISC in October 1933, and while the RF also interrupted its funding for the Deutsche Hochschule in that same year, it nevertheless tried to have the Germans return to the ISC or at least have them continue their participation[76] and maintained contacts as long as possible with its former fellows holding positions in German institutions.[77] Until 1936, the CEIP and RF planned to provide funding for the Institut für Auswärtige Politik in Hamburg, before renouncing the initiative due to the shifting political situation.[78] The RF nevertheless maintained contact with certain local academics until 1940.

In France, the situation was very different from Germany and Great Britain, as in the early 1930s an institution specializing in international relations did not exist. This was a concern for the RF, which opened its wallet to fill the "French gap"[79] by creating an institute based on those existing in Great Britain and Germany. The ISC's 1932 meeting in Milan provided an opportunity for the French to discuss this with Rockefeller officers, as the meeting was attended by a number of academics who were at the same time holding discussions with the foundation for a grant to develop the social sciences in France,[80] of which international relations was only one part. The negotiations led to the creation in 1935 of the Centre d'étude de politique étrangère, which became the headquarters of the French ISC Committee, and whose activities would be entirely funded by the RF until 1940. In 1936 a first fellowship was awarded to the young political scientist Gilbert Maroger to perform scientific secretariat duties for the French committee and to conduct research on the production of raw materials in the colonies.

The German defection and French weakness in the study of international issues convinced the RF not to limit itself to the major powers of Western Europe and to support the emergence of other research centers, especially in Northern, Central, and Eastern Europe. Between December 1935 and January 1936, Kittredge, who was now a member of the ISC's Executive Committee, made multiple trips to Europe, especially to Belgium, Germany, and Italy, where he met with many researchers. He informed Bonnet that the foundation's fellowship program could be used for the ISC by involving former fellows in its work and by awarding future fellowships to young researchers from national committees to travel abroad and collaborate with other committees.[81] This once again meant that this part of the ISC's program would be directly administered by the foundation, even though it chose its fellows in consultation with the Executive Committee. During the Executive Committee meeting in January 1936, Kittredge sent Secretary Leo Gross a list of 23 former fellows—primarily from Sweden, Norway, Denmark, Holland, and Belgium, most of whom were jurists, economists, or historians[82]—and suggested he involve them in the ISC's work.[83] With this information in hand, Gross made a trip through Northern Europe to meet with them[84] and encourage them to create national committees in view of the plenary conference of 1937. In doing so, the RF sought to influence the reconfiguration of the social sciences in almost all countries of Europe. Indeed, the national academic landscapes were marked by profound changes due to the emergence of new research topics and the development of new disciplines (especially economics, political science, international relations, and sociology), which the RF sought to institutionalize and make permanent. Its activity was thus indissociably financial, intellectual, and institutional and represented one facet—that of the social sciences on the national level—of its global project of government through science.

The Danish committee was one of the first to be created. An Institute of Economics and History was created in Copenhagen in 1927 and was funded the following year by the LSRM and then by the RF until 1940, in the amount of one-third of its budget. Already integrated within the networks of experts working with the LoN on business cycles, in early 1936 the institute transformed into an organization of research in economics and political science with a focus on international relations, with the objective of uniting all Danish institutions. It planned to create a department dedicated to international relations, to be directed by the former fellow Franz Wendt.[85] The

RF awarded it a new grant to launch its research. The reorganization became official in September. The institute's governing board included representatives from various Danish institutions, and it was managed by the Minister for Foreign Affairs, with three former fellows among its six members: Franz Wendt, who was a Lecturer at the University of Copenhagen; Johan Plesner, who was a professor of history at Aarhus University; and Kaj Müller, who worked at the Ministry of Finance and Commerce, and was in charge of the institute's bulletin. It was decided that the Danish ISC Committee would be located at the institute and that Franz Wendt would be entrusted with the Secretariat. At the same time, the institute received a four-year Rockefeller grant (1936–1940) to develop its research program, which would be followed by a new grant in 1938 to develop the international relations department. Two other fellows joined the committee that year, one of whom, Thorkill Kristensen, took over the management of the institute's economic department.[86] A doctoral student began to work at the institute in 1936 and was awarded a fellowship in 1939 to study the theory of business cycles in the US, before pursuing his career in that country. In total, there were six former fellows at the institute, often holding key positions.

In Norway there was a different process, since there was no permanent institution devoted to the study of international matters. A national committee was constituted in December 1935 to conduct a study for the ISC's 1936 session. When Christian Lange, the committee director and winner of the 1921 Nobel Peace Prize, and Henri Bonnet evoked the possibility of securing more funding than what was provided by the ISC, the IIIC director advised him to directly solicit the RF, mentioning that the creation of a permanent institute would no doubt be a strong argument for obtaining funding.[87] However, the local situation was difficult, due to the division between the Michelsen Institute of Economic Research, which was private and supported by conservative businessmen, and academic economists, most of whom were socialists. The foundation initially awarded a modest grant in 1936 to launch the committee's organizational phase. Lange would do everything he could to unite these fraternal enemies in order to convince the foundation to pursue its efforts.[88] While in December 1935 the committee only included researchers on an individual basis, it reorganized them to include representatives from all Norwegian institutions involved with international relations: the University of Oslo, the Nobel Academy, the Michelsen Institute, and the Norwegian School of Economics in Bergen.[89] This sent a clear signal, namely that the conflicts had been solved and that the institutes henceforth would seek to work together. This hit the mark with Rockefeller officers, as the foundation renewed its grant in December 1936.[90] The following year, when the institute developed a research project independent of the ISC, the RF awarded a grant of $25,000 until 1940 to promote its long-term establishment. While the Norwegian committee did not originally include a fellow, three of them became members in 1937 and conducted studies in view of the 1938 and 1939 meetings of the ISC.

There was a similar process in Sweden with the creation of a committee in the spring of 1936, to which the RF awarded a grant.[91] In fact, in late 1936 there were discussions among Danes, Norwegians, and Swedes regarding the creation of an inter-Scandinavian Committee.[92] In an effort to promote this process, the RF provided a grant in March 1939 for a study on neutrality under the coordination of Wendt. The inter-Scandinavian committee took shape between December 1939 and March 1940, with both the RF and the CEIP providing grants. Housed at the Michelsen Institute in Oslo, it was led by two former fellows, including Halfdans Olans Christophersen, who in the meantime had completed his contract with the British national committee.

The second geographic sector in which US philanthropy spared no effort to promote the emergence of a vast network of economic experts versed in international issues was Central and Eastern Europe. The process observed for Northern Europe was reproduced identically, with the foundation initiating discussions with the organizations it was already funding or promoting the creation of new structures. It also attempted to unite the various researchers working in each country and used substantial funding to create *ad hoc* teams and even permanent institutes, in which it endeavored to secure key positions for its former fellows, who were often in charge of the scientific secretariat of national committees. This pattern was more or less present in Austria, where the AIBCR was already being funded by the RF. Led by former fellow Oskar Morgenstern, it was home to the national ISC committee, which was created in early 1936 thanks to Rockefeller funding used to establish a secretariat.[93] In Czechoslovakia, a committee was created in March 1936 under the management of former fellow Leipold Sauer, who had become the director of a division of the National Statistics Office.[94] In the spring of 1936, committees were also created in Hungary, Poland, and Yugoslavia, and in Bulgaria in 1937. Each time the creation was accompanied by Rockefeller funding to conduct empirical studies whose results would be presented at future sessions of the ISC.

The Rockefeller tried to promote the grouping of Scandinavian committees and tried to do the same with Central European countries through its support for a project to study the commerce of Danubian countries, which offers a good example of the synergies that the foundation sought to promote among European economic experts. In 1935, when the AIBCR asked for the renewal of the grant awarded in 1930, Morgenstern submitted a new project to the foundation proposing to study Danubian economic problems, which would be coordinated by his institute, and would involve former Rockefeller fellows now working in Central European institutes.[95] Kittredge jumped at the opportunity to connect this project to the ISC's activities; in January 1936, the Executive Committee decided, at his suggestion, to create a Study Group for Danubian Problems and to conduct a study for the plenary conference of 1937. At exactly the same moment, it received a project from Leipold Sauer[96] to create an institute dedicated to international economic issues that would unite the research conducted in Czechoslovakia.[97] In March, Kittredge and ISC

158   *From Cooperation to Expertise*

Secretary Leo Gross visited him in Prague to discuss the project. The decision was made to first create a Czechoslovakian national committee. The partners slated to work together on the Morgenstern project held their first meeting a few days later in Vienna, with Austria, Czechoslovakia, Romania, Bulgaria, Yugoslavia, and Hungary being represented. Of the seven individuals present, four were former Rockefeller fellows, and the meeting was coordinated by Davis, Kittredge, and Gross.[98] The participants agreed on a collective research project—the first of its kind in Danubian Europe—to compare the post-1918 economic evolution of six countries that "represent an interdependent zone, albeit one that is fragmented on the political level."[99] In 1937 the RF awarded it $12,000,[100] and the CEIP-CE most likely around $6,000.[101] The creation of this group was an excellent move for the Rockefeller, as it helped constitute three national committees at once (Czechoslovakia, Hungary, Yugoslavia), united them around a shared project, and integrated them into the work of the ISC. In December 1935 Kittredge asked Gross to involve Morgenstern in preparations for the plenary conference of 1937. He attended his first meeting on January 15, 1936. From that point forward, Kittredge and Condliffe made sure to include the Study Group of Danubian Countries, even though in theory it was independent of the ISC, with Condliffe ensuring this by personally supervising the group's work.[102]

In addition to the increasing number of European committees, the Rockefeller also supported the creation of a US committee that would play a major role in the ISC's plenary conferences in 1938 and 1939. In the US, there were numerous institutions that took an interest in international relations, often in competition with one another. The US social science landscape was no more monolithic than national European landscapes, with the Rockefeller struggling just as much to coordinate it. The US participated in the ISC's founding meeting in 1928, being represented by the Council on Foreign Relations (CFR), which was given the task of identifying US representatives for plenary conferences. However, the CFR's monopoly created discontent in other institutions. It was at this point that the Rockefeller decided to fund the creation of a committee to reinforce US presence at the ISC.[103] It awarded $30,000 in the spring of 1936, a sum much larger than that given to the ISC to fund European national committees.[104] While the CFR initially balked at abandoning its monopoly, it ultimately accepted in principle. Led by Shotwell[105] until 1938, the committee consisted of the primary organizations studying international relations: the Foreign Policy Association, the IPR, the CFR, and the American Commission on Intellectual Cooperation, along with representatives from universities. All of these organizations were financially supported by the RF or the CEIP for their regular research programs. The committee's objective was not only to promote coordination among US research centers but also to ensure US presence at the ISC. While it is difficult to draw conclusions regarding the first objective, given the substantial individual and institutional conflicts between these organizations,[106] the second one was quickly met, for Shotwell presided over the debates at the plenary

From Cooperation to Expertise 159

conference in Madrid in May 1936.[107] Americans were also highly active in the discussions during the Paris conference the following year and would be even more so in 1938 and 1939.

Foundation investment, administrative reorganization, and the creation of national committees coordinated by the ISC's Executive Committee had an important impact on the ISC, as they helped autonomize it with respect to the IIIC and contributed to the growing decentralization of the League system. This phenomenon was similar to those of the HO and EFO, which Rockefeller funding helped autonomize in relation to the Secretariat by providing the means for their virtual financial independence from state funding. One could generally conclude that the funding of technical sections by US philanthropy helped make them into bodies that were practically independent of LoN central management. This was incidentally an objective formulated by Shotwell during the Second Conference of National Commissions on Intellectual Cooperation held in Paris in July 1937: Shotwell came out in favor of creating an "autonomous body for intellectual cooperation, representing a chamber for intellectual relations, which would especially be freed of all ties to foreign affairs services subject to the policies of governments."[108] In other words, an organization separate from the LoN. This is ultimately what would occur, as the International Act Concerning Intellectual Cooperation signed in December 1938 by 28 states ratified the autonomy of the ICO, which was henceforth removed from the administrative supervision of the LoN Secretariat. While the intended objective was to attract the US to join the ICO, the effort drew a blank, for in August 1939 the US government officially communicated its refusal to ratify the International Act Concerning Intellectual Cooperation. Foundations, on the other hand, were firmly installed at the IIIC via their control over the ISC.

From Collective Security to International Trade

When foundations joined the ISC, this did not solely have an impact on its organization and that of the League system, but it also had direct consequences on its work by changing its intellectual, thematic, and methodological orientations. With regard to working methods, the general discussions of the first plenary conferences gave way to an organization into thematic working groups, in addition to individual and collective empirical-quantitative research coordinated by Condliffe. Research subjects evolved toward analysis of international trade, which became the center of the conference's activity in 1938.

The first topic addressed by the ISC was "The State and Economic Life," and occupied the sessions in Milan in 1932 and London in 1933, when the ISC set itself the goal of becoming a laboratory for reflecting on international issues, especially those stemming from the Great Depression. It held its sixth session from May 29 to June 2, 1933, in London, a few days before the opening of the Monetary and Economic Conference held by the LoN in the

British capital. The participants discussed all of the issues on the agenda of the monetary and economic conference: the most-favored-nation clause, the open door policy, the regulation of international capital flows, customs duties, commerce in wheat, etc.

Following the session, the ISC's Executive Committee sent a summary memorandum to the Secretary-General of the Monetary and Economic Conference to provide the opinion of experts "on certain aspects of the current economic situation and certain constructive proposals for international measures designed for a return to prosperity."[109] Duly noting the global economic disorder engendered by the crisis, participants in the ISC agreed that *laissez-faire* policy had seen its day, a

> conclusion [...] that was all the more remarkable given that it was generally adopted only reluctantly. Most economists, who remembered the teaching of the founders of their discipline and were marked by the harmful consequences of state intervention in many past cases, naturally tended to count instead on the free play of economic forces than on the intervention of political factors.

However, faced with the situation created by the international crisis, all experts recommended "the adoption of remedies by states and the international community." Given the "complete and imperative interdependence of various elements of international economic life," it is important to take "concerted international action, not just in a particular domain, but across all domains simultaneously," including trade law, customs barriers, capital flows, etc. To do so, the ISC proposed creating [permanent] "impartial and expert bodies" entrusted with "arbitrating the conflicts arising from the interpretation and application of customs agreements," "developing rules of conduct for economic matters," and fostering the emergence of a "code of political morals in international trade relations." The existence of such courts of economic arbitration would "set international trade in motion again," notably by reflecting on the possible elimination of the most-favored-nation clause; while none of the experts present came out for its immediate removal, they all wanted to abandon it eventually, "a universal lowering of customs barriers being a pressing need" that should be organized in connection with "bilateral and multilateral negotiations dominated by the general and absolute clause of the most favored nation." In the summer of 1934, the EFO's economic and financial committees pursued this idea by proposing a systematic study of state intervention in economic life, especially in order to assess the impact of public works programs.

The ISC's two following plenary conferences, held in Paris in 1934 and London in 1935, focused on collective security, a topical subject due to Hitler's rise to power in Germany. The debates bear witness to the difficulty in constructing a discourse of expertise within an international context as tense as that of the mid-1930s, in which the strict separation between scientific discourse and political matters proved almost impossible. During its final session held in London in June 1935, the ISC came up against two problems that led more to political rather than intellectual confrontations.

The first involved the legal validity of the notion of "collective security," which was initially challenged by the Italian delegates Francesco Coppola, a professor of international law at the University of Rome and a member of the High Commission for the Press, and Roberto Forges-Davanzati, a senator and the former Secretary of the National Fascist Party from 1921 to 1925. The former called it a "false idea" and a "nightmare with blurry outlines" and concluded that it "is absurd and impossible to establish a universal guarantee of what is called collective security through a universal statute."[110] Forges-Davanzati underscored the weakness of the League of Nations, observing that Japan and Germany had left the organization and that it was "unable, even in normal times, [...] to ensure that the articles of the Covenant were quickly and effectively carried out." After challenging the principle of implementing global rules to the detriment of the state, he questioned the very principle of a meeting of experts devoted to studying problems "with an abstract process" and "establishing them into a series of rules." The Italian position was supported by the German Fritz Berber, who was a professor at the Deutsche Hochschule für Politik and the director of the German ISC Committee. While Germany had left the LoN in October 1933, he was authorized by his government to participate in the plenary conference as an observer and intervened in the debates.[111] As this discussion was unfolding, two events struck a major blow to the notion of collective security: the reestablishment of compulsory military service in Germany (March 1935) and the aggravation of the situation in Ethiopia, where Italian incursions had increased since the machine-gun fire of the Walwal incident in November 1934. In March 1935 Haile Selassie brought the matter before the LoN, but France and Great Britain, who were careful not to offend Mussolini, whom they still saw as a possible ally against Hitler, did not react when he began to concentrate his troops on the Ethiopian border in early summer, or when he invaded the country in October.

The second problem that the experts discussed in London in 1935 was the organization of procedures for improving collective security. While the participants were almost unanimous in considering that "the individualist system of security had failed"[112] and that it should be organized collectively, the discussions led to no more than a declaration of principle seeking to reinforce the legal procedures for resolving international problems. Similarly, while almost all of the participants agreed (with the exception of the Italians and the German) on the need for military sanctions in the event of a breach of the peace, the principle of creating an international force was quickly ruled out. They were content with calling for a permanent investigative commission "whose task would be to study"—at the request of governments or at its own initiative—"any situation likely to compromise peace." This idea of an "impartial" commission had already been launched on many occasions since the beginning of the LoN's history. The idea was formulated once again in

London by several participants, especially Lord Lytton, who presided over the Commission of Inquiry in Manchuria in 1932, as well as by Malcolm W. Davis and Allen Dulles. Such a commission "would gain the advantage of speed, a weapon that is so formidable in the hands of those preparing for war, and make it into an instrument for peace."[113] Speed of execution would be accompanied by the systematic publication of its work, which would be sent to all signatory states of the Kellogg-Briand Pact and members of the LoN, in order to provide them with the information needed to undertake activity in favor of peace. However, the ISC was ultimately unable to provide a definition for collective security that could act as a counterweight to the Italian challenge or to make concrete proposals for its implementation, at a time when Hitler and Mussolini were in the process of giving it the final blow. The powerlessness of experts was equal to that of politicians.

In 1936–1937, the selected topic was "peaceful change in international relations," with the two conferences being held in Madrid and Paris, respectively. It was following this session that US criticism grew the sharpest. US delegates were present, especially during the 1937 session, at which they presented six research memoranda.[114] After the plenary conference, they were highly critical of how it had proceeded. When consulted by Kittredge, John Foster Dulles noted that many of the participants behaved as though they were at an international negotiation, expressing their government's positions rather than producing an analysis of the problems. Dulles also criticized the overly general nature of the debates and a lack of framing for the topic, pleading for the ISC to adopt a much more scientific approach in the future by working empirically on specific subjects, in order to allow genuine debates and arrive at concrete proposals.[115] This was the opinion of Condliffe as well, who was also consulted by Kittredge. These consultations reaffirmed the dissatisfaction that Rockefeller officers had with the ISC. In January 1937 Kittredge expressed to his colleagues at the foundation his doubts that the ISC could establish itself with economic study institutes as a linking and coordinating body for collective projects, despite being created for this purpose.[116] The barrage of criticism from US representatives at the Paris conference raised the foundation's most recent doubts and prompted it to proceed with the administrative reorganization mentioned above in order to take over control.

The 1936 and 1937 editions were organized when foundations were still not particularly involved in the permanent conference. The only part of its activity where the RF had a role during those years was the Study Group of Danubian Countries. Rockefeller support for this group was the first step in its assumption of power within the ISC, for it promoted what would become the major topic for the years 1938 and 1939: international trade and its potential role in ending the Great Depression and stabilizing the international context. The Danubian project involved the creation of a chronicle of political and economic events, as well as a statistical study of the population, geographic conditions, agricultural and industrial production, forests, mines, the analysis of monetary and banking problems, balance of payment, and capital. The project was ambitious and would result in a map of activities for the area's countries as well as their economic exchanges, with the group planning to collect information during 1938 and publishing its results in 1939. The data used for this purpose had to be gathered from the administrations of the countries involved and then undergo statistical processing.

In January 1938 a transitional meeting was held to provide an update on the project, attended by the secretaries of national committees in addition to Condliffe, Kittredge, Bonnet, Gross, and the young French economist André Piatier, a fellow of the GRC and Condliffe's assistant. However, Anschluss took place in March, and Czechoslovakia was dismembered in the fall of 1938; work was interrupted, with only the first part being published as a 6-volume compilation of an economic and social chronology of the countries studied.[117] Two months after Anschluss, the group's key players, Morgenstern in particular, left for the US. The Austrian Committee was dissolved in June,[118] signaling the end of the Danubian Group's work.

In the meantime, the preparatory meetings for the plenary conferences of 1938 and 1939 were held. While the RF was unable to impose the topic of the preceding editions, these two editions fully bore its mark. The selected topic was "international trade and peace," which was an extension on the international level of the work that the Group of Danubian Studies was supposed to complete for the Central European area. The choice of this topic was significant in terms of the ISC's evolution, for it was understood in 1938 that collective security could not ensure peace, and that other means had to be found to attain this objective. The reorganization of international commerce along new bases could be one such means. To do so required analyzing the mechanisms of the phenomenon on a global scale, which would be the objective of the 1938 and 1939 conferences.

The funding provided in the fall of 1937 by the RF was given not only to the Secretariat but also to fund research on the subjects identified by the General Rapporteur and undertaken by the young researchers selected by the Executive Committee. Two plenary conferences punctuated this collective work, the first in Prague in May 1938 and the second in Bergen in August 1939. The framework for collective work and research topics were identified during the Prague meeting. When he inaugurated the conference's work, Condliffe observed that "for the first time [...] we have a program committee that has assumed the responsibility of acting as a liaison and ensuring greater research coordination [...] and providing them with an overall plan,"[119] an implicit criticism of the lack of organization in the preceding conferences according to him and the RF.

The work was indeed considerable, with the Bergen meeting being attended by 45 participants from 14 national committees in Europe, as well as other countries such as Mexico, Canada, and Australia. Among them were ten former Rockefeller fellows. These committees produced a total of 89 memoranda on various subjects.[120] They produced a document on changes to their country's trade policy during the 1930s, and a presentation of domestic political, economic, and social conditions, along with the legislation in effect in the country. It should be noted that Japan and Germany, whose committees were not part of the ISC, also produced memoranda. Taken collectively, this research provided a panorama of the foreign trade of the world's major countries. However, most committees also produced multiple memoranda, such that many other subjects were raised, including foreign exchange control, the economic consequences of limitations to migration, the influence of cartels over the organization of international trade, international loans, regional economic agreements in Europe, migration, and international monetary organization. The objective of the meeting in Bergen was to produce a summary of this work and especially to extract a global vision of international trade from the accumulation of national trade policy.

The results of the meeting were published in late 1939 and 1940 in the form of multiple books, with Condliffe playing an essential role in their development.[121] Experts once again emphasized that *laissez-faire* policy in international trade had definitively been discredited[122] and that international cooperation had to be improved by increasing the role of existing international organizations, and if necessary, through the creation of new ones.[123] When war broke out, the analysis they provided for the future of the world economy was based on a clear alternative: either totalitarianism would win out and the world would take shape around a series of regional blocs, some of which would be dominated by such regimes (Russia, Germany, Italy, Japan) and the other one by the US, with a British Empire destined for collapse for lack of support from a sufficient internal market; or the democracies would win and the opening of international trade would give rise to a globalized system in which the US would most certainly be the dominant power. In the troubled situation of 1939–1940, these books went completely unnoticed. However, they included a good portion of the ideas that would structure how the postwar world economy would be organized. In particular, some of the conclusions and recommendations that would be adopted in the Bretton Woods agreement were already formulated in this report, especially the creation of new institutions for regulating the world economy. This data suggests we should put into perspective the notion that the international postwar economic order was an "American" order solely conceived by experts from the State Department and the CFR. The reality was much more complex, in that the results of the Bretton Woods conference were in many ways the result of expertise activities conducted since the mid-1920 by the specialists gravitating around the EFO and the ISC. The discredit of the latter, which was severely criticized by US experts, no doubt helped obscure the reality of its work and its general diagnosis of the world economic situation, some of whose conclusions appeared four years later in the Bretton Woods system.

The Bergen meeting (August 25–29, 1939) took place in the dramatic context of imminent war. Initially planned to begin on August 27, it started two days early due to the heightened tension generated by the German-Soviet Pact signed on August 23 and ended on August 29 instead of September

2. A number of delegations were absent (such as Great Britain) or present with limited staff (France) due to the exceptional context; the US delegation included ten individuals, with representatives from the CFR, the Foreign Policy Association, multiple universities, in addition to four representatives from the CEIP and two from the RF. This delegation dominated the debates.[124] Three days after the end of the conference, Germany invaded Poland.

Conclusion

All told, the development of interwar economic expertise was broadly supported financially, technically, and intellectually by US philanthropy, as demonstrated by the history of the EFO and even more so by that of the ISC, whose administrative takeover and intellectual reorientation—and peopling with Rockefeller fellows—bear witness to the depth of the RF's involvement and influence over its activity. It also shows that this involvement should not be analyzed exclusively in terms of intellectual influence, but also in terms of the metamorphosis of the League system, as foundation investment in the EFO and the ISC resulted in their autonomization from the LoN Secretariat, undermining its authority and the coherence of a system already highly affected by the discredit of its activity in the field of politics. In other words, US participation translated into an important change in the organization's morphology, one that corresponded to a project formulated in 1919 and pursued throughout the interwar period by philanthropic officers. From this perspective, these officers successfully shaped the League system into a largely decentralized ensemble beginning in the early 1920s, a development that facilitated its dismantling in 1940, as we will see in Chapter 6.

Notes

1 An Institute of International Research, 1925, RBF-PU 21/7.
2 Abraham Flexner, Remarks Concerning *A Proposal to Establish an Institute of International Research*, 1926, RBF-PU 21/8.
3 Fosdick to John D. Rockefeller, Jr., December 8, 1926, RBF-PU/21/8.
4 Drummond to Fosdick, April 13, 1927, RBF-PU 21/8.
5 Gunn to Vincent, March 30, 1927, RBF-PU 21/8.
6 Arthur Woods (Laura Spelman Rockefeller Memorial President) to Fosdick, June 10, 1927, RBF-PU 21/8.
7 RF Minutes, December 10, 1930, RF 1.1/705/4/36.
8 Bjerkholt Olav, "A Turning Point in the Development of Norwegian Economics. The Establishment of the University Institute of Economics in 1932," University of Oslo, Department of Economics, Memorandum n°36, 2000.
9 Tournès Ludovic, "L'institut scientifique de recherches économiques et sociales et les débuts de l'expertise économique en France (1933–1940)," *Genèses. Sciences Sociales et Histoire*, 65, 2006, pp. 49–70.
10 The concept of "field" (*champ*) is borrowed from Pierre Bourdieu.

11 Hubbard Ursula, *La collaboration des Etats-Unis avec la Société des Nations et l'Organisation internationale du travail, des origines à 1936*, Paris, Centre européen de la dotation Carnegie, 1937, p. 602.
12 Convention multilatérale pour éviter la double imposition, SDN 10E/R2994/20141/20141.
13 Carroll Mitchell B. & Jones Ralph C., *Taxation of Foreign and National Enterprises*, Geneva, League of Nations, 1932, 5 vols.
14 Rapport d'activité pour la période 1938–1939, SDN 10B/R4520/4072/4072.
15 Alexander Loveday, *Note on Work Done under Rockefeller Grants*, September 25, 1937, RF 1.1/100/18/150.
16 League of Nations. Fiscal committee. Adaptation of tax systems to economic fluctuations, avril 27, 1939, RF 1.1/100/18/152; Farquet Christophe, "Lutte contre l'évasion fiscale: l'échec de la SdN durant l'entre-deux-guerres," *Economie Politique*, 44, 2009, pp. 93–112.
17 The acronym EIS was used in Chapter 3 to refer to the Epidemiological Intelligence Service but will be used in this chapter to refer to the Economic Intelligence Service.
18 Sweetser to Gunn (and forwarded to Fosdick), December 13, 1930, RF 1.1/100/18/148.
19 John B. Condliffe, League of Nations Search Engine (LoNSEA), www.lonsea.de/pub/person/4279, accessed August 19, 2021.
20 Note de E. Felkin (Section financière et Service de l'intelligence économique), 12 octobre 1933, SDN 10B/R4520/4072/4072.
21 Library of Congress legislative reference service, "The Reciprocal Trade Agreement Program," *Public Affairs Bulletin*, 33, Washington, April 1945, p. 4 and 47; Beckett Grace, *The Reciprocal Trade Agreement Program*, New York, Columbia University Press, 1941; Tasca Henry Joseph, *The Reciprocal Trade Policy of the United States. A Study in Trade Philosophy*, PhD dissertation in economics, Philadelphia, 1938; and Butler Michael A., *Cautious Visionary: Cordell Hull and Trade Reform, 1933–1937*, Kent-London, Kent University Press, 1998.
22 Clavin Patricia, *Securing the World Economy. The Reinvention of the League of Nations 1920–1946*, Oxford, Oxford University Press, 2013, pp. 103–104 and 126–128.
23 *Ibid.*, pp. 133–135.
24 Van Sickle to Loveday, May 3, 1933, SDN 10B/R4520/4072/4072. The grant was officially accepted by the League Council in May (Drummond to the Board of Trustees of the Rockefeller Foundation, May 29, 1933, SDN 10B/R4520/4072/4072).
25 Day to Gunn, January 18, 1932, RF 1.1/100/18/148.
26 Day to Fosdick, December 8, 1933, RF 2–1933/100/78/623.
27 MM's Diary. Visit in Europe, Summer 1933, RF 2–1933/100/78/623.
28 Endres Anthony Mark & Fleming Grant Alan, *International Organizations and the Analysis of Economic Policy, 1919–1950*, Cambridge, Cambridge University Press, 2002, p. 30.
29 Grant-in-Aid Form, August 5, 1932, RF 1.1/705/4/41.
30 Haberler Gottfried, *Prosperity and Depression. A Theoretical Analysis of Cyclical Movements*, Geneva, League of Nations, 1936.
31 Rapport d'activité pour la période 1938–1939, SDN 10B/R4520/4072/4072.

From Cooperation to Expertise   167

32 John Van Sickle diary, October 4–8, 1935, RF 1.1/100/18/149.
33 Tinbergen Jan, "An Economic Approach to Business Cycles Problems," *Actualités Scientifiques et Industrielles*, 1937.
34 Alexander Loveday, *Note on Work Done under Rockefeller Grants*, September 25, 1937, RF 1.1/100/18/150.
35 SDN. Service d'études économiques. *Vérification statistique des cycles économiques. 1. Une méthode et son application au mouvement des investissements*, par Jan Tinbergen, Genève, 1939, pp. 163–175.
36 Tinbergen Jan, *Statistical Testing of Business Cycles Theories: I. A Method and Its Applications to Investment Activity*, February 1939; *II. Business Cycles in the United States of America, 1919–1932*, Geneva, League of Nations, 1939.
37 Van Sickle to Kittredge, December 4, 1936, SDN 10B/R4548/27741/27741.
38 Kittredge to Loveday, May 19, 1938, SDN 10B/R4548/27741/27741.
39 Rosenborg to Loveday, December 22, 1936, SDN 10B/R4548/27741/27741.
40 Letter of August 25, 1937, SDN 10B/R4548/27741/27741.
41 Rosenborg to Loveday, December 22, 1936, SDN 10B/R4548/27741/27741.
42 Tournès, *L'Institut…, art. cit.*
43 Conversation between Loveday and Kittredge, June 17, 1938, SDN 10B/R4548/27741/27741.
44 Statistical study tours, report sent by Loveday to Kittredge, September 28, 1939, SDN 10B/R4548/27741/27741; this document is also in Rockefeller Archives (RF 1.1/100/32/251).
45 Vanoli André, *Histoire de la comptabilité nationale*, Paris, La découverte, 2002, pp. 37 sq and 173–175.
46 Note du service des relations internationales et des sciences sociales relative à la subvention Rockefeller 1935–1937, UNESCO-IICI A/II/28.
47 Conférence permanente des hautes études internationales. Dixième réunion du Comité exécutif, Paris, 15 janvier 1938. Annexe B: subvention de la fondation Rockefeller, UNESCO-IICI K/XI/1/23; Kittredge to Bonnet, April 21, 1939, UNESCO-IICI A/II/28.
48 Renoliet Jean-Jacques, *L'UNESCO oubliée: la Société des Nations et la coopération intellectuelle, 1919–1946*, Paris, Publications de la Sorbonne, 1999, p. 316.
49 *Ibid.*, p. 227.
50 Trautwein Hans-Michael, "Haberler, The League of Nations, and the Quest for Consensus in Business Cycle Theory in the 1930s," *History of Political Economy*, 38–1, 2006, p. 62 and 76 sq.
51 SDN. IICI, *L'Etat et la vie économique, rapports sur les travaux de la sixième conférence d'études internationales (Londres, 29 mai–2 juin 1933)*, Paris, juin 1933, pp. 28–29.
52 Van Sickle to Bonnet, March 21, 1934, UNESCO-IICI K/I/4.
53 Chalmers Wright to Kittredge, November 9, 1935, UNESCO-IICI K/I/4.
54 Montenach to Davis, November 5, 1936, CEIP-CE I/32/1; Davis to Bonnet, December 1, 1938, CEIP-CE I/34/2.
55 Davis to Bonnet, December 1, 1938, CEIP-CE I/34/2.
56 Kittredge to Walker, October 28, 1937; Kittredge memorandum, September 28, 1938, RF 1.1/100/105/955.
57 Kittredge to Walker, October 28, 1937, RF 1.1/100/105/955.
58 Bonnet to Condliffe, July 7, 1937, CEIP-CE I/33/2.

168 *From Cooperation to Expertise*

59 Conférence permanente des hautes études internationales. Dixième réunion du Comité exécutif, Paris, 15 janvier 1938. Annexe B: subvention de la fondation Rockefeller, UNESCO-IICI K/XI/1/23.
60 Malcolm W. Davis, *Note on Organization*, January 15, 1938, CEIP-CE I/34/4.
61 Condliffe to Kittredge, September 16, 1937, CEIP-CE I/33/2.
62 Condliffe to Bonnet, January 26, 1938, CEIP-CE I/34/3.
63 Kuehl Warren F. & Dunn Lynn K., *Keeping the Covenant: American Internationalists and the League of Nations (1920–1939)*, Kent, Kent State University Press, 1997, pp. 81–83.
64 RF Minutes, April 12, 1933, RF 1.1/100/5/45.
65 See Chapter 2.
66 Application on behalf of the Geneva Research Centre, February 27, 1936, RF 1.1/100/5/47.
67 RF Minutes, September 25, 1936, RF 1.1/100/5/45.
68 Centre d'étude de politique étrangère, Rapport moral portant sur l'exercice 1er octobre 1936–30 septembre 1937, Paris, 1937.
69 Application on behalf of the Geneva Research Centre, February 27, 1936, RF 1.1/100/5/47.
70 RF Minutes, May 21, 1937, RF 1.1/100/5/45.
71 Geneva Research Centre, Minutes of the third meeting of the governing board, January 6, 1938, RF 1.1/100/6/51.
72 Report on new program, March 10, 1938, RF 1.1/100/6/51.
73 Meeting of economists (Paris, April 29–30, 1938), May 6, 1938, RF 1.1/100/6/51.
74 See also the collective research project on the Rockefeller Foundation fellowship programs coordinated by Ludovic Tournès, Thomas David, & Davide Rodogno, "Rockefeller Fellows as Heralds of Globalization: The Circulation of Elites, Knowledge and Practices of Globalization," at http://heraldsofglobalization.net/.
75 Grant-in-Aid form, May 20, 1936, RF 1.1/100/110/998.
76 Kittredge to Predhöl, November 26, 1936, RF 1.1/100/111/1010.
77 Kittredge to Toynbee, February 4, 1936, RF 1.1/100/111/1010.
78 Kittredge interview with Fritz Berber, April 6, 1936, RF 1.1/100/111/1010.
79 Day to Gunn, July 13, 1932, RF 1.1/100/105/952.
80 Tournès Ludovic, "La fondation Rockefeller et la construction d'une politique des sciences sociales en France (1918–1940)," *Annales. Histoire, Sciences Sociales*, 63-6, 2008, pp. 1371–1402.
81 Kittredge to Bonnet, December 9, 1935, UNESCO IICI K/I/4.
82 S. Rioland (Kittredge's Secretary) to Gross, January 22, 1936, UNESCO-IICI K/I/4.
83 Kittredge to Gross, February 3, 1936, UNESCO-IICI K/I/4.
84 Gross to S. Rioland, February 15, 1936, UNESCO-IICI K/I/4.
85 Kittredge, May 1, 1936, RF 1.1/713S/6/68.
86 RF Minutes, May 20, 1938, RF 1.1/713S/6/68.
87 Bonnet to Lange, December 4, 1935, UNESCO-IICI K/I/4.
88 Norwegian Co-ordinating Committee for International Studies, December 1938, RF 1.1/100/111/1020.
89 Conférence permanente des hautes études internationales, onzième session, Prague, 23–27 mai 1938, ordre du jour de la réunion administrative, UNESCO-IICI K/XI/1/23.
90 Grant-in-Aid form, December 18, 1936, RF 1.1/100/111/1020.

91 Grant-in-Aid form, May 20, 1936, RF 1.1/100/111/1027.
92 RF Minutes, September 25, 1936, RF 1.1/713S/6/68.
93 Grant-in-Aid form, June 25, 1936, RF 1.1/100/110/996.
94 Kittredge, March 20, 1936, RF 1.1/100/110/1000.
95 John Van Sickle, *Summary of Oskar Morgenstern's Report on Past and Proposed Future Activities of the Austrian Institute of Trade Cycle Research*, March 2, 1935, RF 1.1/705/4/37.
96 European Fellowships, 1917–1943, RF 1.2/100/43/319.
97 Sauer to Kittredge, January 22, 1936, UNESCO-IICI K/I/4.
98 RF Minutes, December 1, 1937, RF 1.1/100/110/1002.
99 Rockefeller Foundation *Annual Report*, 1937, p. 279.
100 Bonnet to Morgenstern, April 16, 1937, UNESCO-IICI K/I/4.
101 Davis to Bonnet, June 24, 1938, CEIP-CE I/34/2.
102 Conférence permanente des hautes études internationales. Études danubiennes. Rapport sur la quatrième réunion du groupe danubien d'experts économistes, Paris, 12–13 janvier 1938, in: SDN. IICI. Annexes au rapport général du Directeur, C.A.61, Paris, 1938, p. 9.
103 Sydnor H. Walker to Kittredge, October 4, 1935, RF 1.1/100S/109/983.
104 The International studies conference, Paris, 1937. Report of the American coordinating committee on the preparation for the conference, CEIP-CE I/33/1.
105 American Committee of Experts for the International Studies Conference, October 22, 1936, CEIP-CE I/32/2.
106 Fosdick to William O. Scroggs (Secretary of the American Coordinating Committee for International Studies), February 16, 1938, RF 1.1/100/109/985.
107 Conférence permanente des hautes études internationales, dixième session, rapport introductif présenté par Maurice Bourquin, Paris, 1937, CEIP-CE I/33/2.
108 SDN. Actes de la deuxième Conférence générale des commissions nationales de coopération intellectuelle, Paris, 5–9 juillet 1937, p. 75 and 82.
109 SDN. IICI, *L'Etat et la vie économique, rapports sur les travaux de la sixième conférence d'études internationales (Londres, 29 mai–2 juin 1933)*, Paris, juin 1933, pp. 6–17, this and the following quotations until the end of the paragraph.
110 Conférence permanente des hautes études internationales, *La sécurité collective (Paris 1934–Londres 1935), publié sous la direction de Maurice Bourquin*, Paris, IICI, 1936, pp. 160–166, this and the two following quotations.
111 *Ibid.*, pp. 409–411.
112 *Ibid.*, p. 459.
113 *Ibid.*, p. 477.
114 The International Studies Conference, Paris, 1937. *Report of the American Coordinating Committee on the Preparation for the Conference*, CEIP-CE I/33/1.
115 Dulles to Sydnor H. Walker, November 12, 1937, UNESCO-IICI K/I/4; The International Studies Conference, Paris, 1937. *Report of the American Coordinating Committee on the Preparation for the Conference*, CEIP-CE I/33/1.
116 Kittredge memorandum, January 7, 1937, RF 1.1/100/105/955.
117 Conférence permanente des hautes études internationales, *Chronique des événements politiques et économiques dans le bassin danubien, 1918–1936*, (Yougoslavie, Tchécoslovaquie, Bulgarie, Hongrie, Autriche, Roumanie), Paris, IICI, 1938, 6 vols.
118 Kittredge, July 7, 1938, RF 1.1/100/110/996.

119 IICI. Conférence permanente des hautes études internationales, onzième session. *Les politiques économiques et la paix. compte rendu des réunions de Prague, 23–27 mai 1938*, Paris, 1938, p. 11–12, UNESCO-IICI K/XI/1/23.
120 See the complete list of participants and memoranda in Condliffe John Bell, *The Reconstruction of World Trade. A Survey of International Economic Relations*, New York, W.W. Norton, 1940, pp. 395–405.
121 International Studies Conference. 12th Session. *Economic Policies in Relation to World Peace, A Record of the Study Meeting Held in Bergen from August 26th to 29th 1939*, Paris, 1940; Condliffe John Bell, *The Reconstruction...*, *op. cit.*
122 Condliffe John Bell, *Markets and the Problem of Peaceful Change*, Paris, International Institute of Intellectual Cooperation, 1938, p. 11.
123 International Studies Conference. *International Monetary Organization*, by M. A. Heilperin, Paris, 1939, p. 56. See also Condliffe, *The Reconstruction...*, *op. cit.*, p. 355 sq.
124 RF Minutes, January 19, 1940, RF 1.1/100S/109/983.

References

Bjerkholt Olav, "A Turning Point in the Development of Norwegian Economics. The Establishment of the University Institute of Economics in 1932," University of Oslo, Department of Economics, Memorandum n°36, 2000.

Butler Michael A., *Cautious Visionary: Cordell Hull and Trade Reform, 1933–1937*, Kent-London, Kent University Press, 1998.

Clavin Patricia, *Securing the World Economy. The Reinvention of the League of Nations 1920–1946*, Oxford, Oxford University Press, 2013.

Endres Anthony Mark & Fleming Grant Alan, *International Organizations and the Analysis of Economic Policy, 1919–1950*, Cambridge, Cambridge University Press, 2002.

Farquet Christophe, "Lutte contre l'évasion fiscale: l'échec de la SdN durant l'entre-deux-guerres," *Economie Politique*, 44, 2009, pp. 93–112.

Kuehl Warren F. & Dunn Lynn K., *Keeping the Covenant: American Internationalists and the League of Nations (1920–1939)*, Kent, Kent State University Press, 1997.

Renoliet Jean-Jacques, *L'UNESCO oubliée: la Société des Nations et la coopération intellectuelle, 1919–1946*, Paris, Publications de la Sorbonne, 1999.

Tournès Ludovic, "L'institut scientifique de recherches économiques et sociales et les débuts de l'expertise économique en France (1933–1940)," *Genèses. Sciences Sociales et Histoire*, 65, 2006, pp. 49–70.

Tournès Ludovic, "La fondation Rockefeller et la construction d'une politique des sciences sociales en France (1918–1940)," *Annales. Histoire, Sciences Sociales*, 63–6, 2008, pp. 1371–1402.

Trautwein Hans-Michael, "Haberler, The league of Nations, and the Quest for Consensus in Business Cycle Theory in the 1930s," *History of Political Economy*, 38–1, 2006, pp. 45–89.

Vanoli André, *Histoire de la comptabilité nationale*, Paris, La découverte, 2002.

6 From Geneva to Princeton
The Dismantling and the Legacy

World War II marked the shattering and dismantling of the League system, facilitated by the organization's political discredit and the growing autonomization of its technical sections in relation to the Secretariat throughout the 1930s. This dismantling took on a very concrete form with the LoN's move to the US in 1940. The period during the war, which is often neglected in the history of the LoN, is important for two reasons. First, in spite of the official deferment of the Bruce Reform due to the German invasion, it was *de facto* implemented through the transformation of the EFO's Economic Intelligence Service (EIS) into an Economic, Financial, and Transit Department (EFTD) tasked with a broader mission. This transformation marked a decisive step in the transition from the League system toward the UN system, which would take up the major principles recommended by the Bruce Reform. Second, during these five years the LoN played an active albeit semisecret role in conceiving the postwar international order, especially in the field of economics. The contribution of philanthropic foundations was important in both these processes, especially that of the Rockefeller Foundation (RF), which was decisive in creating the EFTD and organizing its move to the US. Interpreting the episode of the war is a complex exercise, as the League apparatus moved within the US sphere of influence, a process that was confirmed with the major role played by the US in developing the UN system. Yet it would be rushing to conclusions to speak of US hegemony over the conception of the postwar international system, as the role played by LoN experts in its development suggests a coproduction rather than an "American" order, even though the US appeared as its creator.

These issues will be discussed in the two sections of this chapter. The first will focus on the Bruce Reform, the final avatar of the Secretariat's strategy of promoting US participation in the League system, and on the move of the LoN's services to the US. The second section explores the expertise work conducted by the EFTD between 1940 and 1945 and its ties with the networks of experts that established the new international economic order.

DOI: 10.4324/9780429021213-7

The Bruce Reform and the Move

The Bruce Reform

In the early 1930s, the League began reflecting on its organization in view of reforming the Covenant, doing so for a number of reasons. The first was the proliferation of the technical sections created since the 1920s, which communicated little with one another even though their activities intersected, creating overlaps and competition. The need to better coordinate their action became clear after 1929, as the economic crisis demonstrated the interdependence of economic, social, health, and intellectual issues. The second reason was the discredit of the League's political activity beginning with the Manchurian Incident, which prompted the LoN to emphasize the successes of its technical sections as a counterweight. This problem became central in 1936, when the failure of sanctions against Italy in the Ethiopian Crisis made the League's impotence even more blatant. The third reason was the desire to integrate the US in its technical activities in order to save the League system from debacle. The reform of the League system thus partly bears witness to the continued strategy of involving the US, one that was implemented quite early on by the Secretariat. The debate regarding the reform of League institutions began in the early 1930s and would continue until the war, culminating in the creation of the UN, in which specialized organizations (the new name of technical sections) played a central role. The transition from the League system to the UN system did not suddenly emerge in 1945 or even 1940 but was the result of a process that lasted fifteen years, one that was accelerated but not triggered by World War II and in which the US played an important role.

The first manifestation of this process was encouraging technical sections to cooperate in order to solve the problems arising from the crisis. As the EIS was conducting a study on economic depressions in the aftermath of Bertil Ohlin's report submitted in 1931, the HO was taking an interest in the consequences of the crisis and the negative impact that standard of living had on health. In 1932 it planned a conference of hygienists in Berlin to address the effects of the food crisis. European experts were joined by two US academics, who took part in the conference with funding from the Milbank Memorial Fund (MMF). The RF was also interested in these matters, as in February and May 1933, George K. Strode attended two HO meetings at which hygienists and insurance representatives studied the effects of the economic crisis on public health. Finally, in October 1933, H.S. Cumming, who was still the head of the Public Health Service, and Edgar Sydenstricker, now Scientific Director of the MMF, presented to the Hygiene Committee the results of a study they conducted in the US with funding from the MMF.[1] In 1935, the ILO's International Labour Conference decided to address the topic of food and launched a cooperative effort with the HO. Three months later, in September, the LoN General Assembly validated this process of *rapprochement* by creating a Mixed Committee on the Problem of Nutrition designed to pool the research of the HO, ILO, EFO, and International Institute of Agriculture. The EFO positioned itself from the outset as the coordinator of the effort, with four representatives in the Committee, as opposed to two for the other sections.[2] Fifteen countries were represented, including the US.[3] The Committee held its first meeting in November 1935 in London, where it "established the physiological basis for rational nutrition" by defining "a sufficient diet in quality and quantity, considering muscle energy expenditure and growth requirements."[4] The coalescence between this research devoted to the noneconomic consequences of the crisis took a step forward in September 1937, when the LoN General Assembly created a Special Delegation for the Study of Economic Depressions, which marked a key moment in the evolution of the LoN project toward a global view of technical work that included economic expertise as well as the social and health matters connected to the crisis.

At the same time, reflections on the organization's structure continued within the Secretariat, Council, and General Assembly.[5] In 1934 the Council proposed creating an intermediary body between the Council and the technical sections in order to promote coordination. The idea did not come to fruition for the time being but reemerged in 1937, as the development of technical activity was henceforth a matter of survival for a League contending with its failure to regulate international relations. During its eighteenth session in the fall of 1937, the General Assembly created not just the Special Delegation for the Study of Economic Depressions but also a committee to reflect on a new institutional architecture for the entire League. In its report submitted on May 7, 1938, the committee recommended creating a single body merging the EFO and the International Labour Office. The Council approved the proposal, and the committee began its work in the summer of 1938 under the direction of the Australian Stanley Bruce and presented more developed proposals to the General Assembly on September 26, 1938, amid the Munich crisis. The central proposal was to develop nonpolitical activities so as to enhance collaboration between nonmember states, thereby making the LoN a truly universal organization. The strategy of Secretary-General Joseph Avenol continued that of his predecessor, namely securing the full participation of the US in an effort to save the League. With this in mind, the message drafted by Bruce to the General Assembly on September 26 paid emphatic homage to the US, notably to its Secretary of State Cordell Hull, who was credited with playing a major role in developing international economic collaboration since the 1933 London Economic Conference. Bruce did not fail to mention that the EFO's work represented one of the finest successes of the LoN and that it was largely due to the "generosity of the Rockefeller Foundation."[6]

While the Assembly was deliberating, the Democratic Senator from Florida, Claude Pepper, who was a member of the Senate Committee on Foreign Relations, was in Geneva. Sweetser seized the opportunity to meet with him and have him visit the Secretariat in order to present the work of the technical sections, whose importance the senator was not aware of, which is not surprising given that since the 1920s, the federal government had hardly publicized its participation in these activities with Congress. Impressed by the scope of the productions, especially in the economic and financial domain, Pepper was amenable to pleading with the LoN's cause before the Senate in order to advance the notion of expanded collaboration. But he indicated to Sweetser that he would need to base it on an LoN resolution that officially expressed a desire to further such collaboration. The two men thus planned a "move," with British collusion, in an effort to precipitate *rapprochement*. That same night during dinner, Sweetser and Pepper, assisted by Gerig, Pasvolsky (the special advisor to Hull at the Department of State) and Carter Goodrich (the US representative to the ILO), drafted a text that Sweetser forwarded to the British delegation. After making a few changes, the latter presented it before the General Assembly on September 30, a few days after Bruce's speech. The text approved the proposals of the Bruce Committee, especially the central one affirming the importance of technical activities, and officially invited all nonmember states to strengthen their collaboration with the LoN.[7] While the US was not cited, it was the primary recipient of this discreet request.

In the meantime, Sweetser sent the proposals from the Bruce Committee to Fosdick. The General Assembly had just completed its nineteenth session amid a tense international context: it began the day of Hitler's speech to the Nazi Party Annual Congress in Nuremberg (called the "Congress of Greater Germany") and ended the day after the Munich Agreement. In a letter to Fosdick, Sweetser noted that in an interdependent world, it was unthinkable that the US would not be affected by a conflict in Europe that was growing ever more probable, and concluded by stating: "the days of isolationism, particularism, and [US] provincialism are numbered."[8] Shortly after the session, he left for the US to help organize the LoN pavilion for the New York World's Fair to be held in the spring of 1939. He met, apparently at his own initiative, with civil servants from the State Department to inquire regarding the federal government's reception of the proposal from Geneva. To his surprise, the federal government was open to collaboration, as confirmed by the official answer sent by Hull to Avenol in February 1939, "the first official American declaration since 1920 with a favorable opinion of the overall work accomplished by the LoN as an international organization."[9] The US affirmed its desire to deepen a collaboration that had steadily developed during the 1930s. In private, Roosevelt supported the idea of granting greater autonomy to technical sections and went even further, indicating to Sweetser that the LoN would have to abandon all political activity in order to concentrate on economic and social matters. This was also the position supported by Shotwell when he met Sweetser in June 1938 in Geneva.[10] The US reaction was all the more remarkable given that it was the only nonmember state to respond to the invitation extended by the General Assembly in September.

In late 1938 the coordination of technical activities and the increasing autonomization of the sections conducting them were two ideas that had gained ground, all the more so as it was henceforth clear to Secretariat members that they corresponded to the wishes of the US government, which now supported the position defended by philanthropic circles since the early 1920s, namely to make the LoN a major organization of expertise detached from states. Avenol accelerated the process in order to seize this opportunity to integrate the US. In June 1939 a new committee was created to make these projects a reality, once again led by Stanley Bruce. His report, known as the Bruce Report, which was made public in late August, proposed the creation of a Central Committee for Economic and Social Questions open to all states that were not LoN members. While this committee's status was not detailed at this stage, this decision opened the way for eventually making it an organization separate from the League. The Bruce Committee followed the directives of Avenol as well as the proposals of Loveday, who had advocated a clear break between the LoN's political and technical activities, which he believed was the only way to ensure the active collaboration of the US.[11] While the report of May 1938 limited its reform projects to technical adjustment with no overall reorganization of the League's machinery, that of August 1939 proposed a deep structural reform: the international diplomatic situation had deteriorated between the two dates, as had the League's reputation; LoN leaders had understood that the only way to integrate the US was to autonomize economic and social questions as much as possible, and hence to recast the Covenant. The path chosen by the Bruce Reform was the one recommended in 1919 by Shotwell, who wanted to make the League into a series of autonomous conferences; it also agreed with the conception defended by the RF, which would play a central role in implementing the Bruce Reform. This path was now all the more obvious given that, on the ground, the technical sections had continued to autonomize in relation to the Secretariat, notably due to the financial, technical, and intellectual participation of philanthropic foundations.

Germany's invasion of Poland on September 1, 1939, and the outbreak of war in Europe that followed, disorganized the League's activities but did not prevent the General Assembly's adoption of the Bruce Report in December. The Bruce Committee now set out to detail the organization of the Central Committee for Economic and Social Questions, which was slated for inauguration in June 1940. When solicited in February to take part, the US refused due to the proximity of the presidential elections, as the majority of the public remained isolationist and hostile to the LoN.[12] While it was politically impossible for the government to participate in the committee, the RF decided to support it, surely in consultation with the State Department,[13] for in February 1940 Fosdick informed Sweetser that the foundation was ready to provide a grant,[14] at a time when the League's finances had dried up. The weeks that passed between February and May were one of the periods of epistolary and telegraphic frenzy that was customary when the RF machinery followed a case closely. In March the French economist Charles Rist, who was a member of the Bruce Committee, traveled to New York as part of a mission from the French government and took advantage of the opportunity to inform the foundation's officers of the most recent developments.[15] At the same time, a reorganization of all of the LoN's technical activities confirmed that the situation was evolving quickly and that the formal creation of the Central Committee for Economic and Social Questions was imminent. The EIS was indeed transformed in March into the EFTD, with Loveday being appointed Director.[16] It was a first step in the centralization toward a single organization including all of the sections addressing economic and social issues, and one could even say that it was the first act of the Bruce Reform's implementation. Loveday, as agreed previously with Rockefeller officers, immediately asked the foundation for a new grant. The Service was awarded a grant in 1938 for the years 1938–1942, but the outbreak of war had sparked new projects. The EFTD's objective was henceforth to reflect on the postwar world by pursuing three directions: the problems of population, migration, and minorities; international monetary questions; and the experiences of reconstruction conducted in Europe after World War I, with a view to drawing lessons in order to plan reconstruction after the war's end.[17] The EFTD requested a grant of $18,000, but the RF wanted to ensure the success of the new Central Committee for Economic and Social Questions, for which the EFTD was a natural nucleus and instead provided $100,000![18] Such an increase over the requested sum was exceptional—if not unprecedented—in the RF's history and shows how central it was for Fosdick. The foundation was even ready to go further, not waiting for the next meeting of the Central Committee for Economic and Social Questions planned for June 1940 in order to envision an even larger gesture.[19] In this new institutional layout being developed, the EFO became the nerve center of the LoN. From this perspective, the ongoing rivalry with the ILO since the late 1920s for the centralization of economic and social issues now turned to its advantage, with the decisive support of the RF.

The EFTD's Move to the US

It was at this juncture that the French debacle occurred in May–June, dashing the project and postponing the meeting indefinitely. France's sudden and unexpected collapse, in addition to German domination over the European continent, subsequently raised the question of the survival of an LoN despised by Hitler, as well as its continuing presence on European territory. On May 28, Sweetser arrived in the US, where between May and July he held numerous meetings with academics, foundations, and State Department civil servants to plan the move of at least part of the League to the US. This is when the lobbying efforts on behalf of the LoN conducted by internationalists since the 1920s, especially in government circles, ultimately bore fruit. In early June, Sweetser met the President of Princeton University, Harold Dodds, the Director of the Institute of Advanced Study (IAS) Frank Aydelotte, and Carl Tenbroeck, the Director of the Rockefeller Institute for Medical Research, part of whose offices were located on the Princeton campus. The four men discussed Sweetser's project. The IAS struck them as the ideal location to house the League: created in 1930 thanks to the industrial philanthropist Louis Bamberger, it had also been funded by other foundations since its beginnings, especially the RF, the Carnegie Institution of Washington, the Commonwealth Fund, and the Julius Rosenwald Fund.[20] After being led from its founding by Abraham Flexner, it was placed under the leadership of Aydelotte in 1939. In the spring of 1940, the Institute also received Rockefeller funding to conduct a study on international financial questions. The potential arrival of the LoN in its offices would reinforce its expertise in this area. The symbolic dimension was no doubt also part of the choice, as Woodrow Wilson had served as President of Princeton University before beginning a political career. It was also there that Fosdick studied and met the man who would become his mentor.

Sweetser also met other figures such as Henry Grady, Chief of the Division of Trade Agreements at the State Department and a member of the LoN's Economic Committee since 1937. In August 1939 Grady was appointed Assistant Secretary of State, a key position that allowed him to advocate for the League with Cordell Hull. Sweetser finally met with Hull, who believed it was politically impossible to repatriate the entire League to the US, but agreed to have the technical sections come,[21] but not by official channels, as an invitation from the US government would involve a risky vote by Congress.[22] Hull thus ruled out this possibility but gave the green light for private organizations to invite part of the LoN. In the meantime, other voices were heard in support of this solution, as Winfield Riefler, a former replacement member at the LoN's Financial Committee and now a professor at the Economic Division of the IAS, sounded out Aydelotte regarding the possibility of welcoming the EFO in Princeton. The Princeton solution would subsequently materialize between late May and early June 1940.

When he opened his mail on the morning of the 12th, Joseph Avenol learned of a letter signed by Dodds, Aydelotte, and Tenbroeck, in which the three men invited all of the technical sections to Princeton, for as long as necessary, to continue their work on the university's campus.[23] Avenol knew that Hull had provided his consent[24] but initially refused the proposal, which would reduce the League's staff present in Geneva.[25] The rout of the French army in June and pressure from British authorities made him change his mind. On July 26 he accepted to send Loveday and members of the EFTD to the US[26]—officially on a temporary basis—to study "global economic problems,"[27] whereas the League headquarters would remain in Geneva. Loveday estimated the EFTD's total operating cost at $60,000 per year,[28] which the RF committed to providing. It also paid for the emergency microfilming of the documentation amassed by the EFO since its beginnings. Preparations for the operation were in keeping with the general context of the foundation's attempt to attract some of the intelligentsia from Europe to the US. It established, to this effect, an emergency program for a few hundred individuals, notably from Germany, Austria, France, and Italy.

Throughout the process, Aydelotte picked up his phone numerous times to smooth out difficulties with the State Department, especially to find a solution for making the invitation as "private" as possible, in other words one that did not involve a political guarantee on the part of the federal government, which did not want to be accused of attempting to bring the LoN to the US.[29] The last problem to solve was transportation, as in July 1940 connections between Europe and the US were increasingly difficult, and finding 23 tickets for the members of the EFTD and their families was not an easy task. At the time Lisbon was the only port in Western Europe maintaining a regular link to the US, with many candidates for departure. Sweetser and his colleague personally contacted the American Export Lines and Pan-American Clippers companies to give priority to his protégés, who traveled to Lisbon by car and then embarked in multiple waves throughout the summer. In early September, the entire team had moved to the Princeton campus. Between 1940 and 1946, all of its operating costs ($260,000) were covered by the RF, which allowed European experts, once they settled in, to continue working in better conditions than they had ever enjoyed in Geneva.[30]

The LoN's Other Services

The EFTD was not the only one to leave, as, between June 1940 and the spring of 1941, a major discussion was held on both sides of the Atlantic regarding moving all or part of the League machinery. Columbia University Press was the first to follow Princeton's example, for when it learned in the press of the invitation extended to Loveday's team, it decided to conduct a similar process for the LoN's publication service,[31] which also crossed the Atlantic during the summer of 1940. At the same time, there was talk of transferring the International Labour Office to Johns Hopkins University, a solution recommended by its director John Winant. But Roosevelt and Hull were opposed, for if it wanted to maintain an appearance of neutrality as an international organization, the International Labour Office could not move to the US, not to mention that Congress would certainly be reluctant for this to happen. Roosevelt, who was in the middle of an election campaign, decided to delay, with the International Labour Office subsequently moving to Montreal, Canada for the duration of the war. Since its finances were in a difficult situation, like those of the LoN, the Carnegie Corporation of New York planned to provide financial support in the fall of 1940,[32] without it being possible to determine whether it materialized or not.

With regard to the Permanent Central Opium Board, Herbert L. May, who was now president of this body controlling the production and distribution of narcotic drugs, also wanted it to move to the US. Princeton University considered extending a second invitation, this time to all of the LoN's technical sections. Hull was reluctant to do so, and the discussions he had with the LoN's new Secretary-General Sean Lester (who succeeded Avenol during the summer of 1940) dragged on until December. While Hull ultimately agreed to move all antiopium activities, it was on the condition that they be physically separated from the LoN's other sections in order to avoid reconstituting the LoN in Princeton. It was therefore decided in December to transfer the Permanent Central Opium Board, the Advisory Commission on Traffic in Opium, and the International Narcotics Control Board to Washington,[33] where they worked directly with the federal government. The move took place in February 1941.[34] However, the LoN could not provide the funds needed for the move due to its dire financial situation, for contributions from states had evaporated with the war, subjecting the organization to radical austerity. The League's various bodies thus turned to foundations. In the summer of 1940, the RF received requests for funding from the International Labour Office, the Permanent Central Opium Board, and the Permanent Court of International Justice (PCIJ), all of which it declined.[35] The government refused to pay to establish the Permanent Central Opium Board in Washington,[36] with the rent ultimately being paid by a Carnegie foundation[37] and another foundation whose identity remains unknown.[38] Other LoN sections moved to London, such as the High Commission for Refugees and the Treasury Department. With regard to the PCIJ, the Germans allowed it to withdraw to Geneva after the invasion of the Netherlands,[39] from where it also probably left for London on an unknown date.

The cases of the IIIC and ISC are more complex. After its final session held in Bergen a few days before the declaration of war, the ISC entered a process of decomposition from which it would not recover. The foundation had funded it abundantly since 1935 but was not satisfied with the result of its investment. A significant portion of the members of its national committees was not trained economists, and the members of the US Committee were reluctant to continue a collaboration with an organization they considered to be unskilled scientifically and incapable of producing valid expertise on the international economic situation. This is essentially what Jacob Viner, the advisor to Secretary of the Treasury Henry Morgenthau, Jr., said to the new Director of the Social Science Division of the RF, Joseph Willits, in July 1939[40] when the latter mentioned the possibility of moving the ISC in the event of a conflict in Europe. The change of leadership in the ISC deepened the gap between it and the RF, as in October 1939 John Bell Condliffe, the foundation's right-hand man, left the London School of Economics (LSE) to take a position as a university professor in California, abandoning at the same time his role as General Rapporteur of the ISC. A new Rapporteur was named immediately, the US jurist Pitman Potter, a Professor of international law at the Graduate Institute of International Studies (GIIS) in Geneva. He was little interested in international economic matters and instead wanted to focus his reflection with regard to the ISC on global government. Shortly after his nomination he sent the RF a research program for preparing a federal organization for the postwar world.[41] At the same time, the foundation awarded a grant to the US Committee of the ISC to initiate reflections regarding US participation in the organization of the postwar world.[42] The first stage would be a conference held in January 1940 under the leadership of Edward M. Earle, a member of the School of Economics and Politics at the IAS. The participants outlined a research program that was not interested in the political organization of the postwar world so much as the role that the US would play in the new economic and geopolitical order following the conflict.[43] The internationalist dimension moved to the background in favor of research into US interests.

This lack of enthusiasm for the ISC's work was also present with regard to the IIIC in general, which in the eyes of the foundation's leadership had two major flaws: it was a vector for French influence, and it wanted to represent a global ministry of culture encouraging multiple projects, instead of concentrating on a few specific fields in order to produce expertise leading to concrete solutions. Here we have the gulf between the concept of intellectual cooperation, which was primarily defended by the French, and that of scientific expertise, which was advocated by the British and Americans. In an internal foundation note dating from the summer of 1939, Fosdick provided his opinion on the IIIC:

> Personally I have little confidence in the Institute of Intellectual Cooperation. I have followed their work for nearly twenty years, and I think they have shown in most cases a distinct inability to come to grips with practical problems in any realistic way. Too much of their work is largely on paper, and they are specialists in calling for conferences that get nowhere.[44]

Despite everything, when the German invasion prompted Bonnet to sound out Fosdick regarding the potential move of the ISC and the IIIC to the US,[45] he did not shut the door right away. In early July, when the Germans who had entered Paris closed the IIIC, the many transatlantic discussions between Bonnet, officers from the RF and CEIP, and the Director of the American ISC Committee, Edward M. Earle, led to plans for its transfer to Princeton.[46] However, Potter refused to make the ISC an annex to the American ISC Committee and its project focused on the US, believing that it was more important to broaden the reflection to include global problems.[47] The discussions continued until April 1941, after a final attempt by Potter to house the ISC in the IPR's offices. Its director Edward Carter declined the proposal, with the tacit agreement of the foundation, believing from the scientific point of view that the ISC had never been able to completely separate itself from the "tradition of the IIIC."[48] There was no doubt among RF officers, who believed that the ISC was now off-limits and that there were already enough competent organizations in international relations in the US to do without it, especially the recently installed EFTD, along with the IPR and the CFR.[49] Nor was the IIIC useful to the US in its strategy of Americanizing intellectual cooperation, which emerged through the organization of the Havana

Conference in November 1941. The RF subsequently selected experts who would work to organize the postwar global order. The members of the EFTD fulfilled its criteria but not those of the ISC.

The Health Section (HS) did not cross the Atlantic either. It had been without a director since the expulsion of Ludwik Rajchman in early 1939, with its activities subsequently coming to a halt. The transfer of the HS to the US had an on-site advocate in the person of Frank Boudreau, the former Director of the Epidemiological Intelligence Service, who had returned to the US in the late 1930s, and now directed the MMF; he tried to organize the repatriation during the summer with Sweester, as Princeton University had on principle agreed to welcome it.[50] However, the situation had not changed in September, as Yves Biraud, a former Rockefeller fellow and now the head of the Epidemiological Intelligence Service in Geneva, once again approached the foundation regarding a potential move. The idea met with opposition from Sean Lester, as the departure of the final technical section still in Geneva risked the definitive closure of the Secretariat—and hence the LoN—by Swiss authorities.[51] The RF was hardly in any rush to pay to move the HS to the US,[52] and the MMF in all likelihood did not have the means to provide financial support indefinitely, not to mention the reluctance if not the opposition of the State Department. In December 1941 the project to move was definitively abandoned, as the HS, or more precisely what was left of it, remained along the shores of Lake Geneva throughout the war. It limited itself to the activity of Biraud, the last member of the Epidemiological Intelligence Service, who continued to gather information from countries who agreed to or were still able to send it to him.

Still, contact was not entirely broken with the US. When the United Nations Relief and Rehabilitation Administration (UNRRA) was created in the fall of 1943 to ensure the first stage of rehabilitation for liberated countries, its Health Division was led by members of the RF,[53] who relied on the experience of the HS. In early 1944, an HS research unit was created in Washington with the consent of the federal government and jointly funded by the LoN and the MMF.[54] The new structure used the data collected in Geneva by the Epidemiological Intelligence Service since 1922 and put it at the disposal of UNRRA, thereby giving it relatively precise information regarding the health situation of the populations in liberated countries in order to guide activities in the field. In the spring of 1944, the HS took part in the work of UNRRA's Health Division, and when the latter decided in December to create an Epidemiological Information Service,[55] the research unit was officially integrated, with its head Knud Stowman becoming the director of the new structure.[56] The department that was created only duplicated on a larger scale the EIS created by the HS in 1922 with Rockefeller funding. In this respect, the foundation passed on the legacy of the HS in what would become the WHO after the war, of which UNRRA's Health Division was one of the nuclei.

The Coproduction of the New International Order

Integration within Networks of Economic Experts

Upon its arrival in Princeton, the EFTD team consisted of nine experts (excluding their families) mostly from Europe, who had spent their careers at the LoN or associated organizations: its Director Alexander Loveday, John H. Chapman of New Zealand, Paul Deperon of Belgium, Folke Hilgerdt and Ansgar Rosenborg of Sweden, Constantin McGuire of Ireland, Ragnar Nurkse of Estonia, and Jacques J. Polak and P.W. van Ittersum from the Netherlands, the latter being the only woman on the team. Once the initial difficulties of moving were resolved, the EFTD set to work, doing so until August 1, 1946, when the transfer of its duties from the LoN to the UN took effect. Thanks to the good working conditions, these years were the most productive for Loveday's team. In late 1940 the team expanded with an additional twenty people on site. Loveday initially approached the RF to expand his staff. Kittredge provided him with a list of former fellows[57] and advised him to also contact the Emergency Committee, which helped place refugee researchers from Europe in the US. However, practically no former European fellows of the foundation were hired, either because their English skills were not good enough, they did not match the profile for the position, did not have a visa, or were already committed to other governmental programs or universities. In the end, the members who were recruited were almost all Americans, with a few exceptions such as John Lindberg of Sweden,[58] who was a former Rockefeller fellow that had worked at the International Labour Office throughout the 1930s.

From the beginning of its stay, the EFTD tried to make the voice of the LoN heard in plans for postwar organizations. It was supported in this effort by the League of Nations Association, which counted Fosdick and Sweetser among its members, and whose new president was Boudreau. In April 1941 they organized a meeting in Princeton between Americans involved in the LoN and members of the federal government, with a view to showcasing the League's work.[59] A few months later, on November 29, the League of Nations Association held a conference on the organization of the postwar world, at which multiple directors of League sections presented. They affirmed five ideas: (1) another international organization had to be created after the war; (2) the US had to participate; (3) all democratic states had to participate; (4) whatever the form of the institution, it would have to take into account the experience of the LoN, whose staff would form the core of the new organization; and (5) it must have a centralized organization in order to address economic, social, and health problems, among others.[60] At a time when the LoN was discredited, the members, on the contrary, affirmed the validity of its experience and its legitimacy in contributing to the implementation of the postwar order. This lobbying effort had little impact, as neither the US government nor any other was ready to bet on an organization that had been powerless to stop the rising dangers.

Acknowledging this situation, Loveday's team quickly distanced itself from those who wanted to resuscitate the LoN as such. The EFTD henceforth pursued its own strategy of carving out a role for itself among the organizations preparing the postwar world[61] by relying on its scientific expertise and building its own networks but being discreet regarding its belonging to the Geneva-based organization. Since they had microfilmed all of the EFO's archives before leaving, Loveday's colleagues had considerable documentation at their disposal, one that would expand during the war with the arrival of 3,000 books and pamphlets, along with 800 periodicals from 50 countries, not to mention the economic statistics that were still being compiled in Geneva and sent to Princeton. On site, the EFTD could count on the documentation available at the Princeton University Library. With the help of this corpus that was second to none, the EFTD continued its work analyzing the international economy and continued publishing the periodicals created during the interwar period, notably the *Monthly Bulletin of Statistics*, *The Statistical Year Book*, and the *World Economic Survey*,[62] even though it now appeared in reduced form due to the ban on publishing economic statistics in belligerent countries, as well as the haphazard nature of postal communication between the LoN offices in Geneva and Princeton. In addition to these periodical publications, the EFTD produced numerous analytical works, publishing at least 22 books between 1940 and 1946 on the different aspects of preparing for the postwar world.[63]

These books were not only the continuation of the research begun in the 1930s, particularly the efforts coordinated by Gottfried Haberler and Jan Tinbergen, but also the culmination of the cross-disciplinary work of the technical sections, which was the objective of the Bruce Reform. With this research far surpassing strictly economic and financial matters, the EFTD made an important contribution to formulating the intellectual project of the UN. While the new organization owed a great deal to the principles announced by Roosevelt in his Four Freedoms Speech, the expertise work led by the Division of Special Research under the direction of Leo Pasvolsky at the State Department, and research conducted by the CFR and the Brookings Institution, it would be inaccurate to say that the organization of the postwar world was solely the product of "American New Deal internationalism,"[64] for it also directly resulted from research conducted by the EFTD during the war, which remained largely invisible due to the LoN's discredit. Considering the architecture developed between 1940 and 1945 as exclusively growing out of the work of "American-style social scientists"[65] neglects the fact that European experts from the LoN gained extensive experience during the interwar period in analyzing the world economy and that Loveday's EFTD team produced important work throughout the war. Its research was on subjects as diverse as international trade,[66] monetary matters,[67] agriculture,[68] industry,[69] economic fluctuations,[70] food rationing,[71] emergency assistance for populations, reconstruction,[72] demographics,[73] migration, the transition from a war economy to a peace economy,[74] and the stabilization of the world economy.[75] From this point of view, the construction of the international postwar order was an international coproduction,[76] even though geopolitical power relations and the LoN's discredit made it seem like a US effort.

The work of Loveday's team was marked by its genuinely global vision, at a time when the conflict had just broken out and was still limited to Europe. When the team arrived in the US in the summer of 1940, there were few members of the federal government or academic experts who approached postwar problems from a global perspective, as most were focusing on how the US could play its cards right after the conflict. It was only in early 1941, and especially in the aftermath of Pearl Harbor, that the administration—the State Department and the Department of the Treasury in particular—created working groups for a global reflection on the problems of the postwar world.[77] As an outgrowth of an international organization, Loveday's EFTD had already adopted this perspective in the late 1920s. It therefore had a unique experience in the world of economic experts, as its team had amassed considerable documentation and knowledge on these issues. A substantial part of its work was based on the historical experience of the interwar period in the domain of the world economy, with a common theme, namely not repeating the errors committed after 1918.

In addition to this team effort, the EFTD endeavored quite early on to establish ties with the other groups working on international economic matters. In the fall of 1940, Loveday traveled to Washington to establish contact with various services of the federal government, especially the Departments of State, Commerce, and Labor, in addition to the Federal Reserve. Discussions were also held with the NBER, Brookings Institution, IPR, and universities,[78] along with the School of Economics and Politics at the IAS. From the summer of 1940 onward, the work of the Special Delegation for the Study of Economic Depressions, which was created in September 1937 by the LoN, continued in Princeton, where it met eleven times between 1941 and 1945,[79] first under the direction of Frederick Phillips of Great Britain, and after his death that of Winfield Riefler, an IAS professor who had become Assistant Secretary of the Treasury under Henry Morgenthau, Jr. in 1939. In July 1941 he developed the first plan for the Board of Economic Warfare and became the director for the Economic Warfare Division the following year. With such a person at the head of the Special Delegation, the EFTD was quickly associated with the leading circle of those conceiving the postwar world. Jacob Viner's cooperation with the Special Delegation led to the same outcome. He had spent part of his career at the University of Chicago, served as an advisor for Henry Morgenthau, Jr. beginning in 1934, and was one of the most renowned specialists on international trade, with a good grasp of the League system after a stay in Geneva in the early 1930s. In 1939 he also became one of the leaders of the economics section of the *War and Peace*

Studies project created by the CFR with Rockefeller funding, in view of identifying postwar US government policy. The EFTD's work thus strengthened the group of experts gravitating around the presidency, who were working to develop postwar scenarios.

Other specialists also joined the work of the Special Delegation, such as Oskar Morgenstern, who had left Austria in 1938 for Princeton University, and Gottfried Haberler, who was now a professor at Harvard University and an advisor to the Board of Governors of the Federal Reserve. While the Special Delegation's work was theoretically supervised by the LoN's Economic and Financial Committees, which were still active, in practice they were under the influence of the State Department, as it was under the presidency of Henry Grady that they met in Princeton in 1942 and 1943.[80] The Special Delegation's work would be published in two volumes, the first in 1943 under the title *The Transition from War to Peace Economy*, and the second in 1945, *Economic Stability in the Post War World: The Conditions of Prosperity after the Transition from War to Peace*. They were the culmination of research that had been conducted since 1933 by the EIS, as well as the synthesis of research conducted by the EFTD between 1940 and 1946. The synergy between the EFTD and Princeton University was also present in the work of the Office of Population Research, which continued the study program on demographics launched in September 1938 by the LoN General Assembly.[81] Loveday's EFTD was tasked with carrying out this work, and during its move to Princeton entrusted its realization to the Office of Population Research, which conducted its research with funding from the Carnegie Corporation of New York and the MMF. As a result, all of the LoN's expertise was mobilized in organizing the postwar world under the supervision of the US government.

The research conducted by the EFTD was immediately recognized by experts as a decisive contribution to preparing the postwar world, especially the work of the Special Delegation for the Study of Economic Depressions, which quickly gained a wide audience in US and foreign governmental circles.[82] This recognition, which was in sharp contrast to the LoN's discredit, explains why EFTD members were part of all the conferences preparing the new economic and social order, albeit as observers or official guests, whereas the LoN as an organization was *persona non grata*. They attended the Hot Springs Conference that laid the foundation for the Food and Agriculture Organization (FAO) in May 1943, the Inter-American Demographic Congress held in Mexico in October, the founding conference for UNRRA held in Atlantic City in November, the Financial Conference in Cairo, the ILO Conference in Philadelphia in April 1944, the conference of the Inter-American Commission for Development in May, and of course the Bretton Woods Conference in July, in addition to the UN's inaugural conference held in San Francisco between April and June 1945. A substantial part of the EFTD's research was distributed to the participants of these conferences as well as to decision makers, sometimes before they were complete, thereby spurring debate between participants.[83] Forced into secrecy, the LoN was no less central to postwar reorganization, which was not built on a political project that matured only in the last months of the war but rather on technical activities in which the LoN had accumulated considerable expertise for years.

Relief and Rehabilitation

The question of rehabilitation was one of the EFTD's major research topics. It was approached in light of the post-World War I experience, especially in two books: *Relief Deliveries and Relief Loans* (1943) and *Europe's Overseas Needs, 1919–1920 and How They Were Met* (1943). The first studied the relief measures taken after the Great War and concluded that this policy had generally failed, for while there were many relief actions, they lacked coordination, which led to inefficient overlap and rivalry between organizations. In addition, most of this relief concentrated on essentials, whereas the EFTD believed that raw materials should also have been provided in order to restart local economies. It was only in 1920 during the Brussels Conference that the Ter Meulen Plan was presented, which provided for international loans enabling devastated countries to buy commodities and thereby reinitiate commerce. However, aside from the fact that it came almost two years late, it only involved private loans, not governmental or intergovernmental ones. Countries in need had to rely on their own resources, which led to the bankruptcy of Austria and Hungary, in addition to skyrocketing inflation in certain countries, such as Germany. The volatility of exchange rates that followed was not addressed on the international level, as no organization tasked with regulating them existed at the time; it was therefore handled on a case-by-case basis and subsequently had little effect over the medium term. The financial rehabilitation plans led by the LoN in Austria (1922), Germany (1924), Hungary (1924), and Poland (1927) were of course successful, for they addressed the problems as a whole: rehabilitation, stable exchange rates, balanced public finances, etc. However, their late and strictly national nature did not provide the lasting stability that was needed throughout Europe. Rehabilitation efforts came late and were incomplete and not coordinated. EFTD experts believed that it was in this latter area where the most errors were made, with the most serious consequences for the global economy.

The two books came to a dual conclusion. First, relief and rehabilitation were two facets of the same problem and should be addressed simultaneously. While it was necessary to conduct relief measures during the aftermath of this new war, they had to be combined with structural activity enabling the economy to start again. Second, because the issue of rehabilitation would be global, this activity would have to result from international cooperation planned by an *ad hoc* organization. This organization must enable countries without the means of attracting capital to restart their economy and create jobs for their population, in the form of loans or the provision of commodities and raw materials. Loveday supported these two leading ideas during the meetings of experts and governmental representatives he attended in 1942 and 1943. These ideas, especially the second one, also served as a common thread in the first volume of the Special Delegation for the Study of Economic Depressions, which affirmed that one of the major elements allowing for a smooth transition from a war economy to a peace economy was feeding and clothing populations, but also and especially enabling them to produce and to trade what they produce, in order to feed and clothe themselves.[84]

These ideas would be taken into consideration and put into practice in November 1943 with the creation of UNRRA, whose remit included the two components of relief and rehabilitation, which most governmental leaders had previously separated, with the British emphasizing the former and Americans the latter. Loveday's team created a synthesis of the two points of view, and its expertise was decisive in developing the UNRRA program, whose charter was jointly drafted by the EFTD and the State Department.[85] Consisting of 44 countries but largely financed and led by the US, UNRRA was the first major intergovernmental agency of the nascent UN system and represented the first manifestation of a new form of international cooperation.[86] It was in many ways the prototype of the development aid that would be one of the major endeavors of international organizations after 1945 and was also the ancestor of the Marshall Plan, which largely relied on the combination of relief and structural measures. During the Atlantic City Conference that saw the creation of UNRRA, one hundred copies of *Relief Deliveries and Relief Loans, Europe's Overseas Needs, 1919–1920 and How They Were Met* and *The Transition from War to Peace Economy* were distributed to participants to spark discussions about how to define the new organization's missions.[87] The EFTD was represented on its executive board, but only as an observer, for at UNRRA, just as elsewhere, the presence of LoN representatives was not official.

The EFTD's work also focused on food, which, as noted above, had been on the LoN's agenda since the mid-1930s. In the context of war, the central issue was to study rationing and the consequences that food rationing had on a population's state of health. This issue was explored in two books, *Wartime Rationing and Consumption* (1942) and *Food Rationing and Supply, 1943/44* (1944). The EFTD's experts showed that in 1943, food consumption decreased by 30% compared to before the war. They also emphasized the highly variable level of consumption per country. In terms of calories, the quantity of food was almost the same as before the war in countries such as Germany and Denmark, where it hovered around 3,000 calories per day. However, in other countries such as Italy, France, the Baltic States, and Czechoslovakia, rations varied between 1,500 and 2,400 calories and were seen as too small to allow for full labor efficiency and optimum health. A third group of countries (Poland, Russia, Yugoslavia, Greece) was practically in a state of famine, with an average of 1,000 calories per day. What's more, in a substantial number of the countries studied, certain diseases that were decreasing before 1939 began to increase once again, such as tuberculosis, diphtheria, scarlet fever, and malaria, which rose considerably in Greece, where the public health system implemented before 1939 was thrown into complete disarray by the Nazi occupation. In many countries, there was also a decrease in the average weight and height of populations. Finally, the study showed the highly variable situation within each country, as cities were much more affected by shortages than the countryside.

The study identified the needs of countries from a food and health standpoint. The data collected during this study guided UNRRA policy on the ground, with the organization concentrating on twelve countries, with Greece, Italy, Yugoslavia, Czechoslovakia, and Poland receiving the most—Greece by far with 1.3 million tons of food between 1943 and 1946 out of a total of 3.8 million distributed by UNRRA.[88] The EFTD's study also underscored the close connection between food and the economy, and hence between relief operations and rehabilitation: without adequate food supplies, rehabilitation could not take place due to a lack of health—and hence the ability to work—among populations. It also pointed to a major danger, namely shortages in fertilizer and agricultural equipment, which risked smaller harvests after the war. The EFTD's experts relied on the precedent of the Great War, for due to shortages the 1919 harvest was smaller than any of those during the war. This was one of the reasons why part of UNRRA's activity also involved distributing agricultural equipment. However, it could hardly solve all problems, since the workforce for harvesting was cruelly lacking in countries where part of the population had been killed from combat, deprivation, or deportation.

The Global Economy, between Liberalization and Regulation

The restart of international trade was another major research topic of the EFTD. Significantly, the first book that emerged from the research conducted after moving to Princeton was *Europe's Trade*, published in 1941. Loveday's team emphasized the fact that most global trade was produced by Europe: with 4% of the planet's surface and 19% of the world population, Europe produced 51% of international trade. What's more, most of this was between European countries. Europe was thus not only a centerpiece of global trade, but its countries were even more interdependent than anywhere else, with protectionism subsequently being more of a destabilizing factor. With the conflict taking place primarily in Europe at the time of the book's publication, it was clear to the authors that Europe would be the global region suffering the most destruction, with its rehabilitation being both difficult and substantial.

Each country's industry had to be developed in order to restart international trade.[89] Europe's central problem resided in the gap between the industrialized countries of Western Europe, which accounted for the majority of intra-European trade, and the agricultural countries of Central and Eastern Europe, which were marginalized in international trade, and whose trade with Western Europe was limited to exporting foodstuffs. Central and Eastern Europe were among the central concerns of LoN economic experts during the interwar period, as well as those of the RF, which initiated a study of Danubian countries to better understand the region's economy. Loveday's team considered it to be a key region for Europe's future stability. With a population rising three times faster than in Western and Northern Europe,[90] experts believed that these countries risked two major problems in the decades to come. The first was that low growth in agricultural productivity would leave them unable to feed their own population due to the small surface area of their arable land. The second is that they were subject to the influence of Western European ideas and standards of living, especially after 1918;[91] the governments of these countries would subsequently have to manage a growing population with new needs, doing so with material means that would not allow increased production to meet future demand. Would they be able to manage this situation? EFTD experts concluded that industry would have to quickly be developed in some of these countries[92] to satisfy the needs of populations, improve their standard of living, and avoid any destabilization that could lead to the inability of governments to meet this demand. Implicitly present here is the full logic of development aid, and also, amid an ideological context that remained blurry, that of the Marshall Plan.

However, while Europe played a major role in international trade, it was only one element in a global whole that had to be analyzed as such. This was the objective of another book published in 1942, *The Network of World Trade*. It developed a topic that had already been discussed in *Europe's Trade*, namely the interdependence of all countries, which made international trade a unified system,[93] dating back to the last decades of the nineteenth century. This system was undermined during the 1930s by unilateral measures by states and bilateral trade agreements that ultimately jammed global trade. Restarting it would require multilateral trade negotiations allowing countries to lower customs barriers based on a preestablished plan on a global scale.[94] This idea was also supported in *Quantitative Controls of Trade: Their Causes and Their Nature*, in which Gottfried Haberler examined the issue of quotas and licenses, whose return after the war he believed would be a disaster for international trade.[95] In *Trade Relations between Free-market and Controlled Economies* (1943), Jacob Viner came to the same conclusion.

In this interdependent world, two prerequisites were fundamental for international trade to function: stability and coordination. This was especially true in the monetary domain, which was studied in *International Currency Experience: Lessons of the Interwar Period*. In this book written for participants in the Bretton Woods Conference, Ragnar Nurkse explains how international gold flows, which were initially designed to avoid sudden variations in exchange as part of the Gold Exchange Standard, became accelerators and transmitters—when the standard ceased to function in the early 1930s—of economic instability from one country to another. At that time, states abandoned the Gold Exchange Standard and used their gold stocks to absorb the shocks connected to fluctuations in the exchange rate, notably during the devaluations of 1931 in Great Britain, 1933 in the United States, and 1936 in France. The EFTD's experts emphasized that when the present war ended, the stability of national income and employment would be an obligation for states. Two major conclusions emerged from the book: (1) the economic stability of a country is necessary for exchange rate stability and (2) exchange rate stability was required for the development of international trade.

Foreign exchange stability could only result from adjustments made on the national level, which had to be synchronized internationally in order to be effective. The coordinated action required to stabilize foreign exchange was central to the work of the Special Delegation for the Study of Economic Depressions, whose second volume, published in 1945, was significantly entitled *Economic Stability in the Post-War World*. This stability required four types of coordinated measures. The first was abandoning trade restrictions such as customs barriers, quotas, and other forms of restrictions; the second was creating a currency to serve as an international reference; the third was creating an international institution to stimulate and encourage international capital flows for productive purposes; and the fourth was to create a second international institution tasked with reducing currency fluctuations.

The philosophy that emerged from these works, whose preparatory versions began to circulate among Allied experts as early as 1942,[96] consisted of giving a new role to public authority—especially of the international kind—in the form of one or more organizations with extended powers, notably in the area of economics. It is this new approach that materialized at the Bretton Woods Conference, which established the framework for postwar economic organization. The effort involved three central measures. The first was the recreation of a Gold Exchange Standard System based on the dollar, which was convertible into gold based on a fixed parity. Other currencies could only be converted into dollars. The second measure was the creation of the International Monetary Fund (IMF), whose objective was to reduce currency fluctuation by constituting an international reserve fund, which unlike a bank could not issue currency but could provide short-term liquidity to countries that temporarily needed it to support their currency. The third was the creation of the International Bank for Reconstruction and Development (IBRD), which was designed to provide the funds needed for reconstruction and industrial development, thereby giving concrete form to the idea of an international loan policy to reconstruct devastated countries. These three pillars were supposed to ensure a regulation of the world economy that the interwar period never successfully achieved. They combined the liberalization of international trade with the creation of institutions to regulate international economic flows. While members of Loveday's team broadly distributed their work among delegations participating in Bretton Woods, they also provided follow-up service for the decisions made at the Conference. They did so by publishing editorials in the press and speaking on radio to raise awareness regarding the utility of new international institutions with both the American public and members of Congress, which would be called on to contribute financially. The process launched at Bretton Woods materialized in December 1945 with the official creation of the IMF and the World Bank.

The Well-Being of Populations

The work of the EFTD largely surpassed economic matters in an effort to broach the question of the well-being of populations. This issue was not born with the war, as it had emerged in the wake of the Great Depression, when the malfunction of economic mechanisms led to social problems on an unprecedented scale. Mass unemployment and the spread of poverty were such that social and economic security, along with an improved standard of living, emerged as leading concerns for LoN experts. In the fall of 1937, the General Assembly tasked the EFO with producing a study to identify the measures needed to "raise the standard of living" of populations with a view to "increasing human well-being,"[97] which was considered as a priority for the future.

A similar conclusion was reached in 1939 by the ISC's General Rapporteur John Bell Condliffe after two years of research on international trade:

> international trade is not an end in itself. Monetary stability and balanced budgets are not either. Today a system based on free private enterprise is even less justifiable if it cannot be proven that it provides greater well-being for society than all other possible forms of economic organization. [...] "Laissez-faire" has discredited itself, too often offering the private economy a pretext for making profits to the detriment of the community.[98]

More fundamentally, the crisis overturned the intellectual patterns with which most Western economists thought until the late 1920s. Faced with the scope of the Great Depression, *laissez-faire* policy proved devastating from the social point of view and showed that the invisible hand of capitalism did not exist, with the economy proving incapable of regulating itself. The question of standard of living and increasing human well-being gave rise to that of intervention by public authorities in economic mechanisms. This upheaval of paradigms ultimately brought about a reorientation of the LoN's program toward an economic liberalism refashioned with public interventionism. This is essentially what Condliffe noted:

> The argument for more free trade and monetary stability should be revised and linked to the general desire for greater social justice rather than a restoration of private enterprise. [...] Nor is it difficult to demonstrate that with some basic legislation ensuring social security, it is in the general interest to give a greater role to private initiative.

Condliffe sketched out, along with other economists at the time, the outlines of a redistributive policy driven by public authority, which involved providing loans to households, coordinating major large-scale works, and creating unemployment insurance systems, in short a series of "measures to encourage consumption by giving it a desirable social orientation."

The emphasis placed on economic and social well-being was of course not specific to the LoN's technical sections, as it was also central to the New Deal policy led by Roosevelt beginning in 1933. In the late 1930s, this topic began to take hold as one of the international issues for the decade to come. It was at the heart of the arguments in the Bruce Report of August 1939, which presented economic and social well-being as a way to prevent wars. It was also central to the project of Loveday's EFTD since its move to Princeton. Roosevelt gave it due form as a political program during the Four Freedoms Speech before Congress and the rest of the world on January 6, 1941. Of the four freedoms (freedom of speech, of worship, from want, and from fear), the third involved the entire field of social and economic security, as well as an improved standard of living. It was one of the major research topics of the Special Delegation for the Study of Economic Depressions, whose members emphasized that the sole purpose of postwar reconstruction should not be to restart production and trade but to also ensure the well-being of populations, whether it be from the point of view of food, lodging, or health. In the introduction to *The Transition from War to Peace Economy*, the Special Delegation highlighted the absurdity of the current economic system, which proved unable to respond to the ravages of the Great Depression, for it was not until the US entry into the war that mass unemployment ended and employment levels from before the Wall Street Crash of October 1929 were restored. The central question that guided the Special Delegation's work was of a philosophical and not exclusively economic order. Its authors emphasized the absurdity that full employment could only be ensured during wartime and that labor was used to destroy others, whereas the period of peace was characterized by mass unemployment. Social and economic organization as it existed when they were writing struck them as much more likely to reduce the standard of living than to increase it. The future economic organization had to provide an answer to this fundamental problem. Its aim was broader and broke out into seven directions identified by the Special Delegation: (1) the objective of economic organization should be a rising standard of living; (2) unemployment must be reduced to a minimum; (3) the economy's organization must provide for the essential needs of all human beings, especially with regard to food, clothing, lodging, and healthcare; (4) society must collectively assume the consequences of an individual's loss of employment; (5) all human beings must have equal access to education and instruction; (6) all countries must have access to global markets thanks to the elimination of customs barriers; (7) all countries must be able to acquire, thanks to a system of development aid, production capacity enabling them to sell on global markets.[99]

As this vast program combining material wealth and respect for freedoms could not be implemented on its own, it had to be coordinated by public authorities. This would take two forms. The first was the state, which experts from the Special Delegation believed should adopt the measures that were indispensable to righting the economic situation when required; production was not only the result of the private initiative of entrepreneurs but also the social responsibility of the state, which had to provide work for its population if private enterprise proved unable to do so. The new role of the state as conceived by the Special Delegation's experts was not only to distribute unemployment benefits, as governments did during the Great Depression but to go further through the intervention of voluntarist policies supporting economic activity and avoiding depression. But the national state could not implement this project on its own; public authority therefore had to also take a second form, namely an international organization coordinating national policies. This was advocated for by multiple books by the EFTD offering support for a series of specialized international organizations.

The first stage in carrying out this program was the Hot Springs Conference convened by Roosevelt in May 1943, after which a temporary committee was created to establish a World Food Organization. Roosevelt's attention was drawn to food-related issues by the MacDougall Report of 1942, which followed directly on research into food conducted as part of the LoN. While the EFTD was not officially invited to the Hot Springs Conference, Loveday was part of the temporary committee that grew out of it[100] and gave rise to the FAO in October 1945. The following stage in carrying out this program for the well-being of populations was the creation of UNRRA in November 1943. During its founding conference in Atlantic City, participating countries agreed for the new organization to rely on the resources of existing organizations such as the HO, the International Labour Office, and the Temporary Committee of the FAO. UNRRA was thus a laboratory for institutionalized coordination between various international organizations.[101] However, it was at the Dumbarton Oaks Conference between August 21 and October 7, 1944, that plans for an organization to coordinate policies for the well-being of populations were made formal. A few months later, during the inaugural conference of the UN that opened on April 25, 1945, in San Francisco, the participants created an Economic and Social Committee to work under the supervision of the General Assembly on these matters. The members thereby tried to fill this original shortcoming of the LoN; as it was initially more focused on collective security, nothing or almost nothing was provided for in the Covenant for other issues, excepting the creation of the ILO. The objectives of ECOSOC, presented in Chapters IX and X of the UN Charter, are almost identical to the provisions of the Bruce Report, which instituted the Central Committee for Economic and Social Questions. Chapter IX presents its general objectives, notably "higher standards of living, full employment, and conditions of economic and social progress and development," in addition to "solutions of international economic, social, health, and related problems." Chapter X presents the organization of the Council, which would be an emanation of the General Assembly and would elect its members, initially numbering 18 but soon rising to 54. It could issue reports and recommendations to the General Assembly, create specialized commissions on certain subjects,[102] and even create specialized agencies. It was subsequently responsible for coordinating all of the organizations in the UN family.[103] The creation of ECOSOC thus confirmed the UN's dual function: to operate a system of collective security under the supervision of the major powers with the right to a Security Council veto and to organize international cooperation across all domains, in which all states would, in theory, have equal standing.

ECOSOC held its first session on January 23, 1946. It immediately created a series of commissions that, for the most part, assumed the duties of committees created by the LoN. This was especially true of the Commission for Social Development, which took on the activities of the Social Section, especially with regard to the trafficking in women and children; the Commission of Narcotic Drugs, which pursued the work of the Permanent Central Opium Board; and the Statistical Commission, which continued the international harmonization of statistics and the publication of the *Monthly Bulletin of Statistics*. With regard to ECOSOC, it included a subcommission on employment and economic stability that continued the work of the Special Delegation for the Study of Economic Depressions.[104] The year 1947 also saw the creation of a Population Commission that took up the research initiated by the LoN in cooperation with the Office of Population Research in Princeton. Commissions on human rights, the status of women, transportation, and communication were also created, with the latter resuming some of the work from the Communications and Transit Section.[105] Finally, regional economic commissions were also created to coordinate reconstruction and the restart of economic exchange in regions devastated by war: the first two were the Economic Commission for Europe and the Economic and Social Commission for Asia and the Far East. Commissions for the Middle East, Latin America, and then Africa were created somewhat later.

The work of these bodies not only had to be coordinated by the Council, but it also had to be conducted in cooperation with the UN's other specialized bodies, especially the FAO (agricultural matters), the International Labour Office (employment), the IMF (economic stability), IBRD (reconstruction), and UNESCO (education and science). In theory, the UN system was much more integrated than preceding ones, and all of the institutions cited were henceforth under ECOSOC supervision. However, in practice the coordination initially planned for was difficult to implement, and the history of the UN is also one of the gradual autonomization of specialized organizations, in particular the Bretton Woods institutions. The ILO, which was a specific institution in 1919, officially became a specialized institution of the UN. It was the only institution from the League system to survive intact after 1945, although Albert Thomas's ambition of making it a pivotal center for economic and social issues never materialized. While the principles contained in the Declaration of Philadelphia in May 1944 were identical to those of the UN, the rivalry between the ILO and the EFO ultimately ended with the latter's victory.

Conclusion

The EFTD's move to Princeton was a meaningful symbol in the history of the LoN and international relations in general, namely a transition of intellectual and geopolitical power from one shore of the Atlantic to the other during the major crisis of World War II. This symbol was all the more powerful, given that this transfer occurred even before the US joined the war. It should nevertheless not lead to the erroneous interpretation of a transfer between the LoN and the UN, for as we saw during this chapter, the transition was more a continuous process than a sudden break. This was notably true because the architecture of the postwar world owed much to the work of European experts who had moved to the US, and because the UN's institutional form was not so different from that of the LoN, proof that it was less an *ex nihilo* US creation than the continuation of the reforms initiated by the LoN in the 1930s, the Bruce Reform in particular. The new geopolitical relations that reflected the sudden rise of the US in 1940 should not obscure this process, which was kept underground due to the LoN's discredit. With the move of Loveday's EFTD, the Americanization of the LoN that Root desired in 1920 had come to pass, although it did not take the form he envisioned. Still, this Americanization was not complete, for European experts made essential contributions to the UN project, which was the result of a transnational coproduction much more than a simple US undertaking.

Notes

1 Hubbard Ursula, *La collaboration des Etats-Unis avec la Société des Nations et l'Organisation internationale du travail, des origines à 1936*, Paris, Centre européen de la dotation Carnegie, 1937, p. 798.
2 Clavin Patricia, *Securing the World Economy. The Reinvention of the League of Nations 1920–1946*, Oxford, Oxford University Press, 2013, p. 161.
3 SDN. Le problème de l'alimentation, vol. I. Rapport préliminaire du Comité mixte pour le problème de l'alimentation, Genève, 1936, pp. 9–10.
4 Hubbard, *La collaboration…, op. cit.*, p. 800.
5 Ghébali Victor-Yves, "Aux origines de l'Ecosoc. L'évolution des commissions et organisations techniques de la Société des Nations," *Annuaire Français de Droit International*, 8, 1972, pp. 469–511; Ghébali Victor-Yves, *La Société des Nations et la réforme Bruce, 1939–1940*, Genève, Centre européen de la dotation Carnegie, 1970.
6 League of Nations. Nineteenth session of the Assembly. Second committee. Speech delivered by Mr. McDougall (Australia) on behalf of Mr. S.M. Bruce, Chairman of the Committee of Coordination, RF 1.1/100/18/151.

7 This episode is mentioned by Ghébali, *La Société des Nations...*, *op. cit.*, pp. 18–20; the text of the resolution is reproduced pp. 15–16.
8 Sweetser to Fosdick, October 19, 1938, RF 2–1938/100/154/1136.
9 Ghébali, *La Société des Nations...*, *op. cit.*, p. 18. The entire letter is reproduced pp. 16–17.
10 Lavelle Kathryn, "Exit, Voice and Loyalty in International Organizations: US Involvement in the League of Nations," *Review of International Organizations*, 2, 2007, pp. 381–382.
11 Ghébali, *La Société des Nations...*, *op. cit.*, p. 34; See also Clavin, *Securing...*, *op. cit.*, pp. 245–246.
12 The shift of public opinion occurred from the Spring of 1941 onward and mostly after Pearl Harbor. See Schild Georg, *Bretton Woods and Dumbarton Oaks: American Economic and Political Post-War Planning in the Summer of 1944*, New York, St. Martin's Press, 1995, p. 3. As to the position of political elites, the shifting point is the collapse of France in 1940, as convincingly demonstrated in Wertheim Stephen, *Tomorrow, the World: The Birth of U.S. Global Supremacy*, Cambridge, Harvard University Press, 2020.
13 Ekbladh David, "American Asylum: The United States and the Campaign to Transplant the Technical League, 1939–1940," *Diplomatic History*, 39–4, 2015, pp. 629–660.
14 Fosdick to Sweetser, February 28, 1940, RF 1.1/100/18/153.
15 Unknown to Willits, March 4, 1940, RF 1.1/100/18/153.
16 Kittredge to Willits, March 16, 1940, RF 1.1/100/18/153.
17 RF Minutes, April 3, 1940, RF 1.1/100/18/148.
18 *Ibid.*
19 Cable from Kittredge to Willits, April 16, 1940, RF 1.1/100/18/153.
20 *Bulletin of the IAS*, October 10, 1941, p. 11, www.ias.edu/library/digitalpubs, accessed August 30, 2021.
21 Extract from the report of the Director to the trustees of the Institute of Advanced Study, October 14, 1940, RF 1.1/100/18/154.
22 Hull to the American Consul in Geneva, June 29, 1940, SDN 40642/R 5025.
23 Dodds, Tenbroeck & Aydelotte to Avenol, June 12, 1940, SDN C1624.
24 Memorandum of the British Consul in Geneva, June 21, 1940, SDN C1624.
25 Avenol to Dodds, June 15, 1940, RF 1.1/100/18/153.
26 Avenol to Dodds, July 26, 1940, SDN C1624.
27 Avenol to Loveday, July 26, 1940, SDN C1624.
28 Willits memorandum, July 3, 1940, RF 1.1/100/18/153.
29 Willits note, July 2, 1940, RF 2–1940/100/187/1339.
30 File reports of the Supervisory commission, SDN 10B/R4520/4072/4072; Norma Thompson to Loveday, September 21, 1945, SDN C1625.
31 Charles G. Proffit (Associate Director, Columbia University Press) to Avenol, juillet 25, 1940, SDN C1624.
32 Willits note, October 3, 1940, RF 2–1940/100/187/1340.
33 Renborg to Lester, December 17, 1940, SDN 40642/R 5025.
34 SDN. Rapport sur les travaux de la Société pendant la guerre, Genève, octobre 1945, p. 85.
35 Fosdick note, February 13, 1941, RF 2–1941/100/205/1448; Memorandum on finances of the League of Nations, February 1, 1941, RF 2–1941/100/206/1452.
36 Lester to Loveday, May 16, 1941, SDN 40642/R 5025.

37 Watterson to Stencek, janvier 15, 1942, SDN 40642/R5025.
38 Anslinger Harry J., "Herbert L. May," *Bulletin on Narcotics*, XV-2, 1963, 1–7, www.unodc.org/unodc/en/data-and-analysis/bulletin/bulletin_1963-01-01_2_page002.html, accessed August 30, 2021.
39 Dubuisson Michel, *La Cour internationale de justice*, Paris, Librairie générale de droit et de jurisprudence, 1964, p. 14.
40 Conversation Willits-Jacob Viner, July 17, 1939, RF 1.1/100/106/959.
41 Kittredge memorandum, October 19, 1939, RF 1.1/100/106/959.
42 Grant-in-aid form, October 27, 1939, RF 1.1/100S/109/983.
43 RF Minutes, January 19, 1940, RF 1.1/100S/109/983.
44 Fosdick note, June 28, 1939, RF 2–1939/100/169/1228.
45 Bonnet to Fosdick, June 5, 1940, RF 1.1/100/106/960.
46 Bonnet to Kittredge, June 26, 1940; Davis to Bonnet, July 10, 1940, RF 1.1/100/106/960.
47 Potter to Earle, July 15, 1940, RF 1.1/100/106/960.
48 Carter to Kittredge, April 29, 1941, RF 1.1/100/106/960.
49 Kittredge to Carter, May 2, 1941, RF 1.1/100/106/960.
50 Unknown to Sweetser, August 17, 1940, AS-LOC 18.
51 S. Deutschmann to Strode, December 27, 1941, RF 1.1/100/22/181.
52 Borowy Iris, "Maneuvering for Space: International Health Work of the League of Nations during World War II," in Solomon Susan Gross, Murard Lion, & Zylberman Patrick (eds.), *Shifting Boundaries of Public Health: Europe in the Twentieth Century*, Rochester Studies in Medical History, Rochester, University of Rochester Press, 2008, p. 94.
53 Tournès Ludovic, "The Rockefeller Foundation and the Transition from the League of Nations to the UN (1939–1946)," *Journal of Modern European History*, 12–3, 2014, pp. 323–341.
54 Collaboration with UNRRA, s.d., SDN 8A/6150/42474/42474.
55 Raymond Gautier to Knud Stowman, December 13, 1944, SDN 8A/6150/42474/42474.
56 Transfert of the Health research unit to the UNRRA Health division, January 20, 1945, SDN 8A/6150/43321/42474.
57 Kittredge interview with Loveday, December 9, 1940, RF 1.1/100/18/154.
58 Clavin, *Securing…, op. cit.*, p. 268.
59 *Ibid.*, p. 269.
60 Kittredge, December 4, 1941, RF 1.1/100/19/155.
61 See a partial list in "Agencies Planning for Peace," *World Affairs*, 105–1, 1942, pp. 32–33.
62 League of Nations. Economic, Financial and Transit Department (hereafter EFTD), *Money and Banking, 1940/42*, Geneva, 1942; *ibid., Monthly Bulletin of Statistics*; *ibid., Statistical Year Book of the League of Nations* (1927–1945); *ibid., World Economic Survey* (9 volumes between 1932 and 1944).
63 For a detailed analysis of the ETFD work during the war, see Clavin, Securing…, *op. cit.*, chs. 8 and 9.
64 Mazower Mark, *Governing the World: The History of an Idea, 1815 to the Present*, New York, Penguin Books, 2013 [2012], ch. 7, pp. 12–13 [Ebook version].
65 *Ibid.*, ch. 7, p. 5 [Ebook version].
66 EFTD, *Europe's Trade*, Geneva, 1941; *The Network of World Trade* (by Folke Hilgerdt), Geneva, 1942; *Commercial Policy during the Interwar*

Period: International Proposals and National Policies, Geneva, 1942; *Quantitative Controls of Trade: their Causes and Their Nature* (by Gottfried Haberler and Martin Hill), Geneva, 1943; *Trade Relations between Free-Market and Controlled Economies* (by Jacob Viner), Geneva, 1943.

67 *Money and Banking, 1940/42*, Geneva, 1942; *Course and Control of Inflation: A Review of Monetary Experience in Europe after World War I*, Geneva, 1946.

68 *Agricultural Production in Continental Europe during the 1914–1918 War and the Reconstruction Period*, Geneva, 1943.

69 *Industrialization and Foreign Trade*, Geneva, 1945; *Raw-Material Problems and Policies* (by Eugene Staley), Geneva, 1946.

70 *Economic Fluctuations in the United States and the United Kingdom, 1918–1922*, Geneva, 1942.

71 *Wartime Rationing and Consumption*, Geneva, 1942; *Food Rationing and Supply, 1943/44*, Geneva, 1944; *Food, Famine and Relief, 1940–1946* (by John Lindberg), Geneva, 1946.

72 *Relief Deliveries and Relief Loans*, Geneva, 1943; *Europe's Overseas Needs, 1919–1920 and How They Were Met*, Geneva, 1943; *League of Nations Reconstruction Schemes in the Inter-War Period*, Geneva, 1945.

73 *The Future Population of Europe and the Soviet Union. Demographic Perspectives 1940–1970* (by Frank Notestein, Irene B. Taeuber, Dudley Kirk, Ansley J. Coale, Louise K. Kiser), Geneva, 1944; *Economic Demography of Eastern and Southern Europe* (by Wilbert Ellis Moore), Geneva, 1945; *Population of the Soviet Union: History and Prospects* (by Lorimer Frank), Geneva, 1946; *Europe's Population in the Interwar Years* (by Dudley Kirk), Geneva, 1946.

74 *The Transition from War to Peace Economy. Report of the Delegation on Economic Depression*, vol. 1, Geneva, 1943.

75 *Economic Stability in the Postwar World. Report of the Delegation on Economic Depression*, vol. 2, Geneva, 1945.

76 I borrow this term from John Krige. See Krige John, *American Hegemony and the Postwar Reconstruction of Science in Europe*, Cambridge, MIT Press, 2006, ch. 1.

77 Schild Georg, *Bretton Woods...*, *op. cit.*, p. 84.

78 Kittredge interview with Loveday, December 9, 1940, RF 1.1/100/18/154.

79 *Bulletin of the IAS*, November 11, 1941, p. 19; *ibid.*, December 12, 1941, p. 22, www.ias.edu/library/digitalpubs, accessed August 30, 2021.

80 SDN. Rapport sur les travaux de la Société pendant la guerre, Genève, 1945, p. 38.

81 *Annuaire de la Société des Nations*, vol. 8, Genève, 1938, p. 344.

82 Clavin, *Securing...*, *op. cit.*, p. 289.

83 SDN. *Rapport sur les travaux de la Société pendant la guerre*, Genève, octobre 1945, p. 43.

84 EFTD, *Transition*, p. 115.

85 Clavin, *Securing...*, *op. cit.*, p. 297 and 302.

86 Reinisch Jessica, "Internationalism in Relief: The Birth (and Death) of UNRRA," *Past & Present*, 210–Suppl. 6, 2011, pp. 258–289.

87 Loveday to Willits, Report of Activities 1943, January 20, 1944, RF 1.1/100/19/158.

88 EFTD, *Food, Famine and Relief*, p. 100.

89 EFTD, *Europe's Trade*, p. 20.

90 *Ibid.*, p. 50.

91 EFTD, *Demography*, p. 28.

92 EFTD, *Europe's Trade*, p. 14.
93 EFTD, *Network*, preface.
94 *Ibid.*, p. 97.
95 EFTD, *Controls*, p. 54.
96 Clavin, *Securing...*, *op. cit.*, p. 285.
97 SDN. Comité économique. Enquête préliminaire sur les mesures d'ordre international visant à relever le niveau d'existence, par N.F. Hall, Genève, 1938, p. 6.
98 Condliffe John Bell, *Les changements fondamentaux dans la vie économique*, Paris, Chambre de commerce internationale, 1939, pp. 5–6, this and the two following quotations.
99 EFTD, *Transition*, 14. Or, in the French version of the text: Société des Nations. Le passage de l'économie de guerre à l'économie de paix. Rapport de la Délégation chargée de l'étude des dépressions économiques, Genève, 1943, pp. 15–16.
100 Clavin, *Securing...*, *op. cit.*, p. 302.
101 Fisher Allan G.B., "The Constitution and Work of UNRRA," *International Affairs*, 20–3, 1944, p. 323.
102 Fisher Allan G.B., "International Economic Collaboration and the Economic and Social Council," *International Affairs*, 21–4, 1945, pp. 459–468.
103 Luard Evan, *A History of the United Nations*, vol. 1, London, MacMillan, 1982, p. 57.
104 Economic and Social Council of the UN, "Economic Reconstruction, Stability and Development," *World Affairs*, 110–4, 1947, pp. 243–247.
105 Riefler Winfield, "The Work of the Economic and Social Council of the United Nations," *Proceedings of the Academy of Political Science*, 22–2, 1947, pp. 74–83.

References

Anslinger Harry J., "Herbert L. May," *Bulletin on Narcotics*, XV –2, 1963, 1–7, www.unodc.org/unodc/en/data-and-analysis/bulletin/bulletin_1963-01-01_2_page002.html
Borowy Iris, "Maneuvering for Space: International Health Work of the League of Nations during World War II," in Solomon Susan Gross, Murard Lion, & Zylberman Patrick (ed.), *Shifting Boundaries of Public Health: Europe in the Twentieth Century*, Rochester Studies in Medical History, Rochester, University of Rochester Press, 2008, pp. 87–113.
Dubuisson Michel, *La Cour internationale de justice*, Paris, Librairie générale de droit et de jurisprudence, 1964.
Ekbladh David, "American Asylum: The United States and the Campaign to Transplant the Technical League, 1939–1940," *Diplomatic History*, 39–4, 2015, pp. 629–660.
Clavin Patricia, *Securing the World Economy. The Reinvention of the League of Nations 1920–1946*, Oxford, Oxford University Press, 2013.
Ghébali Victor-Yves, *La Société des Nations et la réforme Bruce, 1939–1940*, Genève, Centre européen de la dotation Carnegie, 1970.
Ghébali Victor-Yves, "Aux origines de l'Ecosoc. L'évolution des commissions et organisations techniques de la Société des Nations," *Annuaire Français de Droit International*, 8, 1972, pp. 469–511.
Krige John, *American Hegemony and the Postwar Reconstruction of Science in Europe*, Cambridge, MIT Press, 2006.

Lavelle Kathryn, "Exit, Voice and Loyalty in International Organizations: US Involvement in the League of Nations," *International Organization*, 2, 2007, pp. 371–393.

Luard Evan, *A History of the United Nations*, vol. 1, London, MacMillan, 1982.

Mazower Mark, *Governing the World: The History of an Idea, 1815 to the Present*, New York, Penguin Books, 2013 [2012].

Reinisch Jessica, "Internationalism in Relief: The Birth (and Death) of UNRRA," *Past & Present*, 210–Suppl. 6, 2011, pp. 258–289.

Schild Georg, *Bretton Woods and Dumbarton Oaks: American Economic and Political Post-War Planning in the Summer of 1944*, New York, St. Martin's Press, 1995.

Tournès Ludovic, "The Rockefeller Foundation and the Transition from the League of Nations to the UN (1939–1946)," *Journal of Modern European History*, 12–3, 2014, pp. 323–341.

Wertheim Stephen, *Tomorrow, the World: The Birth of U.S. Global Supremacy*, Cambridge, Harvard University Press, 2020.

Conclusion

A number of conclusions have emerged during this study.

The first is that it is no longer possible to claim that the US was not a member of the League of Nations (LoN). It was of course not a *de jure* member of the LoN as a political entity, but it *de facto* belonged to the League system, which was a larger whole partly tailored for it. It belonged to the League system because the latter's technical sections were made up of US experts sent by their government; because it joined the ILO in 1934; because foundations abundantly and continually funded technical activities, and even ensured their survival during the war by playing an important role in the transmission of the LoN's legacy to the UN;[1] and finally because its presence played an important role in the evolution of its technical activities, and more deeply in the organization's very morphology. US involvement even became more substantial beginning in the 1930s, at a time when the US was increasingly detaching itself from European affairs. If we add that the US had judges at the Permanent Court of International Justice throughout the interwar period, that it managed the International Academic Union, and had an important position in the International Council of Scientific Unions, it is clear that the country's involvement in the system of international organizations was already quite high during the interwar period. With this in mind, the break between the interwar period and the postwar world was much less important than the traditional historiography suggests. Examination of its participation in the LoN instead points to a gradual entry into the international system, which intensified during the 1930s, such that the order established in 1945 was not so much a break with that of 1919 as the culmination of a process that began with US involvement in the aftermath of the Treaty of Versailles.

Given these conditions, one could speak of an Americanization of the LoN, for while the Covenant was never Americanized as Root wanted, the organization's functioning was in the sense that the agenda of the technical sections was partly financed by US contributions, especially by foundations. This was true of the HO, whose programs for the development of health statistics and collective study tours would not have existed without the funding, technical assistance, and intellectual partnership of the RF. This was

Doi: 10.4324/9780429021213-8

202 Conclusion

also true of the research programs conducted during the 1930s by the EFO, as well as for the ISC, whose agenda was completely reoriented in 1935 under the joint effect of Rockefeller and Carnegie funding, and by the colonization of the ISC by Rockefeller fellows. This also applied to the Social Section and the Permanent Central Opium Board, in which US prohibitionist conceptions largely set the tone. Finally, this was also true of the EFTD, all of whose work between 1940 and 1946 was conducted with RF funding. The obvious conclusion is that in the late 1930s, the organization for collective security was transformed into a body of expertise, some of whose components were largely autonomous from the Secretariat, mostly due to the strategy of philanthropic foundations.

This Americanization was a complex process because the participation of foundations in technical activities helped shape a very different LoN than the one imagined by Wilsonians or by legalists such as Root and the internationalist wing of the Republican Party. Both failed in their endeavor: Wilson saw "his" treaty rejected by Congress, and Root neither succeeded in making the PCIJ the center of the League system nor in convincing Congress to join it. It was actually a third conception of the LoN that philanthropists helped bring forth through the strategy they pursued in collaboration with the Secretariat, namely a League system focused on technical sections that were largely autonomous from the central organization. The federal government ultimately validated this approach that saw the League system as a large technical organization, as demonstrated in 1934 by its membership in the ILO and its support in 1940 for moving the EFTD. In short, the activity of foundations toward the LoN during the interwar period consisted of depoliticizing it as much as possible and making it a purveyor of expertise and standards rather than a forum for political decision-making. All in all, a kind of think tank *avant la lettre*.

While US participation helped shape the LoN, it was also one of the major causes of the explosion and dismantling of the League system by promoting the autonomization of technical organizations in relation to the central administration. This process was the consequence of the strategy of the RF and the CEIP. They both supported a decentralized system that modified the structure and hierarchies within the League system by promoting the development of organizations that were autonomous or that wanted to be (HS, Scientific Organization of Labor Institute, the ISC, the EFTD, etc.). The result of this process was to accelerate the delegitimizing of the central administration in relation to the technical organizations. The LoN's discredit did not only come from its powerlessness to solve collective security problems in Europe but also from pressure from US actors—foundations in particular—who, in seeking to strengthen technical activities, helped undermine the authority of the Secretariat. The LoN was undermined by the powerlessness of European democracies but also paradoxically by the emerging globalism of the US, which translated into the activity of foundations. The Americanization of the LoN thus went hand in hand with its weakening.

It should be noted that the role of foundations in the LoN was pursued after World War II, as it was partly in the US where the memory of the LoN was built. The RF and the CEIP continued to consider their participation in the LoN as one of their most significant international activities and underscored that the LoN was a founding moment in the implementation of a global order. One reflection of this was that after the war—at a time when almost everyone wanted to forget the LoN—foundations emphasized the value of its activity. In 1934 Sweetser proposed the idea of writing its history and secured funding from Francis P. Walters, who was the organization's undersecretary at the time, to write a book on the subject.[2] The idea did not go anywhere, but it resurfaced in 1946, when the RF provided a $17,500 grant to the Royal Institute of International Affairs to allow Walters to write his book,[3] which would be published in 1952 and remains a fundamental work on the history of the League today.[4] In 1945 and 1946 the RF also awarded a $56,000 grant to Columbia University and the Woodrow Wilson Foundation (whose president was Sweetser) to produce an exhaustive bibliography of the documents published by the LoN, which would be completed in 1949[5] and published by Columbia University Press in 1951.[6] Finally, in 1970 the CEIP awarded a grant to write books for the LoN's 50th anniversary.[7] This investment in the organization's heritage on the part of foundations, albeit involving small sums considering their usual budgets, reveals the importance that the LoN had in the eyes of US internationalists.

The second conclusion of the book is that this Americanization had its limits and that it would be too hasty to interpret it in terms of hegemony. First, in spite of its move to the US, or more precisely because of it, the European experts who had taken refuge on the other side of the Atlantic contributed, along with the RF, to transmitting the LoN's legacy by developing a new international postwar order, especially in connection with the UN. Beginning in the mid-1930s, the League system initiated a transformation process of which the Bruce Reform was the most visible aspect and whose broad outlines reappeared in the UN in almost identical fashion through the creation of ECOSOC. The work of EFTD experts was an important contribution in the coproduction of a postwar economic order, notably the Bretton Woods system but also the general philosophy of the UN, which was just as much an heir to the reconfiguration projects of the League system following the Great Depression as the New Deal and the Four Freedoms. These two facts were obscured by the inversion of geopolitical power relations before and after World War II, one that propelled the US to the rank of a military and diplomatic superpower between 1940 and 1945. However, they show that the creation of the UN system was a transnational process, in spite of being naturalized as "American" due to its completion on US territory under the coordination of the federal government, at a time when the LoN was limited to secret action due to its discredit.

The interpretation in terms of hegemony is all the more dangerous if we adopt a *longue durée* perspective by viewing the history of the international system on the whole. This is true for three reasons. First, because the US did not hesitate from the beginning to short-circuit the UN when it did not accede to its interests, such as when the US did not ratify the creation of the International Trade Organization provided for in the Havana Charter (1948), and replaced it with the GATT, which gave it greater room for action than a global organization that included its Soviet rival; or when the US created the Marshall Plan, which made the US a major actor in the reconstruction of Europe, whereas this mission was originally supposed to be carried out as a priority by the World Bank; or when it preserved control over the Bretton Woods institutions (IMF and World Bank), over which the UN only had theoretical administrative supervision.

The second sign of the absence of US hegemony over the UN stemmed from the geopolitical situation of the Cold War. In the context of the world's division between two superpowers, the UN was largely paralyzed for a large part of the Cold War, which notably translated into the USSR's intensive use of its right of veto on 118 occasions between 1945 and 1989, as opposed to 66 times for the US. While the US was the dominant power in the Western world, its global hegemony was entirely contestable, if by that we mean a universally accepted domination with no power sharing.

The third reason was that US influence at the UN began to decline in 1960, when decolonization brought newly independent countries to the organization, thereby changing the power relations within an organization that had hitherto been highly centered on the West, not to mention the membership of communist China, which replaced Taiwan as a permanent member of the security council in 1971. This change translated into the gradual distancing of the US, which took concrete form in 1977 when the country left the International Labour Office, before rejoining in 1980. It continued in 1984 with its departure from UNESCO, where it returned in 2003 only to once again suspend its participation in 2011. Finally, since the end of the Cold War, the supposed Wilsonian moment when it assumed the leadership of the coalition that led to the Gulf War should not hide its constant distancing throughout the 1990s, as demonstrated by its recurring bad faith in paying its contribution to the UN budget or taking part in peacekeeping operations after 1994. Other signs of a unilateralist predilection were the refusal to ratify the Kyoto Protocol in 1997 or the status of the International Criminal Court created in 1998, and of course the Iraq War in 2003, which was waged without a UN mandate, along with the summer 2020 decision by the Trump administration to withdraw from the WHO based on accusations of Chinese influence over the organization.

Finally, the third conclusion of this study is related to the project of government through science pursued by the RF, the CEIP, and LoN experts. Once again, this project was not exclusively a US invention, although foundations were among its most ardent promoters and devoted considerable sums to the LoN and others to implement. While the Americanization of the LoN occurred, this was also precisely because the project was shared on both sides of the Atlantic. Did the project succeed? The answer is complex. On the one hand, the LoN amassed an enormous quantity of information, which enabled important advances, especially in health and the prevention of epidemics, thereby inaugurating the concept of today's universally accepted health monitoring. It also developed expertise on economic matters, which represented the basis of its work during wartime to prepare for the postwar world without committing the same errors as after 1918. One could also say that this expertise work allowed for a better understanding of the mechanisms of the world economy, even though it did not avoid all crises. Finally, the postwar period showed that the UN confirmed the importance of experts and technical activities by creating ECOSOC and developing specialized organizations that were heirs to this dream of the scientific and rational government of world affairs. However, expertise quickly proved its limits when not accompanied by political decisions, for instance, with the study commissions created by the LoN as part of the Manchurian Crisis. The same was true of the ISC's debates in which the legitimacy of collective security was challenged by totalitarian regimes. This was also the case after 1945 and remains so up through today, where the work of specialized organizations is often undermined by geopolitical rivalries and nationalist policies. Seen from this perspective, the dream of world government through science, which was entertained during the interwar period by an aristocracy of white men representing the East Coast philanthropy-university complex, proved to be a chimera.

Notes

1 Tournès Ludovic, "The Rockefeller Foundation and the Transition from the League of Nations to the UN (1939–1946)," *Journal of Modern European History*, 12–3, 2014, pp. 323–341.
2 Arthur Sweetser interview, October 10, 1934, RF 1.1/100/22/185.
3 RF Minutes, October 18, 1946, RF 1.1/100/22/186.
4 Walters Francis P., *A History of the League of Nations*, New York, Oxford University Press, 1952.
5 RF Minutes, May 26, 1950, RF 1.1/200S/320/3800.
6 Aufricht Hans, *Guide to League of Nations Publications; a Bibliographical Survey of the Work of the League, 1920–1947*, New York, Columbia University Press, 1951.
7 De Azcarate Pablo, *La Société des Nations et la protection des minorités*; De Azcarate Pablo (ed.), *William Martin: un grand journaliste à Genève*; Sloutzky Naoum, *La Société des Nations et le contrôle du commerce international des armes de guerre, 1919–1938*; Ghébali Victor-Yves, *La Société des Nations et la réforme Bruce, 1939–1940*; Piétri Nicole, *La Société des Nations et la reconstruction financière de l'Autriche, 1921–1926*; Deutschmann, *Le Comité d'hygiène de la Société des Nations, 1920–1946*, Genève, Centre européen de la dotation Carnegie pour la paix internationale, 1969–1972.

References

Aufricht Hans, *Guide to League of Nations Publications; a Bibliographical Survey of the Work of the League, 1920–1947*, New York, Columbia University Press, 1951.

De Azcarate Pablo, *La Société des Nations et la protection des minorités*, Genève, Centre européen de la dotation Carnegie pour la paix internationale, 1969.

De Azcarate Pablo (ed.), *William Martin: un grand journaliste à Genève*, Genève, Centre européen de la dotation Carnegie pour la paix internationale, 1970.

Deutschmann, *Le Comité d'hygiène de la Société des Nations, 1920–1946*, Genève, Centre européen de la dotation Carnegie pour la paix internationale, 1972.

Ghébali Victor-Yves, *La Société des Nations et la réforme Bruce, 1939–1940*, Genève, Centre européen de la dotation Carnegie pour la paix internationale, 1970.

Piétri Nicole, *La Société des Nations et la reconstruction financière de l'Autriche, 1921–1926*, Genève, Centre européen de la dotation Carnegie pour la paix internationale, 1970.

Sloutzky Naoum, *La Société des Nations et le contrôle du commerce international des armes de guerre, 1919–1938*, Genève, Centre européen de la dotation Carnegie pour la paix internationale, 1969.

Tournès Ludovic, "The Rockefeller Foundation and the Transition from the League of Nations to the UN (1939–1946)," *Journal of Modern European History*, 12-3, 2014, pp. 323–341.

Walters Francis P., *A History of the League of Nations*, New York, Oxford University Press, 1952.

Archival Sources

1 Rockefeller Foundation Archives, Rockefeller Archive Center, Pocantico Hills, NY.
   In the notes to this book, references to archival documents are abbreviated as follows: Record group/Series/Box/Folder. Example: Rockefeller Foundation Archives Record Group 1.1, series 500 T, box n° 25, folder n° 246 is abbreviated as RF 1.1/500T/25/246.
2 Carnegie Endowment for International Peace, Columbia University, New York, NY.
   The references are abbreviated as follows:
   - for the American headquarters in New York: CEIP Series/Box/Folder.
   - for the European Center in Paris: CEIP-CE Series/Box/Folder.
3 League of Nations Archives, Palace of Nations, Geneva.
   The call numbers of the LoN archives are complex, with series often changing names and numbers. For more information, see the *Guide to the Archives of the League of Nations* published by the archive service. The references are abbreviated as follows: SDN Section of the Secretariat/Box/Folder/document.
4 International Institute of Intellectual Cooperation, UNESCO, Paris.
   The references are abbreviated as follows: UNESCO-IICI Series/Sub-series/Box.
5 Department of State, Geneva Consulate, National Archives of Recorded Administration, College Park, MD.
   The references are abbreviated as follows: NARA RG 84/Volume.
6 Arthur Sweetser Papers, Library of Congress, Washington, DC.
   The references are abbreviated as follow: AS-LOC Box.
7 Raymond B. Fosdick Papers, Princeton University, Princeton, NJ.
   The references are abbreviated as follows: RBF-PU Box/Folder.
8 James T. Shotwell Papers, Columbia University, New York, NY.
   The references are abbreviated as follow: JTS-CU Box.
9 Philip C. Jessup Papers, Library of Congress, Washington, DC.
   The references are abbreviated as follows: PCJ-LOC Volume/Box.

10 International Labour Office archives, International Labour Office, Geneva.
The references are abbreviated as follows: BIT Series/Box/Folder.
11 Ludwik Rajchman Papers, Institut Pasteur, Paris.
The references are abbreviated as follows: RAJ-IP Box.
12 Emile Brumpt Papers, Institut Pasteur, Paris.
The references are abbreviated as follows: BPT-IP Box.

Index

Abbott, Grace 38–9
agriculture 32, 35, 77, 142, 189
American Council of Learned Societies (ACLS) 119–20, 122
American Federation of Labor (AFL) 40, 42, 45
Americanization 4–6, 23, 195, 201–5
American Red Cross 27, 31, 75
American Relief Administration 75, 88
Anschluss 142, 163
arbitration 46–7, 59, 66–7, 72, 160
Austrian Institute for Business Cycle Research (AIBCR) 141–2, 157
autonomization 2, 5, 139, 147, 159, 165, 171, 174–5, 194, 202
Avenol, Joseph 43, 50, 173–5, 177–8
Aydelotte, Frank 176–8

Babcock, Earle 123, 131
Bergen meeting 154, 163–4, 179
Bergson, Henri 116, 124, 129
bibliographical coordination 124–6
Blue, Rupert 31, 36
Bonnet, Henri 129, 131, 152–6, 180
Bonnevie, Kristine 116, 125
Boudreau, Frank 94–5, 101, 181–2
Bourgeois, Léon 21, 116
Bretton Woods conference 164, 189–91, 194
Briand, Aristide 68–9, 96, 116
Bruce Reform (and Report) 94, 171–6, 183, 195, 203
Bruce, Stanley 173, 175
Bureau of Social Hygiene (BSH) 37, 39, 61, 74, 76
Butler, Harold 41–3, 77–8
Butler, Nicholas Murray 30, 65, 67, 69–70, 118

capitalism 3, 7, 191
Carnegie, Andrew 59, 75–6
Carnegie Endowment for International Peace (CEIP) 1, 3–5, 8, 28, 30, 46, 57–61, 69–78, 96, 113, 118, 122–4, 129–33, 139–40, 150–1, 153–4, 157–8, 180, 202–4
Carroll, Mitchel B. 34–6, 144
Cecil-Réquin plan 64–6
Central Powers 114–15
Chamberlain, Austen 96
Chatham House 153–4
China 61, 89, 102–3, 141, 204
'citizens without a mandate' 28
Clark, John Bates 59–60, 65
Clémenceau, Georges 21
Cold War 2, 7, 204
collective security 24, 64, 68–9, 139, 159–65
Condliffe, John Bell 145, 148–9, 152–4, 158, 162–4, 179, 191–2
Congress of Industrial Organizations (CIO) 45
coproduction 171, 182–95, 203
Council on Foreign Relations (CFR) 5, 130, 158, 164–5, 183, 185
Cumming, Hugh S. 31–3, 87, 93, 95, 100, 106, 172
Czechoslovakia 89–91, 103, 157–8

Danubian project 157–8, 162–3, 189
Davis, Norman H. 27, 34
Davis, Malcolm W. 122, 131, 151–3, 162
Day, Edmund 147
Declaration of Philadelphia 185, 195
Democratic Party 22, 50, 62, 71, 173
Denmark 155–6, 187
Depression *see* Great Depression

210 Index

Drummond, Eric 23–6, 35–6, 41, 46–8, 65, 71, 74, 100, 123, 128–9, 147

Earle, Edward M. 180
Economic Committee 28, 32–5, 94, 177
economic crisis 50, 74, 141, 151, 172–3; *see also* Great Depression; Special Delegation for the Study of Economic Depressions
Economic and Financial Organization (EFO) 32–5, 74, 77, 139–40, 145–9, 152, 159, 164–5, 173, 177, 195
Economic, Financial, and Transit Department (EFTD) 171, 176–80, 182–95
Economic and Social Council (ECOSOC) 193–4, 203, 205
Economic and Social History of the World War 60, 64–7, 140
economic institutes 142–4
Economic Intelligence Service (EIS) 145–9, 151, 171–2, 176, 185
education 40, 61, 72, 86, 89, 105, 115, 118, 121–2, 124, 192, 194
Einstein, Albert 116, 128
Embree, Edwin 86
Epidemiological Intelligence pamphlet 94
Epidemiological Intelligence Service (EIS) 85, 91–6, 99, 181
Ethiopian Crisis 30, 161, 172
European Center of the Carnegie Endowment for International Peace (CEIP- CE) 122–3, 131, 153, 158
expertise activities 77, 139, 147, 164–5, 171, 183, 205
Eyre Hunt, Edward 34, 145

Financial Committee 32–4, 144, 177, 185
Fiscal Committee 34–6, 144
Flexner, Abraham 123–4, 140, 177
Food and Agriculture Organization (FAO) 185, 193–4
Ford Foundation 3
Fordney McCumber Act 1922 146
Fosdick, Raymond B. 62–3, 71–5, 91, 96, 123, 140–2, 174–7, 180
Fourteen Points 21
France 21–2, 30, 68–9, 71, 88–9, 93, 113, 115–7, 122, 129, 146, 149, 151, 154–5, 176

General Agreement on Tariffs and Trade (GATT) 204

Geneva Research Centre 152–3
Geneva World Economic Conference 33
Gerig, Benjamin 25, 153, 174
Germany 21–2, 27, 30, 68, 115–17, 146, 154, 160–1, 164–5, 175, 187
Gilbert, Prentiss 28–9, 43
gold 32, 76, 144, 189–90
Graduate Institute of International Studies (GIIS) 35, 130, 141, 153, 179
Grady, Henry F. 35–6, 177
Gramscians 3–6
Great Britain 21–2, 30, 32, 37, 71, 88, 98–9, 117–8, 127, 130, 143, 146, 150, 154, 161, 190
Great Depression 42, 139–41, 145–6, 159, 162, 191–3, 203
Greek Refugee Settlement Commission 27
Gross, Leo 155, 158
Gunn, Selskar 89–91, 98, 101, 103, 131, 145

Haberler, Gottfried von 142, 148, 151, 183, 185, 189
Hackett, Lewis 105–6
Hagerstown Morbidity Survey 93
Hague, The 36–7, 46–8, 73, 75, 99, 143
Hale, George Ellery 119–22, 125
Harding, Warren 1, 22–3, 26–7, 30–1, 34, 36, 39, 49, 87
Havana Charter 180–1, 204
Health Committee 30–1, 87, 98, 105
Health Organization (HO) 31, 74, 85–8, 92–7, 159, 172, 201
Health Section (HS) 75, 87–8, 90–1, 98, 101–7, 181
hegemony 6–8, 144, 171, 203–4
Herriot, Edouard 66
Historiography of the LoN 2–3, 20
Hitler, Adolf 160–2, 174, 176
Hoover, Herbert 41–2, 50
Hubbard, Ursula 28
Hughes, Charles Evans 26–7, 31, 36–7, 48, 67
Hull, Cordell 29–35, 72, 146, 173–4, 177–8

industry 40, 44, 58, 77, 118, 142, 188–9
Institute of Advanced Study (IAS) 176–7, 184
Institute of Economics and History in Copenhagen 143

Institute of Economic Studies at the University of Oslo 142–3
Institute of International Education (IIE) 5, 72–3, 118
Institute of Pacific Relations 130–1, 145–6, 158, 180
intellectual cooperation 2, 113, 115, 117, 122–4, 128–33, 150–1, 159, 180
Intellectual Cooperation Organization (ICO) 129–31, 150–1, 159
International Academic Union (IAU) 115, 119–20
International Association of Academies 114–15
international associations 114–15
International Commission on Intellectual Cooperation (ICIC) 113, 116, 118–33
International Conciliation 73
International Council of Scientific Unions (ICSU) 115
international harmonization 44, 92, 98, 125, 149, 194
International Health Board (IHB) 86, 89–90, 105
International Health Commission (IHC) 86
International Institute of Intellectual Cooperation (IIIC) 25, 73, 113, 116–18, 122–4, 127–33, 152, 159, 179–80
International Labour Organization (ILO) 29, 39–46, 63, 68, 77–8, 139, 173–4, 176, 185, 194–5, 201–2
International Monetary Fund (IMF) 190–1, 194, 204
International Narcotics Control Board 38, 179
International Office of Public Hygiene (IOPH) 87–8, 92, 95–6, 107
International Opium Convention 36–8
International Relations Clubs 73, 153
International Research Council (IRC) 114–15, 119–20, 124–5
International Studies Conference (ISC) 5, 130–3, 139–151, 162, 165, 179–80, 202, 205
Italy 30, 89, 99–100, 146, 172

Japan 39, 95, 99, 103, 161, 164

Kellogg-Briand Pact 49, 69, 162; *see also* Pact of Paris

Kellogg, Frank 37, 46, 69
Kellogg, Vernon 121–2
Kittredge, Tracy 97, 148–9, 151–8, 162–3, 182
knowledge proliferation 61, 125, 127, 184

Lansing, Robert 21, 60
Latin America 86, 88–9, 94–5, 103, 105
Laura Spelman Rockefeller Memorial (LSRM) 120, 130, 140–2, 145, 148, 155
League of Nations Association (LNA) 72, 74
League of Nations Covenant 1–2, 23–4, 30, 32, 48–9, 57, 63–7, 71, 115, 161, 172, 193, 201–2
League of Nations library 75, 96–7, 102, 120, 141
League of Nations Secretariat 20–8, 35, 46–50, 76, 96–7, 123, 144, 149, 151, 159, 171, 173–4
Leland, Waldo 120, 122
leprosy 25, 103–4
liberal democracy 7, 58
liberals 3, 6
Lisbon 178
lobbying 43, 57–8, 69–73, 78, 115, 176, 182
Locarno Treaties 67–8, 96, 115, 123
London School of Economics (LSE) 130–1, 140–1, 143, 179
longue durée 203
Loveday, Alexander 145–6, 148–9, 151–3, 175–8, 181–95
Luchaire, Julien 118, 123–4, 128–9

MacMillan, Margaret 2
malaria 101–7, 188
Malaria Commission 85, 105–6
Manchurian Incident 28–30, 38, 43, 162, 172, 205
Marshall Plan 44, 187, 189, 204
Martin, Percival 77
May, Herbert L. 37–8, 178
Mazower, Mark 6
Michelsen Institute of Economic Research 156–7
Milbank Memorial Fund (MMF) 75, 94, 101–2, 172, 181, 185
Millikan, Robert A. 120–2, 124–5, 132
Monthly Bulletin of Statistics 149, 183
mortality statistics 99, 104

Index 211

212 Index

Murray, Gilbert 129, 132
Mussolini, Benito 161–2

narcotics 36–8, 178, 194; *see also* International Narcotics Control Board; International Opium Convention; Permanent Central Opium Board
nationalism 6, 58
National Academy of Science 119
National Research Council (NRC) 119–21, 126
Near East Relief 27
neutrality 30, 50, 139, 157, 178
Neutrality Act 30
New Deal reforms 29, 43–5, 101, 143, 146, 183, 192, 203
The New York Times 70, 96
Nobel Peace Prize 69, 156
nongovernmental actors 4
Norway 156
Nurkse, Ragnar 182, 189
nutrition 99, 104, 172–3, 187–8

Ohlin, Bertil 147–8, 172
The Old Savage in the New Civilization 62
opium *see* narcotics

Pact of Paris 69–70; *see also* Kellogg-Briand Pact
Pan-American Union 42, 100, 103, 127
Paris Peace Conference (1919) 1–2, 21–2, 25, 32, 36, 39–40, 60–3, 76, 114, 133
Parmar, Inderjeet 6
Pavolsky, Leo 35, 183
Peking Union Medical College (PUMC) 61, 89, 103
Pepper, Claude 173–4
Perkins, Frances 43–4
Permanent Central Opium Board 37–8, 76, 178–9, 202
Permanent Court of Arbitration (PCA) 46–8
Permanent Court of International Justice (PCIJ) 43, 46–50, 65–6, 69–70, 75–6, 179, 201–2
physics 125–6
Pittsburgh Survey 93
Poland 88–90, 165, 175, 187–8
Porter, Stephen G. 36–8
Princeton 176–195
professional associations 118–19

"professionalized meritocracy" 6
Prosperity and Depression 148
public health 85–94, 98–100, 102–5, 172, 188
Public Health Service (PHS) 29–32, 93–5, 100–1, 103, 106

Rajchman, Ludwik 32, 87–8, 90–4, 99–100, 103–7, 181
rapprochement 26–30, 41, 47, 63, 87, 123, 132, 147, 172, 174
Reciprocal Trade Agreement Act (RTAA) 34–5, 146
relief measures 186–8
Republican Party 21–2, 26, 29, 31, 45, 47, 49, 123, 202
research coordination 144–7
Riefler, Winfield 177, 184
Rist, Charles 141–3, 149, 175
Rockefeller Foundation (RF) 1, 3–8, 57–61, 73–5, 77–8, 85–99, 101–7, 124, 127, 130–3, 139–51, 153–8, 162–5, 175–82, 201–5
Rockefeller, John D. Jr. 37, 61–2, 74–6, 86, 96, 120, 140–1
Roosevelt, Franklin D. 29–30, 34–5, 43–6, 72, 128, 146, 174, 178, 183, 192–3
Root, Elihu 1, 22–3, 46–9, 70–1, 118, 122, 201–2
Rose, Wickliffe 90, 92, 104
Russell Sage Foundation (RSF) 58, 93
Russian Revolution 39, 90

Saint-Simonianism 6
Scandinavia 157
scientific associations 127
Scientific Organization of Labor Institute (SOLI) 75
scientific philanthropy 58, 86
security *see* collective security
Senate Committee 22–6, 28, 40, 43, 45–50, 71–2, 173–4
Shotwell, James T. 40, 57–60, 63–70, 73, 119–20, 122–3, 131–3, 158–9, 174–5
Shotwell Plan 65–7
Singapore Bureau 92, 95–6
Sklodowska-Curie, Marie 116, 125, 128
Social Science Research Council 5, 118, 126–7
social sciences 6, 61, 93, 115, 119, 121, 125–6, 139, 155

Special Delegation for the Study of Economic Depressions 173, 184–5, 187, 190, 192–3
Statistique générale de la France (SGF) 149
Stresemann, Gustav 68, 96
study tours 97–104
superpower 5, 57, 118, 203–4
Sweden 157
Sweetser, Arthur 25–6, 29, 96–7, 123, 142, 145, 153, 173–8, 203
Swellengrebel, Dr 101, 106
Sydenstricker, Edgar 93–5, 172

taxation 33–4, 144–5
technical activities 2, 4–6, 24–9, 32, 36, 39, 45, 50, 57–8, 64, 73–4, 77–8, 91–4, 97, 100, 102, 104, 107, 115, 117, 120–1, 123, 139, 141, 147, 159, 165, 171–8, 181, 183, 186, 192, 201–5
Thomas, Albert 41–2, 68, 194
Tinbergen, Jan 148, 151, 183
Treaty of Lausanne 27
Treaty of Versailles 1, 22, 25, 30, 40–1, 47–9, 90–1, 114–5, 201
Trump, Donald 8, 204
tuberculosis 89, 93, 100–1, 187
Twentieth Century Fund 42, 75–6

unionism 45, 78
Union of International Associations (UIA) 115, 124

United Nations (UN) 2, 5, 7, 45, 171, 182, 187, 193–4, 201–5
United Nations Educational, Scientific and Cultural Organization (UNESCO) 194, 204
United Nations Relief and Rehabilitation Administration (UNRRA) 181, 187–8, 193

Van Sickle, John 77, 97, 148, 151
Vincent, George E. 61, 86, 91, 104
Viner, Jacob 35, 179, 184–5, 189

Wall Street Crash 192
Walters, Francis P. 203
Warsaw Conference (1922) 90
What the League of Nations Is 73
Wilson Harris, Henry 73
Wilson, Hugh 30, 38
Wilson, William B. 40
Wilson, Woodrow 21–7, 40, 60, 62, 64–5, 71, 177, 202–3
Winant John G. 45–6, 78, 178
Winthrop Young, Geoffrey 129
Woodrow Wilson Foundation 75–6, 203
World War I 2, 5, 20, 30, 59–60, 62, 73, 86, 98, 113–4, 118, 130, 140, 186, 188
World War II 4, 36, 39, 72, 150, 164, 171–2, 176, 183, 195, 202–4

Zimmern, Alfred 118, 123–4, 128, 130

Printed in the United States
by Baker & Taylor Publisher Services